THE LOST ART OF V

also by GEOFF NICHOLSON

Gravity's Volkswagen
Sex Collectors
The Hollywood Dodo
Bedlam Burning
Female Ruins
Flesh Guitar
Bleeding London
Footsucker
Everything and More
Still Life with Volkswagens
The Errol Flynn Novel
Day Trips to the Desert
The Food Chain
Hunters and Gatherers
Big Noises
What We Did on Our Holidays
The Knot Garden
Street Sleeper

The Lost Art of Walking

The History, Science, Philosophy,
Literature, Theory and
Practice of Pedestrianism

Geoff Nicholson

Harbour

First published in paperback original by Harbour in 2010
Harbour Books (East) Ltd, PO Box 10594,
Chelmsford, Essex CM1 9PB
info@harbourbooks.co.uk

This edition published in 2011

This is a revised and extended edition of
The Lost Art of Walking
published by Riverhead in the USA in 2008

A CIP catalogue record for this book is available
from the British Library

ISBN 978 1 905128 174

Typeset by Antony Gray
Printed and bound in Finland by Bookwell

Contents

1 *An Introduction: The Lost Art of Falling Down, when Bad Things happen to Good Walkers, some Fellow Travellers and Stumblers* 7

2 *Nicholson's London, Your London, Anybody's London* 39

3 *Los Angeles: Walking Wounded with Ray and Phil and Others* 67

4 *Eccentrics, Obsessives, Artists: Imaginary Walks with Richard Long, Captain Barclay, Werner Herzog et al.* 91

5 *The Ballard Horizon* 116

6 *A Psychogeographer Walks into a Bar: New York, the Shape of the City, Beauty, Order, Convenience* 130

7 *Death and Pedestrianism* 159

8 *As I Tripped Out One Morning: Music, Movement, Movies* 179

9 *Some Desert Walkers, Walking in and out of Nature, with and without God, with and without Water* 203

10 *Walking Home* 225

11 *Perfect and Imperfect Walks, Last Walks, the Walks We Didn't Take* 249

A Walking Bibliography 265

An Introduction: The Lost Art of Falling Down, when Bad Things happen to Good Walkers, some Fellow Travellers and Stumblers

He who limps is still walking.

Stanislaw J. Lec

'A journey of a thousand miles begins with a single step,' or so Lao-Tzu, the Chinese Taoist sage, is often quoted as saying. In fact, this is a rather free translation of what he actually said, which was more like, 'The journey of a thousand miles begins beneath your feet.' I've spent a lot of time wondering whether those words express a deep spiritual truth, or whether they're just stating the blindingly obvious. My own feeling is that with most journeys, and especially the metaphoric sort, it's extremely difficult to decide where and when that first step occurred. We're already in motion before we know where we're going, before we even realise we're on a journey. Designating a particular step as first, or for that matter last, is a tricky and often arbitrary business.

People make a lot of 'baby's first step' but I suspect in most cases it's a photo opportunity rather than an authentic developmental moment. Is there ever truly one step that's absolutely, unmistakably identifiable as the first? Aren't there a lot of attempted steps, failed steps, almost-steps, sort-of-steps, steps taken while the baby's being supported or holding on to something? Paradoxically if a baby is a very proficient crawler he or she may be slow to start walking, because they already have a satisfactory way of getting around. Last steps are easier to identify in some cases; the step under the bus or in front of the train, the step off the bridge into fresh air. Even so, there may be problems of definition. When does a step become a leap, or a stumble, when does a stumble become a fall?

In my own case there was one particular step that was very different from any of the other steps I've ever taken in my life. It was certainly a misstep, a disagreement with gravity that resulted in a bone-breaking coming together of all too fragile body and all too solid earth.

Christmas was two days away, I was in Los Angeles, where I lived at the time, and still do, and I was feeling optimistic. I'd decided to write a book called *The Lost Art of Walking*, my publisher had agreed this was a fine idea, a commission was in the offing, and I was doing what might be called practical research. It was a warm, sunny California winter afternoon, and I was taking a long hard walk in the Holly-wood Hills; intriguing and glossily strange territory, the craggy high ground up above the flatlands of the city, a place with ascents and descents that are steep enough to get your heart and lungs pumping, which is the whole point. From up there you get panoramic views over the city, and some-times you can see all the way to the ocean, and you regularly catch sight of the Hollywood sign. There are palm trees, cactus, bougainvillaea, and sometimes you turn a corner and are confronted by a coyote or deer crossing the street, as though they, and you, were still out in the wilds.

I walked there often but I didn't meet many fellow pedestrians. I encountered a few dog walkers, couples pushing prams, the occasional jogger, a Mexican maid who didn't have her own transport, but I rarely saw anyone who was simply walking for the hell of it, the way I was. I never saw anyone fall down.

Of course, I take full responsibility for my own actions and my own accident, but there remains something inscrutable about it. True, I was thinking about how I was going to write my book, but I wasn't so self-absorbed as to be oblivious of where I was putting my feet. And although I was in good spirits, I don't think there was any hubris involved. I certainly didn't think that nothing bad could happen to me.

I was walking along briskly, the street had a downward slope, but there was nothing treacherous about it, nothing I hadn't successfully negotiated hundreds of times before. But this time, incomprehensibly, the negotiations broke down. I lost it. I tripped, I stumbled, I began to fall.

The older you get, the bigger a deal it is to fall down. When you're a kid you can hit the deck, skin your knees, bleed, and be up playing again in five minutes. The older falling man is so much more vulnerable. He's less supple, less resilient, less accustomed to the experience. He feels far more pain and humiliation.

Even as I was falling I thought, Oh crap, I'm not really going to go all the way to the ground, am I? I'll stop myself somehow. I'll keep my footing. I'll regain my balance. And then I knew I was mistaken about that. I was going all the way. I'd passed the tipping point. Oh crap indeed.

Then there was the impact, a much greater, more generalised blow than I'd been anticipating. I was on the ground, winded, hurting all over, feeling like a fool, trying to breathe deeply and regularly, and thinking, possibly saying aloud, 'Oh man this really, really hurts, this is a bad one.'

Even so I didn't imagine I was actually going to do anything other than get up, dust myself off and carry on walking. I thought I might have torn a hole in my jeans, but that was as much damage as I was expecting. So I made all the moves you'd make in order to stand up, using my arms to push myself up off the ground, and then I realised I couldn't possibly do that; my right forearm was hurting far, far too much. And then I looked at it, and saw that it appeared soft and spongy and was bent like a boomerang made of dough. It was obviously, spectacularly broken.

Naturally, I've since tried to work out exactly what happened, and in the absolute sense I don't know, and never will. But as far as I can tell, as I started to pitch forward I stuck out my right arm to break the fall. I had a camera in my left hand, and I was trying to protect it: a big mistake. All my weight and inertia honed in on my right wrist, with what were all too predictable results.

I lay on the ground unable to get up, and considered my options. If I'd had a mobile phone with me I might have called 911, or more likely my wife, begging her to come and pick me up, but I had no phone, just a camera. I began to wonder if I could use the built-in flash as a distress signal.

I wasn't there very long before a guy getting into his car across the street saw me lying on the ground, decided I wasn't a derelict or junkie, and came to my assistance. He hoisted me up and drove me to the nearby fire station. This was the smart way of doing things, he assured me. The firemen would be able to give me some immediate first aid, then get me to a hospital where, having arrived in an emergency vehicle, I'd be able to jump the queue in the emergency room. All this proved to be true.

I was taken care of by a young fireman who had his surname stitched on to the pocket of his uniform: the name was Finger. He was grimly impressed by the look of my arm. 'Howdya do that?' he asked. 'Just walking,' I said. He shook his head. It didn't seem right to him. It seemed downright weird. Normally they only saw breaks like mine on people who'd fallen off ladders. He got me on a stretcher, put my arm in an inflatable splint, gave me enough morphine to disorientate me without quite killing the pain, and ferried me to a hospital, where everyone continued to respect the extremity of the break.

The X-rays showed there wasn't just one break but three, with huge displacement all round. I'd have to have some serious surgery, was the opinion of the X-ray guys, and I'd end up with metal pins in my arm. They were right about all this. And they too were impressed. They thought my injury was something out of the ordinary, as though I must be one wild and crazy dude to have done that to myself by whatever method. They said it looked like a skateboard injury, and this made me feel just a little better. Another dose of morphine made me feel better still.

That may be one of the reasons I can't really remember what happened next. I seem to recall I was about to set off walking home. There is a fine literary tradition of walking while experiencing opiate-induced sensory derangement – Baudelaire, De Quincy, Coleridge. But the medical advice was that I should call my wife and have her come and pick me up. I followed that advice.

*

A week later I had surgery at the Good Samaritan Hospital. As in the parable, they did have compassion on me, though they also charged me many thousands of dollars. Once I'd been operated on, splinted up, sent home, and begun to recover, I started meeting more people who asked what I'd done to myself. I sensed that they wanted to hear stories of knife fights, car wrecks, overturned jet skis, and I didn't want to disappoint them, though I didn't want to lie. I found myself saying, 'The break was spectacular, even if the cause was pedestrian.'

And there was always the big LA question, 'Are you OK to

drive?' Drive? Hell, I had problems enough walking. As a man working on a book on the subject, I knew I had a duty to try to keep pounding the streets, even with a broken arm, and walk I did. It didn't sound so hard. But walking with a broken arm is much harder than you, or certainly I, would imagine. For one thing, despite serious quantities of pain-killing opiates, the arm itself continued to hurt like hell. This was not sensory derangement, just unalleviated pain. And even if the arm didn't hurt when I set off walking, by the time I'd gone a few hundred yards the blood was circulating faster, setting off fresh twinges and spasms.

More than that, walking while nursing an injured arm, in a cast and sling, throws off your balance, distorts the geo-metry of the walking body, creating various tensions and asymmetries that in themselves created further pain. My broken arm ached and it made the rest of my body ache too. And that didn't stop even when the cast came off. I was left nursing this tender, half-formed thing, something soft and without muscle: it was like having a week-old puppy dangling at the end of my arm, although in this case the puppy actually *was* the arm.

Worse, having fallen down once, I feared that I could all too easily do it again. It seemed my walking capabilities were no longer to be trusted. I still went out walking, but with a new attention to detail. I wore ground-hugging, butt-ugly shoes, and I walked more slowly, obsessively looked where my feet were going, regarded curbs, steps and changes in gradient as obstacles set specifically to undo me. Who knew walking was such a confidence game? Who knew it was so complicated and risky?

Well, quite a few people it turned out. I suddenly dis-covered that falling down while walking wasn't such a rare event. My friends and acquaintances revealed themselves to be a poorly balanced crowd: many of them had stories about getting a foot caught in a hole in the street, or losing their footing on slippery or uneven pavements, tumbling off wet stones, having prat-falls while walking across gravel drive-ways or car parks. Sometimes, like me, they fell for no apparent reason whatsoever.

By some accounts, walking itself was a series of falls, a precarious balancing act that had the walker standing on one leg for most of the time, constantly pitching himself forward, transferring energy and weight in a reckless and dangerous manner, only avoiding disaster by getting a foot down in the nick of time.

Others said that spending your whole life on two legs was a downright odd thing to do. Plenty of mammals stand on two legs once in a while, but humans are the only ones ridiculous enough to do it all the time. The body just wasn't designed for it. All those bad backs and knees and feet and hips: we'd have had none of those things if only we'd remained on all fours. If a quadruped misses a step with one foot, there are three others right there to make up the difference. What was the big deal about walking on two feet anyway?

*

Theories of bidepalism change constantly. Once explanation for bipedalism seemed simple enough, and was demonstrated in that old familiar graphic, a line of rising, ever more human-looking creatures: an ancestral ape at the far left-hand side; some chimp-like thing walking on his knuckles in the middle; and a fully upright spear-carrying *Homo sapiens* at the far end. The image illustrates the basic idea that being able to stand and walk on two legs is one of the things that makes us human.

The text that accompanied this drawing would have told you that our ancient primate ancestors lived in trees and moved on all fours until a more sophisticated primate appeared, called *Rampithecus*, who could stand up at least part of the time and could pick up things with his hands; probably rocks to throw at his enemies. He was around from eight and a half to twelve and a half million years ago. About five million years ago *Australopithecus africanus* came on the scene, tiny brained but a proper upright walker who probably used stones or bones for specific tasks, though these didn't quite constitute 'tools'. Then, two and a half million years ago, along came '1470 man', with a bigger brain than any ape, and with the genuine ability to make and use tools. Standing on two legs really helps when you want to use tools. *Homo erectus* arrived about two million years ago, able to walk upright but also a tree climber. And then, half a million years ago, *Homo sapiens* arrived, someone like us. The move was always onward and upward: four legs good, two legs better.

This narrative went along with the 'savannah hypothesis', which suggested that our ancestors were perfectly happy living in trees, and would have remained there, but some profound ecological change occurred, leading to a cata-strophic deforestation. Swinging or leaping from one tree to another was no longer possible because the trees were too far apart, and so a new form of travel was required. At first we scrabbled on all fours, then raised ourselves a little, using our forearms and knuckles as necessary, and finally we made the breakthrough: we stood up and walked on two legs because that was the most efficient way of getting from tree A to distant tree B, and evolution favours efficiency.

Other theories suggest that walking on two legs simply uses less energy than walking on four, or that standing up-right is advantageous because it keeps the body cooler. Some attribute bipedalism to changes in social and reproductive habits. At a certain point in human development males acquired the nurturing urge. They wanted to care for their families and to provide for them. They went out foraging and brought back what they'd gathered, carrying it in their arms. Since two limbs were engaged in the carrying, they were forced to walk on the other two.

Clearly not all these theories are mutually exclusive, but everything is now being reassessed since the unveiling in 2009 of Ardi, a more or less complete, female, *Ardipithecus ramidus* fossil skeleton, found in Ethiopia in the early 1990s and painstakingly put together over fifteen years. Ardi is 4.4 million years old, by far the oldest hominid ever found, and she is a biped; not a great one, but probably a match for 1470 man. Her existence is certainly a problem for believers in the savannah theory since she lived in woodland and couldn't have developed bidepalism as a response to deforestation.

In the fuss over Ardi (and admittedly her discovery has significance way beyond new theories of bipedalism), research done by two English scientists, Robin Crompton and Susannah Thorpe, has been neglected, research that seems to upset the whole bipedal applecart even more thoroughly. In the early 2000s, Crompton and Thorpe spent a year in the rainforest of Sumatra, studying orang-utans, a species that spends its entire life in trees, and therefore, one might have thought, a species with absolutely no use for bipedalism.

But it turned out the Sumatran orang-utans are *extremely* bipedal. They may not walk on the ground, but they constantly stand on two legs and walk along to the outer edges of tree branches, using their arms for balance and for gathering food. The conclusion is that we didn't come down from the trees and gradually adapt to walking on two feet, but that bipedalism was already part of the tree dweller's repertoire. Knuckle walking therefore wasn't an intermediate stage but a later development, necessitated in chimpanzees and gorillas because they're anatomically unable to straighten their legs. If Crompton and Thorpe are correct, our ancestors didn't start walking upright five million years ago, they started doing it ten or fifteen million years earlier than that.

*

I wasn't much cheered by my research in these areas. Fifteen or twenty million years really ought to be sufficient to get the hang of it, I thought, ought to be time enough to build the skill into the race memory. It was a thing any damn fool could do without falling over. Things only got worse when I spoke to Dr Martin Bax, an English paediatrician with an international reputation, and a friend.

Martin confirmed there was nothing difficult about walking. For instance, he told me, you can see the legs of unborn babies moving in the womb, making walking motions, from about seventeen weeks. This is a good sign and proof that the baby is healthy, mobile and not tangled up in anything, but there's nothing very advanced about it: at seventeen weeks, the baby's cortex isn't fully formed, indicating that walking is a function of the spine or mid-brain.

In the 1920s and 1930s in Oxford, Martin said, a don called Sherington did experiments with decorticated cats. He removed their brains and found they were still able to walk perfectly well. Martin was also aware of some unpublished research done in the 1970s on aborted foetuses, and scientists had managed to get them walking too. In other words, walking could be, quite literally, a brainless activity, and you didn't even have to be alive to do it.

Once babies are out of the womb, Martin continued, they achieve 'primary walking' at about six weeks of age. This isn't real walking because the babies have no sense of balance and no strength in their legs, so they can't stand up, but once you support them, they can make all the motions that are needed for walking. There are some extraordinary films and photographs, by a German called Peiper, in which he gives babies this kind of support, and not only do they walk on the ground, they also walk up walls and on the ceiling.

Well, a man might be forgiven for losing his footing while walking on the ceiling, but what excuse did I have? If I couldn't even walk down the street without falling down and breaking my arm, then I had to ask what my qualifications were for writing a book about walking.

The overriding one was that I liked walking: I liked it a lot. And I didn't just like it in the abstract, I liked *doing* it, and all through my life I'd done it a lot, usually in an unorganised but nevertheless enthusiastic way, on four continents, at home and abroad, in town and country, in conditions that could be favourable or adverse.

Walking had certainly always been a pleasure, but it was more than that. For me walking has to do with exploration, a way of accommodating myself, of feeling at home. When I find myself in a new place I explore it on foot. It's the way I get to know that place. Maybe it's a way of marking territory, of beating the bounds. Setting foot in a street makes it yours in a way that driving down it never does.

Often I've walked for the simplest reasons, sometimes because I've had no choice. When I was younger and poorer, unable to afford taxis, a three-mile walk home was frequently the way I rounded off an evening out. Sometimes walking was simply the most efficient way of getting from A to B. If you live in a big city, and for large chunks of my life I've lived in London or New York, walking is often preferable to using public transport. You don't have to wait for trains and buses that may not arrive. You don't find yourself subject to delays and cancellation. You don't find yourself pressed up against some undesirable. You don't risk being stuck in a tube tunnel in the event of a power failure. When you walk you're your own boss.

On a very small number of occasions I've walked as an act of political protest, though I suspect my fellow protestors might have said they were on a 'march' rather than a walk. These events pertained to the usual sort of things – nuclear proliferation, the British poll tax, the 'gate hours' at my old college, which prevented you from having girls in your room over night. Actually the second and third of these protests might be thought to have been successful: both my college's gate hours and the poll tax were duly abandoned. The nuclear issue is evidently going to require a bit more walking.

I've also walked for charity, but that was some time ago, and even back then it struck me as a peculiar thing. If people want to give money to charity, if they want to help fund a cure for AIDS or cancer or whatever, they should go ahead and do it, but I don't understand why they have to wait for somebody to promise to walk thirty miles and then sponsor them to do it. I'm not such a misanthrope that I'd denounce the charity walk, but it seems to me it places the act of walking in a dubious and undesirable category. The implication is that walking is some eccentric and out of the ordinary activity, so rare that people would only do it for money, even if the money is going to someone else. There's also the sense that walking is a form of suffering: by walking we share the pain and sorrow of the AIDS sufferer or the cancer victim. I object to both these propositions. Walking is special but it's not strange; it may be arduous but it's not a form of suffering. It's definitely not a stunt. It's something entirely worth doing for its own sake.

*

There is, of course, an environmental argument in favour of walking. Undoubtedly there would be Green benefits if we all walked to work rather than drove there in our cars. Undoubtedly also, we'd do less harm to the environment if we spent our leisure hours walking in quiet places rather than, say, off-roading in SUVs. However, the changes needed to convert us into a nation of walkers rather than car users are so colossal that it seems to me we're not talking about promoting pedestrianism here but about attempting to change human nature itself, which strikes me as, at best, an over-ambitious project. Yes, there was a time when everybody walked: they did it because they had no choice. The moment they had a choice, many of them chose not to.

The main problem I have with the activist walking lobby is that its members like to make a hard and fast division between walkers and drivers: walkers are saints, drivers are pure evil. This doesn't match my experience of humanity. Most of us are both walkers and drivers. Sure, I find drivers annoying when I walk, but I also find pedestrians annoying when I drive. It's not clear to me that absolute complete virtue resides on either side.

More than that, even the most environmentally conscious walkers sometimes get in their cars and drive considerable distances in order to go walking. I can see the obvious contradiction in this, but I don't find it genuinely pernicious. Sometimes the neighbourhood just isn't enough. In any case, my walking isn't intended to save the planet. I walk when I can, but when I have to drive I don't feel guilty about it.

Great claims are also made for the health benefits of walking, for its capacity to make us lean and fit, but I have serious doubts about this. Clearly walking is better that nothing, and in general it does the body no harm (unless you happen to pull, sprain, twist or break something, or get run down by a car). But the number of calories burned while walking is really unimpressive. A hundred-and-eighty-pound man walking at four miles an hour burns up about a hundred calories per mile. True, a three-hundred-pound man walking at five miles per hour burns two hundred and eighteen calories per mile but I suspect there are rather few three-hundred-pound men who are capable of walking at five miles per hour even for brief periods.

The fact is, to the dismay of anyone who's ever tried to lose weight, a pound of body fat contains three thousand five hundred calories. In other words, to lose a pound of flesh, you need to walk an extra thirty-five miles. There must be easier ways of doing it. In any case, I don't walk in order to get or stay fit. If there's any such thing as a desirable 'walker's physique', I have yet to see it.

*

I've never walked professionally, though I've had jobs that required me to do a fair amount of walking: garbage man, gardener, security man, drone in a department store. Actually, in the last case the walking wasn't so much work as a way of avoiding work. I was employed by Harrods: vast, labyrinthine, many floors, many departments, like a city ripe for exploration. I discovered, as many had before me, that a man who displayed a sense of purpose and carried a piece of paper in his hand, could walk just about anywhere in the store and everybody would always assume he was going about his legitimate business.

And so at Harrods I walked relentlessly through air-conditioned departments, up and down escalators and staircases, moving just purposefully enough to avoid giving the impression that I was loafing. I circulated through the pet department, ate samples in the food hall, went to the musical-instrument department where I admired the grand pianos. I investigated book and record departments, checked out men's suits. Sometimes I lurked in the electrical department and watched TV: on the odd occasion I even found myself in the bridal department admiring empire bodices and táffeta trains.

And although I wasn't being paid to walk, I did earn money while I was doing it, in the sense that I earned the same amount of money whether I was doing anything useful or not. Since I hated the job so much, every moment that I wasn't doing what I was supposed to be doing became a victory; a modest victory to be sure, but I took my satis-factions where I could find them. When I eventually returned to my own desk after what might have been an hour-long walking expedition, it was rare for anyone in the office ever to notice I'd even been away, though one Australian colleague did accuse me (not with complete disapproval) of going walkabout, like Jenny Agutter in the movie of the same name, though without the nudity.

*

The idea of being a professional walking guide fills me with horror, but I did once lead a walking tour of Munich, a city I had absolutely no knowledge of. It was part of a literary festival about the writer and the city, and I was there because I'd written a novel in which a character sets out to walk every street in London.

It's nice to be invited to a literary festival, but of course you have to sing for your supper. As well as doing a reading and sitting on a couple of panels, the invited writers had to conduct walking tours of Munich, the city seen through fresh foreign eyes, sort of thing. Of course it's unlikely if you're only in a place for a few days that you're going to show the natives anything they haven't seen before, but that was the challenge. I accepted this challenge, but as the date of the festival approached I wished I was something other than a writer: a performance artist possibly, or at least somebody with an act that could be done in the street while walking.

I took it too seriously, as is my way. I was living in New York at the time, and I spent a lot of time fretting. I walked the streets of Manhattan thinking I needed a concept, a plan, an idea. And as I walked I looked for signs of German influence in New York. In a perfect world, I might have come across the Lederhosen district or the Munich Bar and Grill, but I was prepared to settle for much less.

Eventually I found a place selling Bavarian pretzels – Munich is capital of Bavaria – and then something clicked. There was one ubiquitous Bavarian product in New York, BMW cars: BMW stands for Bavarian Motorwerken. I spent a day walking, and taking snapshots of every BMW I saw in New York. Then I had these images printed and I took them with me to Munich.

I had time on my hands at the festival, and so I walked, explored the city. It was what I'd have done anyway, but I was still fretting, and I used these walks as 'rehearsals' for my tour. It was cold and it rained a lot of the time, so I bought a hat. It had 'Hat' written on it, imitating the Gap logo. I'd have preferred it to say the German word 'Hut', but that was OK. It gave me an idea.

On the day of reckoning at 5 p.m., twenty or so people, fans of literature and walking no doubt, gathered in the Odeonsplatz to be led by me. They were a mix of the arty young and the arty middle-aged, but there was one young man, not arty at all, who in a simpler age we'd have described simply as mad. There were also a couple of journalists and a crew from the local TV station. Some of the people definitely spoke English, others just as definitely didn't. There was no translator.

My simple idea was that I'd guide my group around

Munich, and each time we saw evidence of American influence, I would deposit next to it one of my BMW photographs. The cars had made their journey from Bavaria to New York and now, in image, they'd come home.

It didn't go badly at first. There was a Woolworths, a Macdonald's, ads for Apple computers, a graffito saying 'Fuck Tha Police' – a universal American sentiment, though the NWA song with that title comes out of Compton, a city in Los Angeles County, rather than New York. I felt especially lucky when I found a clothing store called New Yorker. As the tour went on the weather got worse, the temperature dropped, the rain lashed down and my audience dwindled. The TV crew slipped away. I didn't blame them. Before long even I was feeling I'd had enough, and I decided I'd end things with the tiniest attempt at something that might possibly be considered performance art.

I'd brought with me three snow globes of New York. I placed them on the tarmac, across the middle of an inter- mittently busy side street. The few of us who were left on the tour watched and waited for the wheels of a German car, a BMW for preference, to crush these fragile miniature plastic versions of New York. This was before 9/11 so it didn't seem quite as crass as it might now, thought I'm sure some would have thought it was crass even then.

It took a surprisingly long time for the globes to be destroyed. Quite a few cars drove along the street and managed to miss them. Another touched a globe with the very corner of its tyre and pushed it gently out of the way. Perhaps this was a metaphor for the elusive, resilient, impermeable nature of America. At one point the mad boy ran into the road and grabbed one of the globes, hoping to take it away as a souvenir. I told him off sternly. I'm fairly sure he didn't speak English, but no doubt the instruction,

'Put the snow globe back in the middle road so cars can crush it,' is the same in any language.

At last a car took out all three globes simultaneously and the stragglers remaining on my tour cheered in absolute, unhesitating delight. Partly I'm sure they were celebrating that the walk was over, and they could now get out of the rain. But more than that, I like to think they were acknowledging that destruction makes a pretty good climax to any activity, even a walking tour.

*

The word 'walking' looks and sounds like a simple, honest straightforward one. The dictionary tells us it has its origin in late Middle English, and therefore doesn't need a Greek or Latin precursor. Maybe that very simplicity is why we need so many qualifiers, so many synonyms, or not-quite-synonyms, for walking, each word with its own shade of meaning. I found it revealing to see which of these words applied to my own walking, and which didn't. Tell me how you walk and I'll tell you who you are.

For example, I've performed all the slack, idle, casual forms of walking. I've strolled and wandered, pottered and tottered, dawdled and shuffled, mooched and sauntered and meandered. I've certainly ambled, and I could be said to have rambled, though I feel the old-style Ramblers' Association (now modernised with less hearty ambitions and called simply Ramblers) would probably regard my walking efforts as trifling. And probably I've shambled, but I don't think I've ever gambolled.

I know I've hiked, since I've definitely been on paths that call themselves hiking trails, but the word 'hiking' conjures up a degree of seriousness, organisation and specialised equipment that's quite alien to me. One of the minor but profound satisfactions of being on a well-known hiking trail is to stroll along in shorts, sneakers and an Acid Mothers T-shirt and to encounter others who are dressed as though for an assault on Annapurna. By the same logic, and with similar reservations, I've also trekked.

I've trudged, tramped and slogged, and in New York I've certainly schlepped. I've marched in the metaphoric but not the military sense. Incidentally, the phrase 'Bolivian marching powder' as a euphemism for cocaine, an eighties phrase if ever I heard one, turns out to have a much earlier origin. First World War British soldiers were given cocaine-based tablets, known as 'forced-march tablets', though I'd have thought all marching is forced; the soldiers wouldn't be doing it if they hadn't been ordered to. Occasionally, I've been given my marching orders.

At the time of the Falklands War, we heard a lot about British soldiers 'yomping' to Port Stanley. It's risky for a civilian to offer an opinion on army slang, but as far as I can tell yomping involves crossing rough terrain carrying a full pack, and is similar to, but significantly different from, 'tabbing'. Marines yomp, paratroopers 'tab' – which according to some sources stands for 'tactical advance to battle'. Tabbing is about speed; yomping is about distance. Unless you've been a British soldier it would be unwise to claim to have done either.

A couple of times when injured I've limped and hobbled. I've waded, which is walking in, though not on, water. I've occasionally, metaphorically, walked on air, and I've probably, again not literally, walked a tightrope. I have never walked, Byronically, in beauty like the night.

I have certainly, in the ordinary sense of the word, drifted. However, that's a word containing various specialised senses too, chiefly coming from psychogeographers, the French Situationists and their followers, who speak of the *dérive*, a word which translates as drift, both as noun and verb. I have never called myself a psychogeographer, except ironically, though sometimes I think I might be a *flâneur*, literally a 'stroller' in French, though a term loaded down with all kinds of baggage, such as this from Baudelaire:

And so, walking or quickening his pace, he goes his way, forever in search. In search of what? We may rest assured that this man, such as I have described him, this solitary mortal endowed with an active imagination, always roaming the great desert of men, has a nobler aim than that of the pure idler, a more general aim, other than the fleeting pleasure of circumstance. He is looking for that indefinable something we may be allowed to call 'modernity'.

Well, that's me only up to a point.

Edmund White wrote a book about Paris called *The Flâneur* in which he describes *flâneur*ism as akin to sexual cruising. I don't think I've ever cruised. I've certainly walked down the street thinking about sex, looking at women and occasionally giving them the eye, very occasionally being eyed back, but I don't think this is the same as cruising. I'm not sure that cruising is a thing a heterosexual man can do. White tells us that whereas in English the word cruise in this sense is an exclusively gay term, the equivalent French word *drageur* is also heterosexual. 'Straight people cruise one another in Paris,' he tells us, 'unlike Americans, who feel menaced or insulted by looks on the street.' Ah those poor, sensitive Americans.

There is, undoubtedly, a sexual component to walking. Actually having real sex while walking, that's just about impossible, but some people are very sexy when they walk, and a great many more people think about sex as they walk. In the days when I had a real job, I'd live for the lunch hour when I could get out and walk the streets and look at all the women who were also walking the streets in their lunch hour. We're talking about the male gaze here, a dangerously ubiquitous phenomenon apparently, and one immortalised in the Frank Loesser song 'Standing On The Corner Watching All The Girls Go By' and its lines, 'Brother you can't go to jail for what you're thinking/Or for that *woo* look in your eye.' Some would probably have it otherwise; and yes, walking is a very different prospect for men than for women.

I'm always fascinated by the female models in fashion shows, the ones who parade up and down on the runways and catwalks. They're sexy all right, and it's got a lot to do with the way they walk, but it's a very specialised form of walking. They strut and stomp, they stride out, hammer their feet down, scissor their legs across each other and look as though they're really determined to get somewhere, but of course they never really do get anywhere. They just get to the end of the runway and then they spin around on their stiletto heels and head back precisely where they've come from. This one just counts as walking. And 'runway' is such a strange term, because it sounds like they're at the airport, taxiing, getting ready to fly. But these fashion models never lift off. They don't even run on the runway.

'Streetwalker' is another term that doesn't quite describe the sexuality or the style of walking to which it refers. Yes, streetwalkers operate in the street, and yes they're on their feet, but how much walking do they actually do? Street-walkers have always been the lowest of prostitutes. *The Oxford English Dictionary* dates the word to 1592, but even if the word was newfangled at the time, the practice surely was not. The streetwalker is, and always has been, the most vulnerable of sex professionals. The sight of a woman walking at night, whether she's selling herself or not, is enough to stir uncontrollable urges in some men. It has required some women to take back the night.

And yet, here and now in the West, women walkers are surely safer than they've ever been. That may not be saying a whole lot, but here's the Spanish feminist Margarita Nelken, claiming that walking was the one thing that separated her, a twentieth-century woman, from her mother and grandmother. 'This footing,' she writes, 'this morning walk – elastic step, rhythmic body in loose, comfortable clothing – of the girls that walk for hygiene in these clear and warm days of early spring . . . they have opened the windows of the sad room in which their grandmothers sat.' She wrote that in 1923 in a magazine called *La Moda Elegante*.

There are, I think, certain ways in which sex and walking closely resemble each other. For one thing, they're both at root basic, simple, repetitive activities that just about everybody does at one time or another. And yet, despite being so ordinary and commonplace, they're both capable of great sophistication and elaboration. They can both be completely banal and meaningless, and yet they can also involve great passions and adventures. They can both lead you into strange and previously unknown territories: tempt you to take a walk on the wild side.

So, if I have never cruised, catwalked nor streetwalked, I'm also pretty sure that I've never trolled or minced. And I hope I've never flounced, as in 'flounced out of the room'. 'Stormed' I think is the preferred manly word here. Sometimes, less forcefully, I may have sloped off or stolen away. I have hit the streets, pounded the pavements, worn out shoe leather, taken Shanks's pony, hot-footed it, legged it, strode out, loped, paced. So far I have never waddled, but as the years pass and the pounds pack on it may be a fate awaiting me.

It may well be that I have promenaded, pedestrianised, peregrinated, ambulated, perambulated, circumambulated, hoofed and locomoted, but these aren't words I'd ever use. And I've never told anyone, as apparently they do, or at least did, in Cockney rhyming slang, to 'go for a ball of chalk', although I've probably done it, that is obeyed what is essentially an injunction to 'get lost'.

I may have strutted, but I'm pretty sure I've never swaggered. In a notorious speech he made at the Republican National Convention in 2004, George W. Bush said, to the delight of the supportive crowd, and the consternation of others, 'Some folks look at me and see a certain swagger. In Texas we call it walkin'.'

I've heard people say they see something light and feline in the way Barak Obama walks, something that reveals his African ancestry. I can just about force myself to see this, but not without some wishful thinking. More usually, and of course I've never seen him walk 'naturally', which is to say when the cameras and the public gaze aren't on him, I get the sense that he's a man walking very carefully, a man who doesn't want to slip up, a man who definitely doesn't want to fall down.

There was a period in Tony Blair's career, when his resignation was certain but the date less so, that he was regularly referred to as a 'dead man walking'. Simultaneously Blair was insisting that he wouldn't just 'walk away' from Iraq. When Gordon Brown came to power it wasn't long before the jackals were out for him too, and he said in a *Guardian* interview, 'To be honest, you could walk away from all of this tomorrow.' He was perhaps remembering Johnny Paychecks's song 'Take This Job And Shove It', with its lines 'You better not try to stand in my way/As I'm walking out the door.'

*

Some of my walking qualifications are literary. A lot of walkers have a strong bookish streak, just like me, and a lot of writers also turn out to be great walkers. Edgar Allan Poe was an 'aqueduct walker', William Wordsworth paced up and down his garden path while composing poetry and, according to Coleridge, walked a hundred and eighty thousand miles in his lifetime. Charles Dickens used to suggest to his dinner guests that they have a walk before eating, and then he'd drag them around the countryside for several hours. This kind of enthusiasm for walking inevitably shows up in writers' work.

If you're a walking enthusiast, and certainly if you're writing a book on the subject, you're alert to the slightest literary mention of walking, and some of these occur in surprising places. In *Gravity's Rainbow*, for instance, you'll read that Oberst Enzian, leader of Pynchon's invented Schwarz-commandos, 'had been walking only a few months when his mother took him to join Samuel Maherero's great trek across the Kalahari', a statement that may well send you dashing off to learn more about Maherero and his trek. *Hamlet* will suddenly seem to be awash in walking references: 'I am thy father's spirit, Doom'd for a certain term to walk the night'; 'Let her [Ophelia] not walk i' th' sun. Conception is a blessing, but not as your daughter may conceive'; 'Sir, I will walk here in the hall' – meaning that Hamlet is ready for a duel and a bloodbath. Even Samuel Beckett, supposedly the great poet of stasis, seems to have things to say about walking. Here, in *Lessness*, 'One step in the ruins in the sand on his back in the endlessness he will make it.'

Perhaps this is not really surprising. Most fictional characters do some walking at one time or another, because that's how it is in life, and much of the walking will be incidental. But in certain works of literature the walking is far from incidental. In *Ulysses* and *Swann's Way*, in Robert

Walser's *The Walk*, in Wordsworth's 'An Evening Walk', in T. S. Eliot's 'Rhapsody on a Windy Night', in Flannery O'Connor's 'The Artificial Nigger' and in Jim Harrison's 'Westward Ho' walking is, in academic parlance, fore-grounded. It isn't something the characters just happen to do, it's one of the subjects of the work itself.

And then there's all the non-fictional literary walking. Here I must confess that though I read plenty of memoirs and travel books that centre around walking they always leave me feeling disappointed in myself, in my own all too humble walking. There's Eric Newby, in *A Short Walk in the Hindu Kush*, walking in areas of Afghanistan where no Englishman has set foot for over half a century. There's Bruce Chatwin devising new theories of nomadism in *The Songlines*. There's Sebastian Snow in *The Rucksack Man*, describing his magnificent (but admittedly unsuccessful) attempt to walk from Patagonia to Alaska. These are fine writers and fine books, but they in-evitably make an ordinary walker feel very inadequate indeed.

Of course the one non-fiction author who absolutely has to be dealt with is Thoreau, the author of 'Walking', originally delivered as a lecture in 1851, and published posthumously as an essay in 1862. I came to this text late, perhaps too late, and one surprising thing is how little Thoreau actually has to say about walking. Chiefly he's banging on about nature, wildness, noble savagery and the 'western impulse', with the occasional digression into squirrels, pigeons and the sweet smell of elands.

In fact, he insists he isn't a walker but a saunterer, a word derived from *sainte-terre* or holy land, so that a saunterer is literally a religious pilgrim. The word was also a term of abuse, precisely for those who *didn't* walk to the Holy Land, but he's happy to embrace the term. He considers himself to be a rare bird, 'I have met with but one or two persons in the course of my life who understood the art of Walking' (Thoreau is a great capitaliser). This, of course, is annoying. It's pretty certain that he wouldn't regard you or me as having that understanding.

Other annoyances come thick and fast. He says that walkers are born, not made; that it 'requires a direct dispensation from heaven to become a walker'. Worse than that, he reckons that *his* walking has a chivalric and heroic spirit: he considers himself a Walker Errant, as opposed to a knight errant. When he tells us that he can't preserve his health and spirits unless he spends four hours a day walking, you might well resent the economic 'dispensation' that allowed him so much leisure, and it gets worse when he delivers some condescending sympathy to 'the mechanics and shopkeepers' who have to keep business hours and therefore can't saunter for four hours. 'I think they deserve some credit for not having all committed suicide long ago,' he writes. I think they also deserve some credit for not seeking out this popinjay and giving him a good thrashing. Robert Louis Stevenson, a man who knew a thing or two about walking, would probably have been happy to assist. He saw 'something un- manly, something almost dastardly', in Thoreau. 'In one word,' he writes, 'Thoreau was a skulker.'

Most readers don't go to Thoreau looking for laughs but there's an entry in his journals that comes close to broad comedy. Writing on 19 March 1856, he tells the story of 'What Befell at Mrs Brooks's', describing events from two days earlier. Mrs Brooks's Irish maid fell down the cellar steps and lay there 'apparently lifeless'. Mrs Brooks ran to the door, saw a passing neighbour, Mrs Farmer, and asked her to go to the blacksmith for help. Mrs Farmer turned on her heel and began walking briskly, too briskly, across the road. She fell down in a puddle of melted snow and came back to the

Brookses' house bruised and wet and asking for 'opodeldoc'. Mrs Brooks went to the door again and called to another neighbour, George Bigelow, and asked him to perform the same errand. He too fell down in the wet snow, but did at least manage to get to his feet and go to the blacksmith. He also summoned another neighbour, James Burke, who went into the Brookses' house and promptly fell down the cellar steps, joining the Irish maid at the bottom. Falling down is always a hoot when it happens to somebody else.

*

Modern literary theory sees a similarity between walking and writing: a walk inscribes space in the same way that words inscribe a text. Michel De Certeau's *Practice of Everyday Life* contains a chapter, 'Walking in the City', in which he writes: 'The act of walking . . . is a process of appropriation of the topographical system on the part of the pedestrian; it is a special acting-out of the place . . . and it implies relations among differentiated positions.' I think this is a fancy way of saying that walking is one way of making the world our own, and that writing is another, a proposition that strikes me as unarguably true. Falling while walking, however, is a great way of discovering that the world is not our own after all. I found myself asking the question: If so many writers are concerned with walking, how many of them are concerned with falling down? Simple answer, as the passage from Thoreau suggests, is more than you might expect.

*

As I sat in Los Angeles, rereading the literature, nursing my broken arm and doing rather little walking, I became aware of one local literary precedent. In the 1950s, Aldous Huxley, author, explorer of inner space, knocker at the Doors of Perception, had lived in the Hollywood Hills, not far from where I did. The Hills reminded him of Greece.

Huxley, who apparently didn't walk until he was two years old, was the man who told us, 'My father considered a walk among the mountains the equivalent of churchgoing.' He went on to write a poem called 'The Walk' that some at the time considered on a par with 'The Wasteland'. Huxley was a walker, writer and thinker in a particular English literary tradition. David King Dunaway's *Huxley in Hollywood* describes a typical day in which Huxley got up, wrote six to ten pages, ate lunch prepared by his maid, then at 1.30 he'd go on a long walk through the Hollywood Hills, getting back in time for tea. He often walked with other people – his wife arranged a series of entertaining but inconsequential mistresses for him – but sometimes he walked alone, and on one occasion, an evening in 1959, had a nasty fall. The Hollywood Hills were considerably less built up then than now and Huxley was walking along a wild canyon path when he stepped off the edge and fell among scrub and cacti. He didn't break anything and he was well aware of how much worse the fall might have been. 'This was so trifling in comparison to what I might have suffered if I hadn't fallen in the most perfect way imaginable.'

I can't swear this fall was a source of literary inspiration. Huxley, who had long had problems with his eyesight, had already described characters who fell down. There's quite a bit of it in *Brave New World* (1932), ' "I fainted after a time," said the young man. "Fell down on my face. Do you see the mark where I cut myself?" He lifted the thick yellow hair from his forehead. The scar showed, pale and puckered, on his right temple.' A character also takes a nasty fall in *Chrome Yellow* (1921) – twisted ankle – but in *Island*, published in 1962, after Huxley's Hollywood tumble, a new kind of fall occurs: a character falls over having nearly stepped on a snake.

*

I found another precedent, though one less local, in Thomas Jefferson, a mad keen walker by all accounts, but also an unfortunate one. In Paris, in 1785, he too fell over while walking and broke his right wrist. There are various accounts of the circumstances, one that he fell while jumping over a fence, in the company of an unnamed friend, though sometimes the unnamed friend is an unnamed married woman and the fence becomes a kettle. Another version has the broken wrist caused by a fall from a horse, which definitely spoils the walking connection. What seems certain is that Jefferson didn't get very good treatment from the doctors of Paris. His arm was completely out of action for several weeks and gave him trouble for the rest of his life. Much later, in 1821, just a few years before his death, he fell again, on a broken step while descending a staircase, and this time he broke the left arm.

And then there is Jean-Jacques Rousseau, he of *The Reveries of the Solitary Walker*. In the second walk described, he's on the road 'down from Menilmontant almost opposite the Galant Jardinière', having spent an afternoon in 'peaceful meditations', when he sees a Great Dane barrelling towards him, running ahead of a carriage, which apparently was the style in those days. Rousseau decides that in order to avoid being knocked down he'll make a 'great leap . . . so well timed that the dog would pass under me while I was still in the air'. History doesn't tell us how big the Great Dane was, but it couldn't have been small if Rousseau thought it was going to knock him down, so say it was three feet tall; I don't know how much of an athlete Rousseau was, but if he was really thinking about jumping three feet straight up in the air from a standing start he must have had a high regard for his own prowess. While he's doing his calculations about when and how to jump, the dog hits him and knocks him over. 'I did not feel the blow, nor the fall, nor anything of what followed until the moment I came to,' he writes.

He was so stunned that he suffered from momentary amnesia, didn't know where he was and couldn't even give his address to the people who helped him up. But eventually he remembered. Someone advised him to get a cab home, but he didn't, he *walked*, 'easily and sprightly, feeling neither pain nor hurt, though I kept spitting out a lot of blood'. And eventually he got home. 'My wife's cries on seeing me made me understand I was worse off than I thought.' I know how that can happen. Fortunately Rousseau wasn't as badly off as *some* people thought. The *Courier d'Avignon* of 20 December 1776 mistakenly reported that he was dead. 'M. Jean-Jacques Rousseau has died from the after-effects of his fall. He lived in poverty; he died in misery; and the strangeness of his fate accompanied him all the way to the tomb.'

Dying while out walking: it doesn't get much stranger than that. It's certainly much stranger and more epic than breaking an arm. And in some ways I found myself wishing that my own injuries had been stranger, or at least more dramatic. Nobody is impressed by or even very sympathetic towards a broken arm. Nobody, and I include myself in that category, understands how it might send you into a tailspin of melancholy. As I recuperated physically, I found myself becoming increasingly, and it seemed to me unjustifiably, depressed. The intensity of the feelings seemed out of all proportion to the injury. OK so I'd broken my arm, OK so I couldn't walk as much as I wanted to, in fact I was walking less and less, but why would that plunge me into the kind of despair I was feeling?

And then I found Oliver Sachs's book *A Leg to Stand On*, in which he describes how he broke his leg while walking, and the long, surprisingly traumatic process of his recovery.

The story of his break offered all the surface drama and stature that my own lacked. He did it while walking on a mountain in Norway, and he fell while being chased by a bull. The injury was serious. He was alone on the mountain and it took him six hours to drag himself to anything like safety. He might have died.

The injury was complicated, the convalescence infinitely more painful than mine. His triggered a personal and professional crisis, and although my own injury wasn't doing that yet, I feared that it might, and I saw all too clearly how an injury that the world regarded as trivial could completely change your view of the world and yourself.

Sachs's own case was complicated because he was a doctor who suddenly became a patient, a change of role and status that I imagine all members of the medical profession would find threatening. But he also experienced an anguish far more general, and from where I was now standing (or slumping) far more recognisable, than that. He writes, 'Almost every patient who had had injury or surgery to a limb, and whose limb had been casted, out of sight, out of action, had experienced at least some degree of alienation: I heard of hands and feet which felt "queer", "wrong", "strange", "unreal", "uncanny", "detached", and "cut off".' Yes, that seemed to be describing my own condition, but I'd have said it was more than that. I didn't just feel detached from my injured arm: I felt detached from the whole world.

As I sat around the house, nursing my broken arm, and doing no walking, I became increasingly dispirited, and although there were some reasons for that, those reasons didn't seem great or serious enough to justify the scale of my feelings. I felt feeble, vulnerable, becalmed. I was spending my time reading books about walking, but I thought I might never walk out of the house again. I considered myself a good and enthusiastic walker, a fully qualified pedestrian. I loved walking: it was source of pleasure, wonder and enlightenment. I was writing a book about walking, yet a walk to the end of the street seemed as impossible as a journey of a thousand miles. I told myself I wasn't doing any walking because I was so depressed and enervated. And then I thought of something. Perhaps I was depressed and enervated precisely because I wasn't doing any walking.

I should have realised it sooner. There was something all too familiar about this. It was something I'd worked out some time ago, then managed to forget. The truth is, the real reason I walk is because I have to. I walk because it keeps me sane. I had proved this to myself a couple of years back when I first arrived in Los Angeles. That was a story in itself.

2

Nicholson's London, Your London, Anybody's London

> When I grew up it seemed to me that the one advantage of living in London was that nobody ever wanted me to come out for a walk. London's very drawbacks – its endless noise and hustle, its smoky air, the squalor ambushed everywhere in it – assured this one immunity.　　　Max Beerbohm

Sometimes I try to imagine a map of the world that shows every walking step I'd ever taken. It would be a curious document. In many locations there'd be a single meandering line: an afternoon's walking in the food markets of Singapore, a meander around some dodgy area of Düsseldorf when I had a couple of hours to kill, the day I decided, for no particular reason, to go and see what Barnsley was all about. There'd be indications of more serious walking in Morocco and Australia, although given the size of those countries my line of footsteps would look minute indeed.

I've never been on a 'walking holiday' (the idea sounds absurd) but I've been on holiday often enough and done plenty of walking on those occasions: in France, in Malta, in Greece. And I've made business trips to Hamburg, Toronto, Paris, and always made sure I had time to walk around these places, simply because that's what I like to do.

For most of the last decade I've lived in the United States, half in New York, half in Los Angeles – and I've done plenty of walking in those cities. I've also done a certain amount of walking in the great American outdoors, parts of it quite often and intensively, especially in the Mojave Desert.

But inevitably the vast majority of my walking has been done in Britain. That's where the densest routes would appear on that imaginary map, clustered around Sheffield where I grew up, in Cambridge where I lived for four years and was a non-bike rider, and in other places where I've lived or stayed for greater of lesser amounts of time: Colchester, Halifax, Yoxford in Suffolk.

Much of this walking was done as part of my daily routine – I didn't really consider it a separate activity – but there was deliberate recreational walking too, in the Peak District, the Yorkshire moors, the Scottish Highlands. And there was lots of regular seaside walking too: Blackpool, Skegness, Bridlington, when I was a kid; Brighton, Southend, and long stretches of the Suffolk coast as an adult.

Even so, despite this far flung, maybe even promiscuous British walking, I've walked far farther and more often in London than anywhere else. In part that's not a huge surprise – it's the place in which I lived longest – but that's not the whole explanation. London is a city that needs, that demands, to be explored on foot. It's also the city where I decided to be, or perhaps more accurately, discover that I was a serious walker.

There was an odd period of my life when I was new to London and I lived in a shared basement flat just off Tottenham Court Road. I used to spend Sunday afternoons exploring the immediate neighbourhoods: Bloomsbury, Fiztrovia, Soho and Oxford Street. These were unknown areas to me, but then so was most of London. It was on one of these jaunts that I discovered I was walking in the footsteps of Thomas De Quincey.

One wet Sunday afternoon in the autumn of 1804 Thomas De Quincey, aged nineteen, and later to become the author of *Confessions of an English Opium Eater*, was walking along

London's Oxford Street and finding it every bit as bleak and depressing then as many still do till this day. In order to cheer himself up he went into a druggist's shop ('The druggist, unconscious minister of celestial pleasure') and bought himself a tincture of opium. That brightened up his day no end. It was the beginning of De Quincey's love affair with opium and a continuing part of his love affair with walking the streets of London. Later he would write:

> And sometimes in my attempts to steer homewards . . . I came suddenly upon such knotty problems of alleys, such enigmatic entries, and such sphinx's riddles of streets without thoroughfares, as must, I conceive, baffle the audacity of porters, and confound the intellects of hackney-coachmen. I could almost have believed, at times, that I must be the first discoverer of some of these *terrae incognitae*, and doubted whether they had yet been laid down in the modern charts of London.

Of course, opium is generally not a big help when it comes to finding your way home, but in any case he may be speaking metaphorically here. It seems impossible that he was the very first person ever to have set foot in any given location, although it remains perfectly possible that he was walking in a place for which a map hadn't yet been drawn.

De Quincey's fantasy of an unknown London is an attractive one, since London is, in every sense I can think of, exceptionally well-trodden territory: a place of walkers, with a two-thousand-year history of pedestrianism. I've trodden it as widely and as well as I know how, but like every London walker, I realise that I'm always walking in somebody else's footsteps. No part of London is genuinely unknown. However obscure or hidden the place and its history, somebody has already discovered it, walked it, staked a claim to it. Your own exploration therefore has to be personalised; you're doing it for yourself, increasing your own store of particular knowledge, walking your own eccentric version of the city.

The first London walkers had to be the Romans, since before them there was no London (or Londinium, as they called it), just expanses of marsh and swamp, thinly inhabited by surly, saturnine Iron Age Brits. Maybe the Brits walked, but they didn't walk in anything called London. When the Romans invaded Britain for the first time in 43 AD, they probably used a pontoon bridge to cross what was to become known as the River Thames; a few years later they built the first permanent bridge across it, thought to have been just east of the present-day London Bridge. People could then walk from one side of the river to the other, if they chose, though then, as now, quite a few probably chose not to. North and South London continue to be inhabited by very different and sometimes warring tribes.

The Romans weren't meanderers. Their walking was straight to the point. Who can walk along a long straight road without thinking of the Romans. You don't need a highly developed sense of history to enjoy knowing that you're taking the same route that some legionary or proconsul walked very nearly two thousand years ago.

Inevitably the growth of London, the change, the decay, plus a certain amount of bombing and urban redevelopment, has tended to obscure the Roman origins of the city, but even in central areas it's not so hard to walk along what was once a Roman road. De Quincey's Oxford Street, now to many minds a crass, soulless, over-commercialised shopping Mecca, was once part of a Roman route connecting Hampshire to Suffolk.

At this very moment somebody is out there, walking their own version of Roman London, trying to make a connection with some real or imagined concept of imperial Rome. I say this without much fear of contradiction, because I know that London's streets contain walkers of every possible description, all of them pursuing separate destinies, pacing out routes of personal need, desire and obsession. At least one of them must think of himself or herself as a Roman London walker.

The mayor's office tells us that seven million walking journeys are made in London every day, and although the majority of these will no doubt be short and mundane (and I do wonder what percentage involve going to or from the pub), that still leaves plenty of more programmatic walking expeditions. At the most modest level, these walks will be done by tourists. Showing the city to visitors is good business, and doing it on foot is a great way to reduce overheads. You see them in progress all over London, walking tours being conducted by rather theatrical guides, who look like would-be or failed or maybe just unemployed actors; gaggles of lost-looking walkers being shown Dickens's London, Sherlock Holmes's London, Jack the Ripper's London or the Beatles' London. Some more serious itineraries have you tracing routes of plague, fire, riot, ethnicity, workers' struggles, terrorism and so on.

In the interests of research – thinking I wasn't going to enjoy it very much – I went on one of these walking tours. Called 'The Blitz: London at War', it happens every Thursday afternoon at 2.15, rain or shine, starting outside exit 2 of St Paul's tube station. The guide, a skinny, intense, blonde woman with one of the most determined strides I've ever seen – rushed, urgent, leaning forward into some fierce wind of her own imagining – led me and twenty or so others on a tight circuit that had St Paul's Cathedral at its centre. We looked at the shrapnel marks preserved in the cathedral's masonry, visited a bombed-out church that's been left in a semi-ruined state as a memorial garden, saw a monument to the Blitz firemen, and as we walked we spotted various incidental pleasures, the preserved ruins of the Roman Temple of Mithras, for instance, and an ice-cream seller without a street-trading licence being collared by the law.

'I haven't got my licence with me,' the ice-cream seller whined.

'Now that does surprise me,' said the arresting copper.

Inevitably, there wasn't much Blitz to see, as such, and so we had to rely on our guide, her anecdotes, and some photographs she had with her in an album. Her anecdotes weren't bad at all. One was about two old ladies who were walking down a London street in the middle of an air raid. This wasn't so unusual; a lot of people simply didn't bother to head for the shelters. As they walked, a bomb landed near the old ladies, not too close or they'd have been killed instantly, but near enough for them to catch the tail end of the blast, which left their bodies unscathed but blew off all their clothes and left them standing in the street, alive, well and completely naked. We also heard the story of a young soldier whose job it was to deal with an unexploded bomb that had landed close to St Paul's Cathedral and vanished into the earth. Dealing with it involved digging down, finding the bomb, then defusing it. Of course the very act of digging might be enough to make the bomb go off, but the young soldier was evidently a gentle shoveller and he successfully uncovered the bomb, at which point he saw that it was booby trapped. Trying to dismantle the fuse was the very thing that would detonate it. The British army boffins were familiar with the type but hadn't yet worked out a method of disarming it. A controlled explosion on site was recommended, but that would have brought down half the cathedral. So a crane was brought, the bomb was pain-

stakingly winched out of its hole, put on the back of a truck
and covered with sandbags. It was then very carefully driven
the six miles from central London to the Hackney Marshes,
where it could be safely blown up; this meant they had to
take it along a main road, evacuating houses and clearing
pedestrians as they went.

I suddenly felt a lump in my throat at this story of unimaginable courage set against the familiar backdrop of a
grubby, everyday city. I suppose courage is to be found everywhere, and especially in cities under attack. Courage seems
to be unattached to ideology, though naturally we want it to
belong to the one we support. To be walking in a London
street where men had taken such terrible risks was both
chilling and infinitely moving. I thought I was going to blub.

Thank God I managed to hold it in. Being reduced to
tears on a walking tour would really not have shown the Blitz
spirit at all. We walked on, not very far and not very fast. It
gradually became obvious, and it was not exactly a surprise,
that two hours of standing around listening to stories, interspersed with rather short walks of no more than a couple
of hundred yards each, was actually very hard work, much
harder than walking continuously for two hours. As the tour
ended, twenty people were rubbing their backs, complaining
about their feet and saying they needed to sit down. I checked
my GPS: in those two hours we'd walked just under a mile.

*

In the end no serious London walker allows himself to be
guided around the city by anything other than his own
instincts and internal compass. The real enterprise is to make
the city 'yours' as opposed to Dickens's or Sherlock Holmes's
or the Beatles'. This is perhaps what that fine London walker
William Blake (or at least his hero, Los) meant when he said,
'I must Create a System, or be enslaved by another Man's.'

To devise your own system of walking in London isn't easy, it requires resolve and maybe even perversity. The true London walkers avoid the obvious even if that means pursuing some grand, illogical, Quixotic, agenda. They walk in search of lines of force, unrecognised symbols, secret bunkers, evidence of conspiracy, seeking the Land of Cockayne or a new Jerusalem. Personally I blame the author Iain Sinclair for a lot of this.

Iain Sinclair, is a poet, novelist, memoirist, occasional filmmaker and publisher, formerly a book dealer and municipal gardener, who dwelled in pretty thorough obscurity until 1985 or so when Peter Ackroyd wrote the novel *Hawksmoor*, a trans-historical detective novel, with a plot that involves the discovery of human sacrifices in the crypts of certain seventeenth-century London churches built by an architect not entirely unlike the historical Nicholas Hawksmoor, although in the novel he's called Nicholas Dyer, and Hawksmoor is the name of a present-day detective.

Ackroyd fessed up – he'd have been a fool not to – that the novel had been partly inspired by Iain Sinclair's *Lud Heat*, a prose poem that invokes, among other things, pilgrim routes, the American avant-garde filmmaker Stan Brakhage, and municipal gardening.

Ackroyd's book was a commercial success and although that still didn't convince throngs of people to start reading Sinclair's work, he did become a contender, a grey eminence, a distant, brooding literary figure, and a sort of guru for London's hipper, more sociologically aware literary walkers. His own commercial success came chiefly from writing non-fiction accounts of walks in and around London, especially his home territory of Hackney, and although the thick, dense allusive prose of these accounts isn't easy reading, it's a whole lot easier than the thick, dense, allusive prose of his poetry and fiction. My favourite of his books, everybody's favourite, and the most accessible, *Lights Out for the Territory* is subtitled '9 Excursions in the Secret History of London'.

Sinclair's project, pretty thoroughly realised, was to connect his personal experiences of walking in the more feral parts of the city (in general the parts where the tour guides don't take you, although Sinclair is a Jack the Ripper maven) with various overlapping historical traditions; the literary, the bohemian, the criminal, the mystical, the alchemical; not so much the sexual. He brings together the worlds of various Londoners, some living, many dead, many of them walkers, some permanent residents, some who just passed through: Daniel Defoe, William Blake, the Kray Twins, Derek Raymond, William Burroughs, Alan Moore, Rachel Whiteread, to name very few. He's also spectacularly good at revealing and connecting historical characters you wished you knew more about: 'Thomas Canry Caulker, son of Canrah Bah Caulker, King of Bompey in West Africa; William Hone, bookseller, prosecuted for blasphemy ... Samuel Sharpe, banker and Egyptologist ... John Swan, originator of the steamship's screw propeller and the self-acting chain messenger.' The text has frequent exciting references to 'secret mythologies', 'psychic landscapes' and 'mystical geographies'.

All this makes Sinclair a psychogeographer, though these days who isn't? For millennia people found it perfectly easy to walk, and to think and write about walking, without having the sense that they were doing anything remotely 'psychogeographical'; indeed the word wasn't invented until the 1950s. But increasingly it seems, and we're certainly told, that walking and psychogeography are inextricably linked.

Psychogeography is described rather elegantly by the author Merlin Coverley as 'what happens when psychology meets geography'. It's essentially a French invention, the brainchild of Guy Debord (1931–94), a Lettrist, then a Situationist, and author of *The Society of the Spectacle*. He defined psycho-geography, in 1955, in a paper called 'Introduction to a Critique of Urban Geography', as 'the study of the precise laws and specific effects of the geographical environment, consciously organised or not, on the emotions and behaviour of individuals'. This is fine as far as it goes, but it doesn't go very far, and Debord himself didn't go much further.

For me, the most obvious problem with Debord's definition is that it's hard to see that there are any 'laws' whatsoever about the way we experience environments as we walk. Rather there's a cluster of imprecise and frequently conflicting personal impressions and preferences. You might think there's a general consensus that walking in the Tivoli Gardens is preferable to wandering along a street filled with dangerous crack heads, but it wouldn't be hard to find some 'urban explorer' who took the opposite view. You and I walk down the street together and come to the opening of a dark alleyway: I think it's intriguing, you think it's scary. Some people think that Disneyland's Main Street, USA is a walk-way of charm and winsome nostalgia: others don't.

These different reactions obviously say something about individual psychologies, preferences and previous experiences in dark alleyways or on main streets, but surely nobody is experiencing the effect of anything as hard and fast as a 'law'. In which case, psychogeography seems to be concerned with a minor statute like the prohibition of jay-walking rather a universal law like gravity.

Walking was, and remains, psychogeography's main mode of operation: specifically, in French, the *dérive*, in English, the 'drift', which Debord defined as 'locomotion without a goal', abandoning your usual walking habits and letting the environment draw you in, letting your feet take you where they will, and where the city dictates. By drifting, he believes, we detect the 'ambiance' of different parts of the city, their special feeling and psychic atmospheres. If we let ourselves drift we are drawn by 'unities of ambiance', although he accepts that these ambiances may not be unified at all, and may change abruptly from one street to the next. All this strikes me as perfectly, unarguably true, but also patently obvious to anyone who's walked though any city. It doesn't seem like something you need to build a theory out of: it really isn't all that *clever*.

Where Debord becomes insufferable is in his insistence that the drift should be a group activity. Yes, he says, you could drift by yourself, but 'all the indications are that the most fruitful numerical arrangement consists of several small groups of two or three people who have reached the same awakening of consciousness, since the cross-checking of these groups' impressions makes it possible to arrive at objective conclusions.' This is obviously twaddle. If they've all reached the same level of consciousness then what kind of cross-checking can possibly go on, let alone objectivity? But the real objection is to that very term 'awakening of consciousness'. It sounds, at best, doctrinaire, at worst positively Stalinist, with a broad hint of the clique and the school playground. 'You can't come walking with us because you haven't reached the required level of awakened consciousness.'

But perhaps I'm taking Debord too seriously. Other members of the Situationist International referred to him as the 'Bore', although coming from any member of the Situationist International this is a bit rich. Then again, the group remained small, because of Debord's practice, as David Bellos puts it, of 'excommunicating members one by one, until he was in fact the only one left'.

In its current form, psychogeography often seems to be a

way for clever young men to mooch around cities doing nothing much, claiming that they're *flâneurs* who are doing something really, you know, significant, and often taking Iain Sinclair as their role model. He has any number of fellow travellers, including Stuart Home, founder of the London Psychogeographic Association (a name that I hope is ironic, but with Home it's hard to be sure), Nick Papadimitriou, who calls himself a 'deep topologist', and Will Self, who seems to have created a rod for his own back by having a series of newspaper columns in the *Independent*, collected in the books *Psychogeography* and *Psycho Too*.

Of course, Iain Sinclair is not to be blamed for any of this. It's not his fault. And to be fair to him, he seems thoroughly amused by the craze he's started. He refers to psychogeography as a franchise, which seems to get it about right; it neatly turns the psychogeographer into the Mac-*Flâneur*.

For anyone to compete with Sinclair on his own terms would be folly. He knows more than you do. He has read more widely, more deeply, more obscurely than you. He's also walked more, walked farther, more often, more observantly, more obsessively. And so, not being an absolute fool, I decided it would be a good idea to have Iain Sinclair (metaphorically, at least) walking on the footpath with me, rather than standing beside it observing my failings. I thought I'd better talk to him. I made contact. He said walk on over, so I did. For a grey literary eminence, he was remarkably welcoming.

Sinclair, as his writings regularly tell us, has lived for forty years in Hackney, in the all too appropriately named Albion Drive. He describes living in one place that long as a sign of dysfunction. I'd walked past his house years earlier on one of my expeditions, and noted that it seemed a good deal less the dark shamanic lair than you might have expected from reading Sinclair's books.

The only other thing I remembered from that walk was seeing a graffito at the end of the street. Painted in blue on a pale-yellow brick wall were the words 'No lips'. I took a photograph of it, and over the years I've regularly looked at it and wondered what, if anything, those words meant.

Photographing graffiti is a suitably Sinclairian thing to do. One of the essays in *Lights Out for the Territory* has him walking from Hackney to Greenwich Hill and back to Chingford Mount, recording all the graffiti he sees on the way. 'These botched runes,' he writes, 'burnt into the script in the heat of creation, offer an alternative reading – a subterranean, preconscious text capable of divination and prophecy. A sorcerer's grimoire that would function as a curse or a blessing.'

When I went back to Hackney, on my way to see Sinclair, I walked around trying to find the 'No lips' graffito again, but either it had been removed or I was looking in the wrong place. So I looked for other clues instead. Sinclair the writer is so preternaturally aware of his surroundings and their histories and meanings, that just going to see him is enough to put you on your sensory mettle. Not far from Albion Drive, for instance, was a street called Vixen Mews: surely that was a name that bespoke a dark past and a tangled, vulpine narrative. Later, Iain Sinclair told me he had no idea where the name came from, though he was intrigued by it too, and I admit I was relieved to find that his knowledge of London wasn't utterly encyclopaedic.

On the other hand, when I mentioned that the previous day I'd been wandering around London and had found myself walking through the Nonconformist graveyard known as Bunhill Fields (where quite a few people go at lunchtime to eat their sandwiches, I discovered), his eyes lit up like Roman candles.

'Oh yeah,' he said, 'the epicentre. Blake, Defoe and Bunyan.' (All three of them have memorials there, though current scholarship doubts whether any of them is actually buried there). 'My theory is that all lines of energy or intelligence move out from that particular cluster. Bunyan's *Pilgrim's Progress* is actually the ultimate English walking book, where the physical journey that he does then becomes fabulated into this Christian mythology, but all the places are actually mappable. And then Daniel Defoe, because he travelled around the whole of England as an intelligencer and spy and double man. And then Blake, with his cosmic and imaginary journeys, with specific wonderful transits of London that are in the Jerusalem poem where he starts on Highgate Hill, through the narrows of the riverside, and he actually lists all these places. So I think any sense of a journey must begin on that spot, in this wonderful cross between the three of them.' I should have known this already. In *Lights Out*, he writes, ' . . . Bunhill Fields. Everything I believe in, everything London can do to you, starts there.'

Sinclair's appearance is professorial, alert, a touch gaunt, unamused, with a very correct posture that might make you believe he's had a spell in the army, which as far as I know he hasn't. There was none of the soft fleshiness that desk-bound writers are heir to. Maybe it came from all the walking. His voice, however, was soft, gentle, of a higher pitch than you'd expect to hear coming from that severe face. He was friendly but reserved, and obviously accustomed to being interviewed, though I insisted I wanted this to be a conversation rather than a Q and A.

'London,' he said, 'is the ultimate walking city, although it's a kind of battle, it has that mysterious labyrinthine quality that keeps it interesting. It's never the same twice, and you duck in and out of alleyways and there's so much *business* going on, and very soon you can negotiate into green spaces, rivers, it keeps it interesting.'

This is what I had come to hear. I was still on my sensory derangement kick. In fact I was still popping opiates for my recovering broken arm, but I wanted to talk about more recreational forms of medication.

Actually I've only once done any walking while under the influence of LSD and it wasn't much fun. I was walking in a crowded street and I believed I could read the minds of the people walking towards me. They were all nightmarish, ugly, grotesque minds, it seemed to me, minds that I'd have very much preferred not to have been able to read. And this was among the dreaming spires of Cambridge. I said I couldn't imagine walking around London on acid.

'Very wise,' Sinclair said, 'because underneath there's a monstrous aspect to it.'

The people I know who support the idea of walking around on LSD say what's so great about it is the way you see all the minutiae and fine detail that an unclouded mind simply skims over.

'But,' said Sinclair 'you can train yourself to log and sense those details anyway. Over the years you can come to recognise aspects and details, down to the smallest particulars and incorporate them into a larger sense of the whole. That's really what walks are about. As well as hoovering up information it's a way of actually shifting a state of consciousness and you get into things you didn't know about, or you begin to find out about, and that's the interesting part, otherwise it's just reportage.'

I sensed that he thought few things in the world were quite as pernicious and worthless as reportage.

In his books Sinclair is seldom a solitary walker. He has a

loose posse of fellow obsessives, mostly male, who share a taste for walking, thinking, recording, talking; especially talking he said.

'It's the only time you've got to have a long conversation, even though it contains a lot of silence. You stop to have breakfast in a greasy spoon, then later in the day you drop into a pub, and you can have different kinds of conversation from the kind you have as you're rambling along, when you're not quite together, or you come together and then you'll do a stretch where one person goes ahead, then you meet up and he notices something, you notice something, and so on over the course of the whole day, and there it is, it's very, very civilised, a perfect philosophical dialogue.'

I wondered if he had a series of set walks.

'Yes, because we've been in this house since 1969 so there are many set-piece walks that I do. I've got different walks for different questions or problems or ideas that I'm dealing with, a whole chain of maybe fifty different walks that I do for different things.

'One would be that short-story walk. If it was a more confused situation, if I was worrying away at something, I'd go down to the river, it would be one of two ways. If it was a seriously difficult thing that needed to be really thought out, I'd go down the canal to Limehouse, get on the river and stay on as far as the problem needed, then loop back. If it was something more straightforward, I'd go to Bethnal Green, through Brick Lane down to Wapping and hit the river there, and that would be enough to resolve this one thing, but if there was something I was looking for still, I'd go up to Waltham Abbey or the New River or Tilbury or something serious.'

Given that he's written so explicitly about where he lives and walks, and since he continues to live and walk in the same place, I wondered whether he was ever recognised by fellow walkers.

'For a period I kept bumping into people somewhere around Shoreditch,' he said, 'who were actually walking about with books of mine, doing various projects from the books, but I haven't of late seen any.'

And did he reveal himself to them?

'A couple challenged me, and one I saw just reading the book and talked to him and pointed something out that he was looking for, and a couple of times on the canal, too, a guy on a bike who was cycling through one of the books and ticking things off. He practically ran into me. But I think there are huge numbers of people walking, not my books, but walking and doing their own endlessly strange projects across London.'

I mentioned that I'd been rereading D. H. Lawrence's *Sons and Lovers*. It had been one of the first pieces of grown-up literature I'd discovered for myself. Reading it again, I realised that it's a book full of walking. I was impressed by the huge distances the hero Paul Morel would walk in order to see his girlfriend Miriam. The fictional Miriam is closely based on Lawrence's own girlfriend, Jessie Chambers. Morel's mother says, 'She must be wonderfully fascinating, that you can't get away from her, but must go trailing eight miles at this time of night.'

And she's right, of course. Miriam is wonderfully fascinating. The evenings together, Paul and Miriam's – D. H.'s and Jessie's – were intense and passionate, and one of their passions was for literature. In Jessie Chambers' memoirs she mentions the books they discussed. Turgenev's *Fathers and Sons* was one of them, its title perhaps an inspiration for Lawrence's own novel.

As I was saying this Sinclair's eyes lit up again. Yes indeed, he said. He got up, left the room and came back a minute or two later with a small, blue, hardback copy of *Fathers and Sons*. He opened it up and held it out to me. There on the flyleaf was the signature 'Jessie Chambers'. This was Jessie Chambers' own copy of *Fathers and Sons*. This book had belonged to the woman for whom Lawrence was prepared to do so much walking. Sinclair had been given the book by a dealer, as a thank-you for carrying a box of books.

It had occurred to me that Iain Sinclair might invite me to go with him on one of his fifty or so routes. I thought it might make for good, if again well-trodden, material. He didn't, but I did do one short walk with Iain Sinclair. It wasn't arduous, and as far as I can tell it was devoid of secret histories and alternate mythologies, although you can never be sure about these things. Our walk together was about twenty feet in length, the distance from his front door to his front gate, from his house, along his garden path to the street. Being a good host he saw me all the way out, escorted me off the premises. This, unarguably, was a walk through Iain Sinclair's London.

*

I was left wondering which particular endlessly strange walking project of my own I should be doing in London. I tried to imagine another map (or perhaps a detail of the one I first thought of) that showed every step I'd ever taken in the city, beginning with my first visit, with my parents when I was eleven years old, and taking in all the visits I'd made when I was a student, thinking myself pretty cool to have friends, even a girlfriend, who lived in Brixton.

Then, as soon as I got out of college, I went to live in London, and began a period of twenty years or so living in one grim, unsatisfactory room, bedsit or flat after another, all over the map: Notting Hill, Shepherd's Bush, Stamford Hill,

Hendon, Baker Street, Greenwich, Bloomsbury, West Hampstead, Earls Court, Upton Park. In those days the approved way to find a flat was by answering an ad in the *Evening Standard*. The ads didn't give the exact address so when you called up the landlord you always asked how near it was to a tube station. If he said it was a five-minute walk away, you knew it would really take ten minutes. A ten-minute walk meant twenty. If he said it was 'a bit of a walk', or a 'good walk', you knew you were really going have to do some hiking. And then when I went to see the place I'd always try to be optimistic. I'd get out of the tube and walk to the place where the flat was, telling myself that this was a nice street, this was a pretty good neighbourhood, that all the buildings looked well kept and decent; and then, some distance away, there'd be this rotting hulk of a house in which, inevitably, the flat was located. It wasn't exactly fun, but I told myself it was a great way to get to know London.

Eventually, and for the longest time, I owned a small flat in Maida Vale; I wanted to move out the day I moved in, and I managed it just over twelve years later. I contemplated doing a pilgrimage walk around all these places I'd lived, but it would have taken for ever, and why would I want to depress myself?

Like Iain Sinclair, I had a certain number of set London walks, and I liked to think that over the years these had got more eccentric and sophisticated, more full of the connoisseurship of walking and experiencing London. Some of them were straightforward enough, various walks along and across and under the Thames, various walks that enabled me to watch the endless, cyclical destruction and reconstruction of London. Some were more consciously obscure: a walk to the six-hundred-year-old Whitechapel Bell Foundry, a stroll along Lombard Street to see where Alexander Pope, Aubrey

Beardsley, T. S. Eliot and Charles Dickens's first love Maria
Beadnall had all lived at one time or another, an expedition
to see where the 'King's Place Nunneries' had once been –
exclusive, expensive eighteenth-century brothels, the best of
them run by a woman from Guinea known as Black Harriott.

Sometimes I just took a shot in the dark: an afternoon
spent on the green cheerless expanse that is Wanstead Flats
wasn't one of the great walks, but it took me to a place I'd
never been before, and will most likely never go again; a walk
to the Horniman Museum – the home of stuffed critters and
primitive musical instruments – was wonderful and I promised
myself I'd definitely go back, but so far I never have.

I had a brief obsession with a book on architecture, written
by Charles Jencks, called *Post-Modern Triumphs in London*. I
spent quite a few Sunday afternoons walking around looking
at new buildings that were all *faux* this and high-tech that,
and saying to my walking pals, 'Well yes, it *is* post-modern,
but is it a triumph?'

All these excursions would be charted on that imaginary
cosmic map of Nicholsonian walks in London. There'd be
thin spidery traces all over the city, some a single line
indicating a route I'd taken only once. There'd be some slight
thickening around the places where I'd gone to visit friends,
the better the friends, the greater the thickening, and even
more thickening in the places where I'd lived: the longer I'd
lived there the denser the markings. Same with girlfriends.
As a result of the decade I spent in Maida Vale, the map
would be positively clotted and embossed along the route
from the tube station to my front door. After that I suspect
Oxford Street was the place I'd walked the most: a street that
so many people hate.

I know plenty of Londoners who go out of their way to
avoid setting foot in Oxford Street. I'd taken to asking people

what they thought was the worst London street for walking. Iain Sinclair said, 'The Rotherhithe Tunnel. Not really a street, but a pedestrian way (or euthanasia path). West India Avenue & Cabot Square (by Canary Wharf) would be right up there as an anti-street, high-level surveillance, suspended liberties, drone crowds, comic-book architecture.' But a great many of them said Oxford Street. It's not that it's especially dangerous or ugly or mean, although pickpockets do operate there, and I've seen a couple of fist fights break out. The problem is more that it's full of people that a lot of Londoners don't want to mix with: tourists, out-of-towners, kids skiving off school, mad shoppers. The real objection is that it's too popular, too full or ordinary, miscellaneous humanity. It's unpopular with one set of people precisely because it's so popular with others.

It's also a street where everybody has walked at one time or another. William Blake must have walked there when he lived in Poland Street and South Moulton Street. Anybody who's ever played at the 100 Club – from Louis Armstrong to the Rolling Stones by way of Archie Shepp and the Sex Pistols – must have walked in Oxford Street. Pistols' manager Malcolm McLaren made an eccentric documentary about it. And I once saw Bob Geldof walking along at the eastern end, by Tottenham Court Road, weighed down with his Christmas shopping.

Before it was Oxford Street, in 1713, it was variously known as the Road from Uxbridge, the King's Highway, the Acton Road and Tyburn Way, the Tyburn being a river that still runs not so very deep beneath the street's surface. In 1941, a German bomb made a crater that briefly exposed it. Tyburn, of course, the place of public executions, was nearly but not quite where Marble Arch now stands. To walk along Oxford Street is to follow the route of the fifty thousand or so convicted criminals who were executed at Tyburn and of the huge crowds who came to watch.

Most of my walking on Oxford Street was not done entirely by choice. I had a couple of day jobs in the street itself, and two more that were close by. Consequently when I went out at lunchtime I found myself walking in Oxford Street. My bank was there. I bought food there. I bought clothes, books, records, spectacles. The truth was that, despite everything, I'd rather enjoyed walking there, and yet I could see there was something troubling and paradoxical to have done so much walking in a place that was held in such contempt by so many. I felt that Oxford Street needed to be redeemed. I thought it might be a good place to do my particular, strange, walking project.

I came to a decision. I would make six transits of Oxford Street, there and back, from Tottenham Court Road tube station at the east end of the street to Marble Arch at the west, and back again. I would spread them out over the course of one day. I would see how the street and my walking changed.

The Oxford Street Shopping Association claims the street is a mile and half long (though I suspect this is an optimistically high figure), so each round trip would theoretically be three miles, building to a total of eighteen. A few unexpected detours and diversions, plus the short distances between the start and finish of the walks, would surely make it add up to twenty miles: that seemed satisfyingly like hard work.

Why six transits? Partly because I was trying to work up a pun about *sic transit gloria mundi*, but more because I was doing the walk on the sixth day of the sixth month of 2006. There were reports in the papers about this date having some relation to the number of the beast, 666, but I couldn't see that. No reasonable way of writing the date could be made to give you that bestial number. In any case, one of the notions being bandied about was that this would be the day the Antichrist was born, which in itself didn't seem to threaten much, at least for the time being. Even the Antichrist surely wouldn't hit his stride on the very day he was born.

In the course of the day I duly walked the length of Oxford Street, six times in each direction, did my eighteen to twenty miles. I set off for the first walk at six in the morning, in bright sunlight, and I completed my last walk a little before midnight. I walked the street when it was all but empty and when it was so packed that I could scarcely walk at all. Chiefly I saw other people, first the workers, then the shoppers, finally the carousers and the drunks and the lovebirds.

At times here was something festive about it all. The weather was as good as English weather ever gets. The people on the street looked as though they were enjoying themselves. Many looked like tourists, and many of them seemed lost. A lot of maps were being consulted, and lots of photographs were being taken. I saw one man scanning the street with binoculars. A woman in full, all-enveloping Arab dress was wielding a video camera. The crowd was diverse in terms of race, age and class. They wouldn't all be going to the same shops or buying the same things or spending the same amount of money, but they were all there to buy *something*, whether designer clothes or cheap T- shirts with a map of the London Underground on them. They were united, made homogenous by the great equaliser of trade, and they all looked essentially happy about it.

I was hassled occasionally, once by a young man in a red T-shirt, smiling far too broadly, who stepped in front of me and demanded, 'Do you have love in your heart?' I couldn't stop myself guffawing at the question. 'I think you know I haven't,' I said. That made him lose a lot of his charm. 'This is a very serious issue,' he said very seriously, which I didn't dispute. He was raising funds for a children's charity, a worthy cause as far as I know, and no doubt they've done some research proving that asking dumb questions of people who are walking in Oxford Street is a good way to suck in money, but I was the wrong demographic.

'Does this ever work?' I asked as I walked away.

'Yes,' the young man called after me earnestly. 'Yes, it does.'

Later, outside Marble Arch tube station, there were two young Muslim men standing behind a stall decked out with leaflets and hand-labelled DVDs. One asked me, 'Now, what's your understanding of Islam?' He had the winning smile and the steady, open gaze favoured by the more appealing sort of zealot, and I said I didn't really have any understanding of it at all. He asked me if I had a DVD player, and offered me a DVD. I said I'd rather have something written. 'Ah,' he said, 'you want the *original.*'

I ended up with two publications, one called 'Jesus, peace be upon him, a Concise Islamic Belief', and another entitled 'Muhammad's Prophethood: An Analytical View' by Dr Jamal A. Badawi, Professor of Business Management at St Mary's University, Halifax, Canada. Dr Badawi is very insistent that Muhammed was not an epileptic nor did he suffer from 'the falling-down disease that was known to his contemporaries'.

A minute after I'd left the Islamic boys, I encountered a Christian preacher, an American from his accent, shouting through a megaphone, who was asking whether I, or anyone else, wanted to know about heaven. He certainly hadn't perfected the winning smile and the steady gaze. I, and everyone else, looked away and walked on.

Halfway through the afternoon I noticed a fragmentation,

people displaying tribal affiliations: retro punks, a pair of Japanese women in kimonos, some Hare Krishna celebrants, and a group of four particularly nasty-looking young skinheads – not quite skinheads actually, they'd left odd patches of velvety hair here and there on their skulls and had it razored into hard-edged geometrical patterns. This wasn't the style I was familiar with from authentic English skin-heads, and when I heard the boys speaking to each other in German I was relieved. It seemed to explain something. And even if the prospect of German skinheads was ultimately no more reassuring than that of English skinheads, I felt some consolation in knowing they were no part of any tribe I remotely belonged to.

In the busiest part of the day, I wasn't so much looking at people as looking out for them, trying to avoid being bumped into, knocked aside, trampled under foot. This, of course, applied to everyone else too, and resulted in some general bad temper. People around me were getting annoyed because walking was becoming so difficult. It was becoming so difficult because of all the other people who were there, also walking, also having difficulties, also becoming annoyed.

You couldn't have called it chaos exactly, since there was no slide towards entropy, no heading towards a state of lesser organisation. In fact, there was a great deal of steely purpose about many of the walkers, and there wasn't anything random about it. Everyone looked determined, like they were on a mission, like they had to get somewhere fast. They wished they were already there, and yet they were thwarted and frustrated by their fellow pedestrians.

As the day ended and the stores closed, garbage bags filled with commercial waste had been built into slack pyramids at intervals along Oxford Street. Each pyramid had its own scavenging homeless person. The bags were semi-transparent, which made it easier to see the contents and determine which bags needed to be ripped open.

The London rush hour came and went. It was a thing I was well familiar with from my days working on and off Oxford Street: a frantic, but not quite genuine, desire to get away, to go home, to draw a line across the day. But this was regularly undercut by a reluctance to engage with the rush at all; and so people chose not to go home, but to find a pub or bar instead, to hang out with people from work and complain about work; delay the inevitable. At eight o' clock there were plenty of people on the street who'd spent a couple of hours in the pub and were now going home a bit drunk, a bit late, dashing along, working up excuses for when they got there, chasing after buses and missing them, and cursing as though this was the worst thing that had ever happened to them in their whole lives.

I set out for my last transit at a little before eleven o' clock at night. Oxford Street was still well populated with people coming out of pubs, restaurants, burger bars, some finally heading home and walking to bus stops and tube stations or trying to flag down taxis. Others were looking for somewhere to carry on partying.

A few people were the worse for drink, but most seemed better for it, mellowed and easy going, strolling, enjoying the warm night air, a lot of couples holding hands, one or two snogging in shop doorways. A lone, lanky, big-eyed, bookish girl was coming out of a Borders bookstore just as it was closing, the kind of girl who gives hope, and then disappointment, to lone bookish boys everywhere. Two excited Italian gay boys had their digital cameras out and were photographing the window displays in some of the clothes shops: they looked deliriously happy.

It could have made you feel melancholy if you were that

way inclined – walking alone and seeing all these people with significant others – and usually that's very much the way I am inclined, but the fact I had a reason to be walking alone, that I was involved in my own endlessly strange project, that made all the difference in the world. It made it all right. I was a walker: I was a writer; I had a double purpose, and no need, now at least, to feel lonely in my solitary walking.

The irony of all this, not lost on me even then, was that I had done the transits, completed my self-imposed mission, walked the journey of twenty or so miles, and I was right back where I'd started. Essentially I had got nowhere.

Had I made Oxford Street my own? Had I redeemed or reclaimed anything? Well, yes and no. Oxford Street remains unpossessed and unclaimed, but that means it's still available. It's yours for the taking. It's promiscuous. It's anybody's. In the course of the day I'd walked with and in the footsteps of a multitude of people, but I knew that I must be one of the very few who had ever walked twenty miles back and forth on Oxford Street in a single day. The perversity of this pleased me no end.

*

At the time when I made my Oxford Street transits, and indeed when I first wrote the above, I was unaware that Virginia Woolf had written an article called 'Oxford Street Tide'. It was one of six essays she wrote for *Good House-keeping* magazine in 1931: they're collected in a very thin volume called *The London Scene*.

Now, Virginia Woolf is not exactly an open book to me. In the past I've forced myself to read her novels, including *Mrs Dalloway* which some regard as a great London walking novel, though not me. Mrs Dalloway is so little of a walker that the very idea of having to walk to the florist is an incredible excitement that sets her off thinking, 'What a lark!

What a plunge!' You'd slap her, wouldn't you? The critic John Sutherland is similarly unimpressed and, devastatingly, calculates that to get round her circuit in the allotted time she must have taken a taxi.

In 'Oxford Street Tide', Woolf knows she shouldn't like Oxford Street; it's so cheap and gaudy and full of plebs, awash with people 'tripping, mincing, in black coats, in satin dresses', so downright vulgar. But then suddenly, to her great credit, she realises she can't sneer at it completely. She notices something appealing in the energy and vulgarity of the place. She detects something Shakespearean about it and that makes it all right.

Then, on a street corner, she writes, 'tortoises repose on litters of grass. The slowest and most contemplative of creatures display their mild activities on a foot or two of pavement ... One infers that the desire of man for the tortoise, like the desire of the moth for the star, is a constant element in human nature.'

Well, I think I saw a few elements of human nature in the course of my six Oxford Street transits, but I had not inferred that the desire for a tortoise was one of them. I'm pretty certain I wouldn't want to spend too much time in Virginia Woolf's Oxford Street, but for the sake of seeing the tortoises, I wish I could walk down it just once. They, as much as a tincture of opium, might be a cure for melancholy.

3

Los Angeles: Walking Wounded with Ray
and Phil and Others

> I took the steps down Angel's Flight to Hill Street: a hundred
> and forty steps, with tight fists, frightened of no man, but
> scared of the Third Street Tunnel, scared to walk through it.
>
> John Fante, *Ask the Dust*

In May 1930, P. G. Wodehouse moved to Los Angeles,
more specifically Beverley Hills, to write for MGM. He'd
organised a deal whereby he worked at home and only went
into the studio for meetings. The story goes that he regularly
caused alarm and amusement by walking the six miles from
his home to the MGM offices in Culver City, and then
walking home again after the meeting. When the executives
got wind of it, one of them told Wodehouse this was foolish
and freakish behaviour, adding, 'Even the hookers don't
walk in LA.'

I think this story is at best apocryphal. Wodehouse was
certainly a keen walker but his letters suggest he was a keen
driver too. That he'd impose four hours of walking on himself just for a tedious studio meeting seems unlikely. As for
whether all 1930s LA hookers really had their own transport,
well, commonsense suggests otherwise. Still, the story con-
firms Wodehouse's reputation for lovable unworldliness, and
more importantly promulgates the myth that 'nobody walks
in LA'.

There are at least two pop songs that express much the
same sentiment, 'Nobody Walks In LA' by Ashford and

Simpson and 'Walking In LA' by Missing Persons, although the deeper message of these songs is not so much that nobody walks in LA, but rather that nobody who's *anybody* walks in LA. In Horace McCoy's *They Shoot Horses Don't They*, the lead characters are immediately established as Hollywood losers. Gloria misses a bus outside Paramount Studios, and Robert offers to walk with her to the next stop. Clearly they're doomed.

John Paul Jones, bass player with Led Zeppelin, has a story that he still trots out in interviews, of how he was arrested in the 1970s for leaving his hotel room and daring to walk the streets of Los Angeles. 'I didn't realise you're not supposed to walk anywhere,' he says.

D. J. Waldie, author of *Holy Land*, writes about the one-mile daily walk from his home to his office (actually in Lakewood, in LA County, rather than the city). He describes being 'stopped by a sheriff's patrol car on a completely empty stretch of suburban sidewalk, at midday, dressed in a coat and tie, and ordered to identify myself and explain my destination. As a pedestrian, I was a suspect.'

Waldie was perhaps citing Ray Bradbury, author of the dystopic science-fiction short story 'The Pedestrian', in which the hero is picked up by totalitarian cops who know he must be up to no good simply because he's a walker.

Jean Baudrillard, in his book *America*, writes, 'As soon as you start walking in Los Angeles you are a threat to public order, like a dog wandering in the road.'

All these add up to a fine and persuasive legend, and as they say in John Ford's *The Man Who Shot Liberty Valence*, 'This is the West, sir. When the legend becomes fact, print the legend.'

*

I moved to Los Angeles, with my then girlfriend, now wife, a couple of years before I had my bone-breaking fall. We'd gone there partly for work, and partly in order to enjoy certain Californian fantasies, both of glamour and apocalypse. I admit I didn't go there for the walking.

We found a place to live and bought a couple of cheap cars. My girlfriend started her job, and I sat in the house, writing as ever, and then doing the sort of things you do when you're first in LA, going to the Musso and Frank restaurant, to the Getty, to a couple of Frank Lloyd Wright sites, to the Museum of Jurassic Technology, to the beach. Life was conspicuously good. I had nothing at all to complain about. And I became completely and utterly depressed.

Now, I know what some of you are thinking, 'Good. Any halfway civilised Englishman who chooses to move to the vacuous wastelands of Los Angeles *deserves* to be depressed by the thinness and emptiness of the culture, by the super-ficiality and prefabricated good looks of the people, perhaps simply by the ease of being in a place where the sun usually shines and the living is too easy.' Well, only up to a point.

I lived with my depression, didn't do the obvious LA thing, which would have been to see a therapist or get some mood-lightening pharmaceuticals. Instead I tried to pretend it wasn't happening. I carried on with my housebound, sedentary writer's life. My writing was going well enough. At the weekend we'd get in the car and drive around soaking up the splendours of LA. I tried to be cheerful but it didn't work.

And then one day I was sitting gloomily in the sunroom of our house reading the newspaper, and I came across one of those 'recent medical evidence shows' type of articles. The evidence came from Duke University and it concerned the treatment of depression. The research said that a twenty-minute walk three times a week was better medicine, did patients more good, than all the anti-depressants in the world.

You know, this shouldn't have surprised them or me. It was an idea that had been around for a while. Robert Burton, author of *The Anatomy of Melancholy* and a hero of mine, realised something similar in about 1621. He regards walking as a cure for melancholy, and says,

> . . . the most pleasant of all outward pastimes is that of Aretaeus, *deambulatio per amoena loca* [strolling through pleasant scenery], to make a petty progress, a merry journey now and then with some good companions, to visit friends, see cities, castles, towns . . . to walk amongst orchards, bowers, mounts, and arbours, artificial wildernesses, green thickets, arches, groves, lawns, rivulets, fountains, and suchlike pleasant places, like that Antiochian Daphne, brooks, pools, fishponds, between wood and water, in a fair meadow, by a riverside . . .

He's free-associating by this point, and you could draw a parallel between the obsessive, indirect yet forward movement of his prose and similar qualities to be found in the act of walking. The effect is slightly spoiled, however, because although Burton says walking is the most pleasant way of banishing melancholy, he doesn't think it's superior to a great many other forms of banishment. He also rates watching a battle very highly.

Robert Burton and Duke University aside, even I was aware that exercise stimulates the production of endorphins, 'nature's painkillers', and the fact was, just about the only exercise I'd ever done, certainly the only exercise I'd ever enjoyed, was walking.

A light went on.

For most of my adult life I'd lived in London or New

York, two of the world's great walking cities. In these places I
hadn't just walked for twenty minutes three times a week,
I'd walked every single day, sometimes for hours. It was how
I got around. It was how I related to the city. In my spare
time I'd head off to some unknown part of town and explore
it on foot, alone or with other people. I frequently met others
who did very much the same. In both places there was a long
and solid literary tradition.

In Los Angeles it seemed to be different. I'd heard the pop
songs, read Baudrillard and a John Paul Jones interview.
As far as I was aware back then there was no tradition, no
history, no literature of walking. I now know that I was
completely wrong, but at the time I thought walking in LA
was a foolish and freakish thing to do.

Still, I wasn't afraid to be thought foolish and freakish.
There were bigger issues at stake. For the sake of my own
sanity, I started walking. And the truth is that the moment I
started walking I saw plenty of other people doing the same.
There were people dog walking, power walking. People walked
with their kids, kids walked by themselves, old people walked
together. There were always tourists walking on Hollywood
Boulevard and in Santa Monica and taking self-guided
walking tours of downtown. Once you started looking, there
were walkers everywhere.

Some, of course, may have been merely walking to their
cars. Some may have walked unwillingly because they were
simply too poor to own a car, because they had lousy jobs or
had recently arrived in the country, or all of these. Some of
the walkers I saw were homeless, some pushed shopping
trolleys full of recyclables, some pushed shopping trolleys full
of junk. A few were simply mad. I joined them. I became an
LA walker.

*

I had first set foot in Los Angeles in 1975. I'd got there by hitchhiking. Yes, when I was twenty-one years old I crossed North America on foot. Sometimes I think I only ever did it so that one day I'd be able to say, 'When I was twenty-one years old I crossed North America on foot.' It also had something to do with having read a lot, arguably too much, of Jack Kerouac.

The received wisdom about Kerouac back then had him as the king of the hippie hitchhikers. This, as we now know, was inaccurate in almost every way. He wasn't a hippie, and he wasn't a king, and although he did a certain amount of hitchhiking, he was just as likely to catch a bus or hop a freight train or be driven by Neal Cassady in a borrowed or stolen car. I was ready to experience all these modes of transport, but my initial plan was to stand by the American roadside with my thumb stuck out and get lifts from Toronto (I had good, dull reasons to start there) all the way to Santa Barbara, where I had a semi-legal job lined up.

Today it sounds to me as absurd, difficult and dangerous a plan as it must have sounded to my father at the time. To be fair to him, he didn't raise any objections on the grounds of personal safety: after all, he'd run off to join the Royal Navy when he was sixteen, in the middle of World War II, and he'd found himself in the thick of it, on a minesweeper in the Mediterranean. His worries were more about the basic feasibility of the project.

I remember him saying to me, 'But what if you don't get any lifts?'

The idea had literally never occurred to me.

'Of course I'll get lifts,' I said.

My father thought about this. 'Well I hope so,' he said. 'I mean, if you had to get from here to London' ('here' was our home in Sheffield), 'then I suppose you could get there eventually just by walking. But getting to California – well, it'd take you for ever.'

There was no denying that; but, of course, I did get lifts, plenty of them, some of them colourful, only one of them with obvious lethal potential, and I'll spare you most of my hitchhiking stories, but the fact is, when you hitchhike you do a lot of walking, far more than you want to. You get dropped off in places you don't want to be, in places where no other car will ever stop to pick you up. So you walk on to the next crossroads where more traffic joins the road, or a little farther to a nice long, clear stretch where a car can pull in easily, or a couple miles farther still to a field where you can sleep for the night.

My best hitchhiking and walking moment came some-where in semi-rural Oklahoma. There was a bleak empty highway on my left and weed-strewn railway tracks on my right, and I admit that my memory may have made the image a little more cinematic than it really was, but the story is as true as I can make it.

A long way up ahead I saw an old black man walking towards me. He was lean, loose, in work clothes. His walk was solid and serviceable, but very, very weary-looking. We were approaching each other for a good long time and we made eye contact long before we got within hailing distance. When we finally came face to face, the old guy said, 'I wish I wus where you just comin' from.' I've spent quite a lot of time over the years trying to think of some witty thing I should have said in reply.

*

Eventually, and a little reluctantly, my hitchhiking took me to Los Angeles. Even before I'd left England everybody had told me that LA was impossible without a car, and I saw no reason to doubt them. I'd even read Kerouac's opinion, in

On the Road, that 'Los Angeles is a jungle,' and though I certainly wished he'd come up with a more interesting metaphor, I again thought it was probably true.

There are plenty of lacunae in my memories of that first visit, but I do remember the lift that took me into LA. The driver, who looked like a hippie from Central Casting, bearded, mellow, softly spoken, and pretty well-heeled judging by his car, proudly pointed out as we approached the city that we were driving on a twelve-lane highway, and he made a detour so that he could drive down Sunset Boulevard and show me the Strip. He was especially keen that I see the huge billboards, and as I remember it they were of the Marlborough man, Peter Frampton and Joe Cocker, but again, time may have improved these memories.

My new pal dropped me off on Hollywood Boulevard, and I found a fleapit that called itself a 'motor hotel', and even so cost far more than I could afford. I'd hoped that somewhere along the way I might have been befriended by fun-loving hippie chicks who'd invite me to stay in their commune in Laurel Canyon, but that hadn't materialised.

Hollywood Boulevard was a scary place in the mid-seventies, though no doubt I scared more easily than I do now. But undoubtedly, contrary to expectations, there were lots of people walking on the street. Many of them looked somewhat like hippies, but you could tell they weren't the mellow, peace-loving type of hippie. They were only there for the drugs and the sex, and you just knew they wanted bad drugs and bad sex.

And there were indeed a lot of hookers walking the streets, hookers of both sexes, but predominantly male. Thanks to John Rechy, author of *City of Night* and *The Sexual Outlaw*, and himself a one-time street hustler, we now know that the real, industrial-strength action was taking place not on Hollywood Boulevard itself but half a block south on Selma, but the main drag was quite action-packed enough for me. The hustlers walked up and down, wearing their cowboy hats and fringed suede jackets looking like extras, or perhaps leads, from the movie *Midnight Cowboy*, or more likely Warhol's *Lonesome Cowboys*. As a matter of fact, I owned a fringed suede jacket at the time, and I was glad I hadn't brought it with me to America.

And I did by chance meet a fun-loving woman, though not a hippie chick, who had a couple of tickets for a David Bowie concert at the Hollywood Bowl, and she offered me one of them, but the journey there seemed unimaginably difficult to both of us. We didn't have a car so we thought it was impossible.

Now I look at the map and see that you can walk from Boulevard to Bowl quite easily in half an hour at most, and I suppose a bit of careful map-reading would have told me that even at the time. But I believed the legend, that you couldn't get anywhere or do anything in LA without a car, and you were wiser not to try.

*

Three decades later, newly arrived in Los Angeles, determined to fight depression, I was ready to defy the received wisdom. In the name of self-medication I began to take regular, long, sometimes arduous walks in LA. In fact there are plenty of places in and around the city where people go walking: Griffith Park, Runyon Canyon, Venice Beach, the shopping streets of Beverly Hills, Santa Monica's Third Street Promenade, Little Tokyo. A long drive may be involved in getting to any of them, but once there, people do actually walk. It seemed to me there was something a bit too obvious about walking in these places, but I didn't want to be completely self-denying or contrarian so I walked in all of them at one time or another.

Then, since I was living in a movie town, it seemed natural enough to visit some movie-related sites; places where Hollywood stars lived or at least *had* lived. Maps were easily available and I bought several, each containing a different and sometimes contradictory set of information.

If the data were to be believed you could, for instance, go along Franklin Avenue, a largely unsung street, and walk past the apartment block in which Dorothy Dandridge had lived before she went bankrupt, past where Gary Cooper had lodged with his parents, the spot where Joan Didion had lived in her yellow Corvette period. Current stars were a bit thin on the ground on Franklin, however. For them you were recommended to go to, say, Aldercreek Place in Westlake Village where you could saunter past the home of Frankie Avalon, or to Folkstone Lane in Bel Air where Tony Curtis still lived, or to Cornell Road, Agoura Hills, and see where Kelsey Grammer called home. I was never sure how accurate this information was. It seemed likely that celebrities moved more often than the maps got reprinted.

Once you started walking in Beverly Hills, the famous, and the ghosts of the famous, were to be found on every street: Greta Garbo on Chevy Chase Drive, Barbara Streisand on North Bedford, everybody and his uncle on Roxbury; mostly they were dead legends, such as Lionel Barrymore, Jimmy Stewart, Lucille Ball, Dorothy Parker, the Gershwins, but there were a few live ones too, including Mia Farrow and Peter Falk.

Perhaps inevitably these walks of mine didn't result in my seeing any movie stars. In many cases I didn't even get to see the houses because of high walls and hedges, and signs promising an armed response. My star maps told me not to go knocking on doors and I certainly didn't, but I did by chance, when not looking for her, meet one genuine movie star on my travels. More than that, I even walked with her.

It was in Valley Oak Drive, a long, quiet, traffic-free dead end, like many of the streets in the Hollywood Hills. I walked all the way to the end of the street then immediately turned and started walking back. It was the only thing to do, but I feared it made me look shifty and up to no good, as if I was casing the neighbourhood.

As I turned on my heel, I saw walking towards me down the middle of the street what at first appeared to be a child, or at most a very young teenage girl. She was incredibly thin, had brassy, dyed blonde hair and was wearing minute hot pants. She was looking lost and she spoke before I had a chance to.

'Have you seen a dog?' she asked me.

'No,' I said, and then, even though I have no interest in dogs, and can barely tell one breed from another, I asked, 'What kind is it?'

Either sensing or sharing my indifference to dog breeds, the little girl said, 'Oh, it's just a little dog,' and she mimed holding a puppy that wasn't much more than a single handful.

It was then that I realised the little girl was a fully-grown woman; was in fact the movie actress Christina Ricci. I'd have realised sooner if she hadn't had the blonde hair. Of course I didn't tell her I knew who she was, but my eyes probably signalled recognition. I'd thought she was great in the Addams Family movies. She evidently lived nearby. Indeed, as I found out later, she had just moved into a Lloyd Wright house in the street.

'Oh well,' said Christina Ricci, and she then seemed to be at a loss. Having reached the dead end of the street she too had to turn back, which meant walking along with me. I like to think I look reasonably presentable when I'm out walking. I don't think I look like a stalker or a pervert, but as Christina Ricci had seen, I was certainly a man who had walked to the end of the street and then turned on his heel and started walking smartly back. Was that a man you could completely trust?

An odd, socially awkward, and in my experience unique, interaction took place. Christina Ricci and I walked half the length of Valley Oak Drive in each other's company. We weren't exactly walking together, but we weren't quite walking separately either, and we both felt obliged to make some polite, stilted conversation as we went. We talked about dogs. It was excruciating. And as we walked, a chorus of canine barking came at us from behind various neighbourhood gates and fences. None of the barks sounded as though it came from a dog of the size she apparently owned.

What I didn't tell her was that as I'd been walking that afternoon I'd seen a lot of handmade signs attached to trees and lamp posts: wanted posters for lost dogs and cats. Some generous rewards were being offered. The fear, a reasonable one, in fact a strong probability, was that these family pets had been snaffled up by the coyotes that roamed wild in the area. If Christina Ricci was going to find her little dog, she had a strictly limited amount of time in which to do it.

*

I felt I was starting to get the hang of walking in LA. My walks became a profound source of pleasure. I was making the city my own, discovering my own version of it, marking territory, beating the bounds, drawing my own map. And I was doing myself good. I was feeling much, much less depressed. I can't say that I finished each walk and thought to myself, Ah yes, this is precisely the kind of serotonin-stimulating activity that those boffins at Duke University were talking about, but then I didn't need to. When you're not depressed you don't spend much time thinking about depression. And that was the state I was in when I went walking in the Hollywood Hills that time two days before Christmas, fell, broke my arm, stopped walking, and got depressed all over again.

It was obvious what had to be done. After a couple of months of nursing my arm, of inactivity and escalating misery, as the opiates ceased to deliver much in the way of pain-killing, I knew I had to start self-medicating again. I did what I had to do, picked myself up, dusted myself down and started walking again.

I undertook a series of long, unfocused but serious walks on the boulevards that run more or less east and west across LA: Pico, Olympic, Sunset, Santa Monica, Beverley, Melrose, Wilshire. I referred to the walks, only somewhat ironically, as 'transits'. There was nothing conceptually rigorous about them. I went at my own pace, without specific expectations or goals and I noticed what I noticed.

One of my enduring memories of Sunset concerns the couple I saw walking along ahead of me, near the Hollywood Freeway. The man was middle-aged, lean, bearded, a bit raddled perhaps but essentially keeping it together. His female companion was not. She was younger than him, as wide as a house, dishevelled, with huge, flopping, untethered breasts, and I guess she was suffering from some mental problems. Suddenly she looked down to the side of the road, at something in the bushes, and she reacted with delight. I looked to see what she'd found. There were twenty or thirty medicine bottles lying there, empty as far as I could tell, but still containing some powdery residue. The woman swooped down on them with absolute joy, and the man wasn't able to stop her, though he tried. About a week later, walking some miles away, I happened to see them again, and I fell into conversation with the man. He told me he liked my shirt. He said it was the kind of shirt worn by men of influence. I said it was the nicest thing anybody has said to me in a long time.

On Wilshire Boulevard I saw a man with no legs, indeed nothing at all below the pelvis, with a sort of thick plastic diaper round the bottom of his torso, and he was not literally walking, I suppose, but he was propelling himself at some speed. He had a block of wood in each hand, like wooden door handles, so that his hands didn't have to touch the sidewalk, and as he moved they made a noise somewhere between the sound of clogs and high heels.

As I was walking down Rampart Boulevard a car pulled up next to me. I looked over and saw the driver was a woman talking on her mobile phone, with an unruly little girl bouncing around in the passenger seat. I thought the woman was lost and stopping to ask me for directions, but no, she'd actually stopped the car so she could give the little girl a good slapping, which she then did, with her mobile phone still at her ear, and quite oblivious of my presence.

Some of my walks could be tough. It does get damned hot in the middle of the day in LA, even in early spring. I did nearly get run down once or twice. Dogs endlessly snarled and yelped at me, and naturally street people hassled me with varying degrees of seriousness.

On Los Feliz Boulevard, a wild young black man who appeared to have all his worldly goods scattered at his feet gave me a bright hello, which I returned, and when I was past him he called after me, 'Dude! Are you in the movies?'

'Nah,' I said laughing.

'You look just like that dude in *Die Hard 2*,' he said.

For no good reason I said, 'I wish,' and then we both had a good laugh.

When I got home I went through the cast list of *Die Hard 2* and I'm damned if I can see anybody there who might look like me. Not Bruce Willis I think we can safely say. It'd be flattering to think it was Franco Nero, but leaving all other objections aside, we aren't in remotely the same age bracket. And surely not Dennis Franz. Surely. Not even my worst enemies would say I looked like him. Whatever my physical failings I do have plenty of hair.

And then there was the time when I was walking in downtown, a place that feels more like a 'real' city than much of LA, where a lot of others walk too. It was a busy weekday lunchtime. The streets were full of people. There was a lot to look at, a lot of distractions, and that was why I wasn't paying much attention to the youngish, hippie-ish white guy who was standing next to me as I was waiting to cross the street. He may have been a hippie, but he was also a beggar, and he thought I was deliberately, pointedly ignoring him. If I'd been aware of him I very well might have done, but I wasn't, my mind was simply elsewhere. After failing to get my attention for a while he said loudly, in a sneering tone of voice that finally did the trick, 'Hey, who do you think you are? Jack Kerouac?' It was a long time since I'd thought of myself as an imitator of Jack Kerouac. As sneering insults go, I couldn't have asked for better. I didn't know what to say, but fortunately the lights changed and I walked across the street smiling fit to bust. I didn't give him any money though.

*

I walked for a while in the footsteps of those two great Angelinos, one real, one fictional: Raymond Chandler and his creation Philip Marlowe. I had a partial list of the places

Chandler had lived, based on information from his selected letters, and the Chandler biographies, plus a certain amount of anecdotal evidence. Chandler seems to have lived *everywhere*: Los Feliz, Santa Monica, Arcadia, Monrovia, Brentwood, Pacific Palisades, and all manner of places in between.

Given that Raymond Chandler first came to Los Angeles in 1906, it can hardly be a great surprise that large parts of Chandler's city have changed beyond recognition. Some of the addresses simply no longer existed. A good natured, dread-locked postman spent a lot of time trying to help me find one of Chandler's old places on 12th Street, but our best efforts put his apartment exactly where there was now an alleyway that ran behind a Korean Presbyterian church. A bungalow court on Leeward Avenue certainly shared an address with a place Chandler had once lived, but Tom Hiney, Chandler's biographer, describes the place as a semi-detached house. When I visited it was a series of tightly packed bunkers, neat enough and recently repainted, but thoroughly austere, and enclosed behind spiked iron railings and barbed wire, evoking captivity as much as security. By now it may be something else again.

I did however find one place that had a thoroughly Chandleresque feel to it. The address was an apartment block on Greenwood Place, Los Feliz, walking distance from where I live. Chandler and his wife Cissy rented there in the early 1930s, when he wrote his first crime stories. Chandler's alcoholism had ended his career as an oil executive, and he had no income whatsoever when he first moved in. Even when Black Mask published his stories, he must still have struggled for money.

Consequently I'd constructed quite a tragic and romantic picture for Chandler, and for myself. There are some very bleak apartment blocks in that area, and I guessed that Ray and Cissy had holed up in one of those. I was quite wrong. There was nothing bleak about 4616 Greenwood. It looked like a very decent place to live. It was a small, two-storey apartment block, Spanish style, with red-tile roofs and coated in creamy off-white stucco. There was a wrought-iron gate, with a huge spreading tree behind it (Chandler would have known exactly what tree it was, I didn't), and behind that was an archway leading through to a central courtyard. Somebody had painted 'El Pueblo' above the arch in a swirly hand.

There were balconies and circular windows and I could hear men's and children's voices coming out through the open windows. I couldn't help thinking, first, how 'very Los Angeles' it all was, and then how 'very Raymond Chandler'. It's not just that he describes places like this, it's that he's made places like this a proper backdrop for fiction. A youngish, hipsterish man came out of the gate and got into a car that was parked in one of the garages at the side of the block. I rather wished I had a reason to tail him. It was easy, all too easy, to imagine I was a private eye on a surveillance job. This is absolutely to be avoided when writing about Chandler. As Tom Shone has so neatly put it: 'What is it about Chandler that compels any writer within a twenty-mile radius to try to out-Chandlerise him?'

Of course, things are only likely to get worse when a writer starts to walk with Philip Marlowe, as I then did. We tend to think of hard-boiled detectives as drivers rather than walkers, but in the course of his enquiries Marlowe does plenty of walking too.

An early scene in *The Big Sleep* has Marlowe, on foot, following a customer from Geiger's bookstore, a sort of porno lending library, located on the north side of Hollywood Boulevard, near Las Palmas Avenue, a place that can be located today with some precision. Some sources place the bookstore in what is now the 'new room' of Musso and Frank, one of Chandler's favourite watering holes, a taste shared by such writer/drinkers as Faulkner, Parker, Hammett and later Bukowski.

Marlowe tails the customer, who gets increasingly panicky as he walks west on Hollywood Boulevard to Highland, then he goes another block, turns right, then left into a 'narrow tree-lined street with three bungalow courts', the second of which is called the La Baba. Eventually the customer cracks, ditches the smut he's borrowed and then saunters away, leaving Marlowe to retrieve the filthy goods.

The first part of the walk is easily replicated, but by the end you'll find yourself walking into 'Hollywood and Highland', a corporate, multi-story shopping mall, that by some accounts is responsible for the revitalisation of Hollywood, but which nevertheless has the look of something that will be a slum in ten years' time. Chandler would have been horrified, and would have revelled in his horror.

The Big Sleep is also the novel in which Marlowe walks to Geiger's house in Laurel Canyon, setting off from the Sternwood mansion in West Hollywood. He covers 'ten blocks of curving, rainswept streets' until he 'comes out at a service station', then adds, 'I made it back to Geiger's house in something over half an hour of nimble walking.' Funny, I always saw Marlowe as stolid rather than nimble.

I've walked various routes between various possible locations for both the mansion and Geiger's house, but convincing though Chandler's (and Marlowe's) account is, the geography of the book is a long way from the real geography of the city. The best guess has Geiger living on Kirkwood Terrace, a street off Laurel Canyon Boulevard, with the Sternwood mansion as ringer for the Doheney mansion, a mock-Tudor extravaganza in Beverley Hills, sometimes used as a movie set (*Murder She Wrote*, *The Witches of Eastwick*, *The Prestige*) and also the site of a real murder. But there are no ten curving blocks and never could have been, and it's hard to imagine exactly where that gas station was. This, of course, is absolutely fine. It's what novelists do, what they're supposed to do. They start with the real world, distort it for their own ends, then sell it back to you and make you believe in it as real, real enough for a man to think he can actually walk in it.

Still, my favourite Marlowe walking moment appears in *Farewell, My Lovely*, where Marlowe climbs the two hundred and eighty steps up to Cabrillo Street in Montemar Vista where he's got an appointment with a fop called Lindsay Marriott. 'It was a nice walk if you like grunting,' Marlowe says when he's got to the top.

Cabrillo Street and Montemar Vista are Chandler's inventions, but if you're looking for a long trudge up a great many steps, Castellammare, on the Pacific Coast Highway, offers a very adequate substitute. I went there and tried to do Marlowe's walk. It's a struggle to find exactly two hundred and eighty steps from beach to clifftop – some lead into dead ends, some are crumbling wood and closed off – but you can do something that's not too far off the mark. The grunting is much as reported, but it really is a 'nice' walk, if you like walking. On the way you pass the house where the actress Thelma Todd was murdered, and the view from the top is just about worth the effort.

*

There is in Los Angeles these days a place called Raymond Chandler Square. It isn't a square in the usual sense, rather an intersection where Cahuenga and Hollywood Boulevards meet. It's pleasing in a way that Raymond Chandler Square is so ordinary, so unfancy. It's the kind of place where the businesses don't seem to be in it for the long haul; but the last time I looked the four corners offered a Greek pizzeria, a Popeye's chicken and biscuits restaurant, a place for cashing cheques and, more substantially, a big serious anonymous bank building which is a contender for the fictional Cahuenga Building, where Marlowe once had an office. To be fair John Fante has a square too, but it's in front of the Central Library, which seems way too literary.

Hollywood Boulevard is one of the places where people *do* actually walk in Los Angeles. When people complain about the lack of street life in LA, other Angelinos tend to say, 'Go to Hollywood Boulevard if you want some street life, man.' They mean that Hollywood street life is all about drugs and sex, runaways, people fresh off the bus, boys up to no good, the improbably and ill-advisedly transvestite, the kind of people who need piercing and tattooing parlours and smoke shops, who find themselves sitting on the sidewalk, with a dog on a string, eating pizza and bumming cigarettes, the mad, the lost, the winsomely deranged. One of my recent favourites was a guy, youngish, clean, healthy looking, pushing a stroller full of his belongings and singing, 'The Devil's been defeated and you can all go to Hell.' Everyone, including me, will also tell you that it used to be a whole lot worse.

These days there are also plenty of tourists walking on Hollywood Boulevard, and many of them look downright bemused. They know they're in Hollywood, they know that they're on the legendary Hollywood Walk of Fame, and yet they don't quite know what they're supposed to be doing there. Taking the names of people you admire and putting them in stars on the sidewalk where people can walk all over them still strikes me as an odd and not very respectful thing to do.

And of course some people do far worse than walk. You can imagine my ambivalent glee when I discovered the existence of something called the Hollywood Entertainment District Public Urination Map, charting every act of public urination observed by the area's security guards. You might think that part of a security guard's job might be to prevent public urination rather than merely observe it, but it's probably a hard thing to stop, certainly once the perpetrator is in full flow. And of course a great deal of unobserved urination must go on too. This is one of the unavoidable facts of walking on Hollywood Boulevard: anywhere you go, not only has somebody walked there before you: somebody has probably pissed there as well.

The Walk of Fame runs east/west along the Boulevard from Gower to La Brea, and north/south on Vine Street from Yucca to Sunset, forming a long thin cross. The names at the far west end are Spanky McFarland and the Dead End Kids. At the eastern end it's Benny Goodman and Stanley Kramer. On Vine Street we run from Jeff Chandler and Texas Guigan in the north down to Franklin Pangborn and Edward Small in the south.

If you say that these are no longer household names, then I suppose I'd say that might be the whole point. The names are written in concrete (actually brass set in terrazzo) but their fame is no more permanent than if they were written in water. The Walk of Fame might remind you that showbiz just isn't the place to look for permanence, but I suspect you know that already.

If there's a journey's end for the Hollywood Walk of Fame, it's Grauman's Chinese Theater, where people congregate and pay a couple of dollars to have their pictures taken with a movie lookalike: a Marilyn, an Elvis, a Charlie Chaplin, a man in a Spiderman suit, a woman dressed as Wonder Woman.

Since changing facilities are limited on Hollywood Boulevard, most of the characters arrive already in costume, and in order to avoid commuting many of them live in the area, within walking distance of work. Marilyn has lived in a camper van on Selma for some years now. One of the best sights I know in Hollywood is that of Wonder Woman emerging from her apartment block on Las Palmas and striding up to Hollywood Boulevard, getting into character as she goes.

*

The most extreme Los Angeles walker I know (and he too is a kind of superhero) is called Mudman, a persona of the artist Kim Jones. In order to become Mudman, Jones coats his body in mud, pulls a thick nylon stocking over his head, puts on a foam headdress and then straps to his back a large lattice structure, made of wooden slats, tree branches, wax, wire, tape, sponge and whatnot. Sometimes he also wears a glove on his left hand from which a number of long wooden spikes protrude all the way to the ground. The effect is visually and conceptually compelling, especially if you see him walking towards you in a city street.

Mudman is a living, walking sculpture, one that invokes a whole raft of visual associations. He looks grotesque yet vulnerable, sinister perhaps but not humourless. The idea of the man made out of mud is as old as Adam or the Golem, and certainly Jones's creation has elements of ancient religion, part shaman, part witch-doctor, part Wicker Man. The structure on his back looks like broken wings or a self-inflicted cross he has to bear. He also looks like something out of pop culture, a blighted superhero, some kin of Swamp Thing or the Incredible Hulk, though it's not clear what powers he has, apart from being able to walk.

Mudman's most famous exhibitions of art-walking con-sisted of two twelve-hour walks he did along the full length of Wilshire Boulevard, about eighteen miles from downtown to the ocean at Santa Monica. He did the first walk on 28 January 1976, which was his birthday, from sunrise to sunset, then a week later, on 4 February, he did it again from sunset to sunrise. Along the way he had the kind of encounters you might expect: with a gas-station attendant who wouldn't let him use the bathroom, a cop who told him to keep moving and an old lady who asked him, 'Does your mother know you're doing this?'

I made contact with Jones and asked if he had any plans to do a Mudman walk in the near future, hoping I might walk along with him, or at least observe other people's reactions. 'I still do Mudman,' he said. 'I haven't done it in a while but I plan to do it as long as I can. My favourite time to do Mudman is when *no one* expects or knows that I'm going to do it.'

Which brings us back to the myth that nobody ever expects anybody to walk in Los Angeles. However, I think I've proved the contrary, to my own satisfaction if nobody else's, and I think the myth is busted. The longer I live in LA the more I become aware of the city's rich tradition of walking: literary, artistic, recreational and, sometimes, political.

There's an annual César Chávez Walk, for example, at which you're invited to 'walk alongside Chávez family members, students, elected officials, celebrities, and community members'. By walking you join 'the call for social justice'. Who could be so churlish as to walk against social justice? When Angelinos wanted to protest against the war in Iraq they closed Hollywood Boulevard and thousands took to it on foot. When they want to demonstrate in favour of Latino immigration, as they do increasingly often, then Wilshire becomes a pedestrian precinct.

Look, LA is never going to be a city where most people

do the majority of their travelling on foot. The distances are too great, the city is too spread out. And yet people who've lived in LA much longer than I have assure me that Angelinos are walking more now that ever before. Partly it's because driving around LA is such misery that if you can accomplish what you want by walking you'll do so. There are also some genuine, if often half-baked, environmental concerns. Walking by itself won't save the planet but it's got to be better than thrashing around the streets in a V8 Range Rover.

Some of us Angelinos keep on walking, and while it seems fair enough to question the essential wisdom and sanity of certain LA walkers, for far more of us it's not only a pleasure, it's a passion, and also a necessary activity that keeps us (more or less) sane. We would be a great deal crazier, and certainly more depressed, if we didn't do it.

And so to return to the nay-sayers, to the likes of Jean Baudrillard and his assertion that: 'As soon as you start walking in Los Angeles you are a threat to public order, like a dog wandering in the road.' The fact is, it takes rather more than a bit of pedestrianism to disrupt the public order of LA. As far as that goes LA can pretty much handle a dog wandering in the road too. Print the legend if you must, but don't expect all us Angelinos to believe it, much less live it.

4

Eccentrics, Obssessives, Artists: Imaginary Walks with Richard Long, Captain Barclay, Werner Herzog *et al.*

Tourism is sin, and travel on foot virtue.
Werner Herzog, *The Minnesota Declaration*

In September 1954, Albert Speer, Hitler's chief architect and then his Minister for Armaments, made up his mind to walk from Berlin to Heidelberg, a distance of six hundred and twenty kilometres. Since he was incarcerated in Spandau prison at the time, and was to remain there until 1966, his walk had to be an entirely theoretical and imaginary one.

He paced out a circular course of two hundred and seventy meters in the prison garden, which he had designed, and he began a journey that would require him to make just over two thousand two hundred and ninety-six circuits of that course. He set himself the task of walking seven kilometers seven times a week. If he fell behind one day he'd try to make it up the next and he kept detailed, some would say obsessive, records of his walking, noting the distances covered, along with daily and overall averages. Rudolf Hess, Hitler's deputy in the Nazi party, also an inmate of Spandau, helped him keep count.

Speer completed his 'journey' to Heidelberg on 19 March 1955, his fiftieth birthday. He then decided he might as well continue and make another imaginary walking trip, this time to Munich and beyond. Again Hess tried to be helpful, suggesting he could walk all the way to Asia, but Speer fretted that almost any route eastward would involve having to walk through some dreaded Communist countries.

According to Speer's diary, he and Hess had some discussions about whether or not this sort of walking was inherently sane. Speer at first claimed it wasn't and writes, 'I insisted on my claim to have a screw loose,' an odd thing to insist on unless he thought that incipient insanity might speed up his release. Hess, however, was having none of it. 'That just happens to be your pastime,' he said, quite reasonably, and this is surely one of the very rare moments in history when one sides with Hess rather than Speer.

By 18 September 1956, Speer had come round to Hess's point of view and was able to record, 'I have walked 3,326 kilometres; counting the winter that makes a daily average of 9.1 kilometres. As long as I continue my tramping, I shall remain on an even keel.'

*

The question of whether walking is a completely ordinary activity or whether it's evidence of incipient eccentricity (if not worse) is one that troubles me more on some days than others. Will Self has said that when he tells people he's about to set off on one of his manically long walks, people ask him whether he's doing it for charity or for a bet. Those are the two of the 'uneccentric' reasons for walking that most people understand. Fitness is another.

In 2005, when Steve Vaught, a four-hundred-pound ex-marine began his walk across America, from San Diego to New York, the media tended to treat him as a weight-loss enthusiast. He did the walk, and he did lose weight, just over a hundred pounds in thirteen months, and he did get to appear on *Oprah*. But his weight loss wasn't enough for some, and you could see their point: at three hundred pounds he wasn't the very best advertisement for walking as a weight-loss strategy. Vaught insisted that weight loss was only part of the story. He was also walking 'to regain his life', he said, and by his own account he has. 'I no longer manage business or pursue money beyond what I need,' he says. 'I've given away all my material things and live life out of two or three carry bags, and I recommend it highly.'

Weight loss was identified as a good reason for walking, 'regaining your life' is an even better one. But it seems that Mr Vaught's walking has led him astray. This, we know can happen. Take the example of an Englishman called Steve Gough, currently our most famous naked walker. He describes himself as 'body positive' and claims that his extensive experience of walking naked in the world has given him a 'connectedness' with others. He has now twice walked naked from Lands End to John O'Groats. He has spent a lot of time in court, and a certain amount of time in jail.

The media only got really interested when he did the Lands End to John O'Groats walk for the second time and took his naked girlfriend, Melanie Roberts, with him. He also had a film crew in tow. Cynics might think that without the naked girlfriend there might not have been a film crew.

The resulting documentary, made by Richard Macer, shows the British public's surprisingly extreme reactions to the naked pair, both positive and negative. Gough encounters a number of people who regard him as a harmless, likable, even admirable eccentric, part of a great British tradition, which is surely the only sensible way to regard him. This includes a group of women he encounters in a pub in Derbyshire who strip down to their underwear in a show of solidarity. By contrast, a working-class mother is seen seething with rage and disgust, afraid that the sight of a naked man and woman will have some hideously damaging effect on her innocent children. Her reaction is alarmingly, frighteningly extreme.

The police and the courts seem to take a similar view. The more time goes by, the more time Gough spends in jail. Every time he gets out he walks naked, gets arrested and is sent back to jail. This has gone beyond eccentricity, surely. Insisting on walking naked even when you know you're going to end up behind bars seems, at best, a little crazy. Given that Gough refuses to wear clothes either in court or prison suggests it's become about something other than walking. Even the media seem to be getting a little bored with him, and the fact that he's started comparing himself with Rosa Parks probably isn't helping.

I wonder what the modern media might have made of the Old Leatherman, a nineteenth-century tramp who for just over thirty years, from 1858 to 1889, was in constant motion, dressed head to foot in leather, walking a three-hundred-mile circuit around parts of Connecticut and New York State. The route took him precisely thirty-four days: you could set your watch by him. In those three decades of walking he wasn't heard to utter a single intelligible word.

The story is that the Old Leatherman began life as young Jules Bourglay (spellings differ) in Lyons, in France. He was a woodcarver who fell in love with the daughter of a wealthy leather merchant, surname Laron. Bourglay asked for the girl's hand in marriage and Laron *père*, perhaps surprisingly, didn't dismiss the idea out of hand. He gave Bourglay a job in his leather business. If the young man proved himself in the first year, he'd keep him on and approve the marriage.

The move was a disaster. The leather business was already in trouble, and Bourglay made some bad decisions that resulted in Laron's bankruptcy. The wedding, understandably, was off. Devastated, Bourglay spent a year in a

French monastery then made his way to America where he tried to expiate his putative guilt by walking.

That sounds pretty thoroughly eccentric to me, and of course it may be untrue, but even as a myth from a different age it's interesting that the story was thought of as a reasonable explanation for why a man might walk regular three-hundred-mile circuits while dressed entirely in leather. Perhaps once eccentricity is understood it is no longer considered eccentric at all.

In fact, the Old Leatherman did receive a certain amount of public attention. He was widely photographed, and his image appeared on postcards. He was also invited to display himself in a New York City freak-show, an opportunity he wisely declined. His reputation as an eccentric walker could surely not have survived long periods as a sedentary museum exhibit. And speaking of museums . . .

*

I once worked for a security company that provided guards for many of London's major art institutions, including the British Museum, the Royal Academy and the Tate Gallery. My job was simple enough, to protect works of art from the public, and a basic level of vigilance was all that was required of me. But I did have to stay literally on my feet, and metaphorically on my toes, and so whole days, and eventually weeks and months were spent pacing up and down one gallery or another, trying to remain alert, looking at art, keeping an eye on the potentially troublesome public. Sometimes I fantasised about where my endless pacing might have taken me had I actually been going somewhere. But, of course, I wasn't being paid to go anywhere: I was being paid to walk back and forth in a gallery.

Some of my colleagues complained about the boredom and the pains in their feet, legs and back, but I never found this a problem. Being able to spend long periods of time in the presence of great works of art, far longer than you'd ever have on a normal gallery visit, made it all worthwhile.

There was a moment in the Royal Academy, before it opened for the day, when I found myself alone in a gallery surrounded by thirty or so priceless Van Goghs, part of an exhibition on Post-Impressionism. And as I walked up and down, waiting for the public to be let in, it was easy to entertain other fantasies: that the Van Goghs belonged to me, that I was some sort of James Bond villain who'd secreted these treasures and that I was walking in my own marble hall, a secret lair that was mine and mine alone and than no others would ever be allowed to walk there.

It was even easier to sustain such a fantasy in a basement gallery at the Tate, where few people came, and where I was guarding a sculpture by Richard Long called *Slate Circle*. It consisted of two hundred and fourteen rough, largish, unworked pieces of Welsh slate, arranged on the floor in a precise circle about twenty feet in diameter. Guarding it wasn't much of a challenge. It was unlikely that anyone was going to slip a large lump of Welsh slate under their coat, and the few visitors who came to that particular room had a tendency to ask, 'Is this the bricks?' meaning Carl Andre's *Equivalent VIII* made from, and consisting of, a hundred and twenty firebricks, which to this day remains an exciting touchstone for art sceptics and Philistines everywhere. I was delighted to be able to say, 'No, it's not the bricks. It's the slates.'

Long's *Slate Circle* explores a tension between art and nature, the indoors and the outdoors, between the created and the found object, between the making of art and the claiming of what's there. It was undoubtedly a sculpture, but the slate had not been 'sculpted' in any conventional sense, it had simply been arranged. Two hundred and fourteen lumps of slate had been extracted from the ground and carefully, artfully placed on the floor in the warm glow of an art gallery where I could see and walk around them. They made my days of pacing very happy.

There were also certain ironies in the work that I only became aware of later. The slate, I discovered, came from a quarry that Richard Long had gone past while walking, 'From the source of the River Severn to the summit of Snowdon, 60 miles'. That was the description of his walk and also the title of a work of art. Long is a sculptor and a conceptual artist, and has said that walking is the real medium of his art.

His first walking piece was made in 1967, a straight line in a field of grass, created by pacing up and down until the grass was flattened and the line was made visible: one of those works of art that any damn fool could make if the damn fool were a conceptual artist. Later, Long's works became larger and more ambitious. Sometimes they involved the stamping out of patterns in earth or ash, sometimes the rearrangement of rocks along the way, sometimes 'painting' with water in the course of the walk. On occasions, Long has collected mud from the area where he's been walking and used it to create works of art on the walls or floors of galleries.

Some of his walks have been lengthy and arduous – across the Sierra Nevada, through the Sahara. The works have titles such as 'Walking a Circle in Mist', 'A Walking and Running Circle', 'A Cloudless Walk', 'A Walk across Ireland', 'A Line of 33 Stones A walk of 33 Days'. He documents the walks using maps, drawings, photographs, texts, or a combination of these things. Some of these works are wonderfully inscrutable, consisting of no more than a few words. Here, in its entirety, is a piece called 'A Five Day Walk':

FIRST DAY TEN MILES
SECOND DAY TWENTY MILES
THIRD DAY THIRTY MILES
FOURTH DAY FORTY MILES
FIFTH DAY FIFTY MILES

In a 2006 article and interview with Long in *Art + Auction*, the writer Roger Tatley admits to doubts about the 'provenance of some of Long's walks', suggesting that maybe they didn't really take place. He puts this to Long and describes the artist's response as 'gracious'.

> My work has to work on all levels, for unbelievers as well. It is of course possible that I don't do any of these walks, and in some ways, if I didn't, they would have to work on the level of true conceptual art, like Lawrence Weiner's. He's a great artist in that his use of language means it doesn't matter whether the work exists or not. But the difference for me is that while ideas are important, it's crucial that I do make my art – that these are real walks, real stones, real mud.

> When you walk through wild places, as I sometimes do, especially in the desert, you often see that people have been there before you and stamped out patterns on the earth or arranged stones or debris into shapes and designs, with greater or lesser degrees of skill and ingenuity, with a greater knowledge of the conventions of art. The best of them look like fake Richard Longs, although of course there's always the possibility that some of them may be real Richard Longs.

*

Much of Long's work is concerned with the human measurement of space and time, with walking as a major yardstick. One of his earliest works, created in 1974, was a drawing and text piece called 'A Thousand Miles A Thousand Hours'. Perhaps Long is invoking Lao Tsu and his remark about the journey of a thousand miles, but if you're at all familiar with the history of sustained eccentric walkers, those words can only mean one thing: Captain Barclay.

Captain Robert Barclay Allardice (1779–1854) was a Scot, a sportsman, an athlete, a soldier, a fan of horse racing, a gambler, a landowner and a 'gentleman'. Sometimes these roles sat uneasily together. For instance, one of the rules of the English class system decreed that, as a gentleman, he was allowed to 'spar' with professional boxers but he wasn't allowed to 'box' against them. Being a landowner, he had no practical need to make money by performing athletic feats: he could have performed them as a gentleman amateur. However, he needed to up the stakes and he bet heavily on himself when he competed. If he lost the bet, as he sometimes did, it could cost him the best part of a year's income.

History, however, has remembered him as one of the very greatest walkers, or at least pedestrians. The two words were not quite synonymous in Barclay's time. To be a pedestrian in the nineteenth century simply meant that you raced on foot, as opposed to on horseback or in a carriage. 'Go as you please' races were popular, sometimes lasting several days, in which competitors were free to walk or run, or indeed hop, skip and jump, and certainly to rest, as and when they saw fit throughout the event. At the end the winner was simply the one who'd gone farthest around a predetermined route.

As a spectator sport, long pedestrian races must have been lacking in all sorts of ways: the competitors weren't necessarily on the track at the same time, if they were they certainly weren't likely to be on the same lap, and you might easily turn up to watch during a prolonged rest period and see no action at all. But large crowds did gather at them, and large amounts of money were staked on the outcomes.

Young blades of the Regency period loved a bet, but the rules of many sports were at that time unfixed so every new contest represented an opportunity for invention, variation, and sometimes bizarrely complicated constraints to make the event, and the betting, that much more of a challenge.

Peter Radford in his book *The Celebrated Captain Barclay* recounts some gloriously eccentric pedestrian contests. One was devised by 'an unnamed Duke' who wagered a thousand guineas that he could find a man to walk the ten miles from Piccadilly to Hounslow within three hours, taking three steps forward and one step back. He wasn't wagering on his own ability to do it, but on his ability to find a man who could, though Radford tells us the contest never actually took place.

Barclay first performed as a competitive pedestrian while still at school. At the age of seventeen he wagered that he could walk six miles 'heel and toe' (the standard definition of race walking, with one part of one foot in touch with the ground at all times) within an hour, on the Brixton to Croydon road. He succeeded, and won a hundred guineas, a good pay day for anyone, and a nice feat for a schoolboy, but not really so very impressive by Barclay's later standards.

His career as a pedestrian began in earnest in 1801. The bet was that he could cover ninety miles in less than twenty-one and a half hours. The contest took place on the Roman Road at Balmby Moor in Yorkshire, and Barclay went back and forth on a one-mile stretch, and completed the distance with over an hour to spare. Radford says, 'He mostly walked but broke into an easy run each time he came to one of the slightly uphill sections.'

Barclay's success in that event wasn't completely un-expected. He'd been training fiercely and had done a trial at the nearby Newborough Priory, where he'd walked a hundred miles within eighteen hours, through the toughest conditions. He walked in the rain, in the cold, in the dark, throughout the night. By daybreak he'd created an ankle-deep circular track in the mud. Richard Long would have loved it.

Barclay performed other impressive feats in this period. In 1803, he wagered that he could cover the sixty-four miles from his quarters in Porridge Island (an alleyway near St Martin-in-the Fields) to Newmarket in Suffolk in twelve hours. He did it in ten, and again this surely must have been a pedestrian race rather than strictly a walking race, and some running or at least jogging must have been involved. In 1807 he challenged Abraham Wood, one of the best-known competitive walkers of the day, to a twenty-four-hour race, the winner simply to be the one who'd walked farthest in that time. Out of what can only have been sheer arrogance, Wood gave Barclay a twenty-mile head start, but then got into physical difficulties, resigned after six and a half hours, and subsequently died.

There was no shortage of other well-known pedestrians in that era, such as a Lieutenant Halifax, who walked six hundred miles in twenty days at thirty miles a day, and then two hundred miles in one hundred hours. There was a pedestrian known as 'Child, the Miller of Wandsworth', who walked forty-five miles in seven hours fifty-seven minutes. There had been Foster Powell, who in 1790, for a bet of '20 guineas to 13', wagered that he could walk from London to York and back in five days and eighteen hours, and he did it with one hour and fifty minutes to spare. In 1808, a Mr Downs walked four hundred miles in ten days, then thirty-five miles a day for twenty successive days.

One thing that separates Barclay from this group is that some of his most impressive walking wasn't done in competition or for money. Often it seems to have been done for the sheer hell of it. In 1802, for example, he set off on a journey from his home in Ury to Kirkmichael and back again. For a lark he returned by the more difficult highland route, but nevertheless clocked up a hundred and eighty miles in two and a half days. This could possibly be construed as part of a training regime but it surely also involved a considerable degree of showing off. Barclay had a reputation, undoubtedly well deserved, but it was buffed by rumour and fantasy, like the story he trained by carrying a load of butter and cheese on his back.

Barclay impressed by combining speed and endurance, but his greatest challenge and success, the walk that was to make his name, involved only the latter. In 1809, Barclay went for the big one (the one that Richard Long's 1974 piece alluded to), and wagered that he could walk a mile in each of a thousand consecutive hours, for a prize of one thousand guineas. The event started 1 June on Newmarket Heath and, if all went well, was due to end on the afternoon of 12 July.

There's something elegant and elemental about those grand, high numbers, but paradoxically there's also something that sounds quite simple and straightforward. An average speed of one mile per hour is insultingly slow: and walking twenty-four miles in a day is not much of a problem for anyone who considers himself a serious walker. Even walking a thousand miles in less than six weeks is well within the range of possibility. The problem is having to walk just one mile in every single hour. Think about it.

If you go at four miles per hour that means that in each hour you're walking for fifteen minutes, and at rest for forty-five. If you join the two miles together, the last fifteen minutes of one hour leading straight into the first fifteen of the next, that still only gives you a maximum of an hour and a half's rest before you have to start walking again. And naturally enough you tend to slow down as the event goes on. The challenge is all about staying power and stamina, but over the course of the six weeks it must have as much to do with overcoming sleep depravation as it does with walking skills.

Barclay succeeded. Once per hour, every hour for one thousand hours, he walked a single mile on a set course in Newmarket, in Suffolk. He actually changed the course part way through the event when he changed his lodgings, on day sixteen, but the rules remained the same. Barclay struggled, he endured, he won. If his stride was a yard long, then he made one million, seven hundred and sixty thousand strides.

It was a huge public event. Vast crowds gathered to see Barclay, though most of them must have seen very little. To a modern sensibility, the sight of a man walking not all that fast for rather short periods of time doesn't sound like rich entertainment, and surely the crowds must have been there for the freak-show element. They wanted to see Barclay's suffering, his agony, perhaps they wanted to see him collapse, even expire *à la* Abraham Wood. Part way through the event the *Edinburgh Advertiser* gleefully reported, 'Captain Barclay was pursuing his extraordinary undertaking yesterday, but as he proceeds, the hopes of his accomplishing it become ever more feeble.' Perhaps they were disappointed when he succeeded and lived. Barclay showed them all. He did the deed, won his money, slept a few hours and then joined his regiment, based outside Deal, and went off to fight Napoleon.

*

Barclay's walking expressed something singular and profound about himself and about the human condition, demonstrating what the human body and the human spirit are capable of. His walking was something in the world and of the world, something natural but also something created and willed. Money was part of his motivation, fame and glory too, but there was surely something inexplicable and irreducible about his obsessive walking, something that remains compelling and admirable, and ultimately mysterious, to this day.

Barclay didn't do drawings or text pieces or mud sculptures as part of his walking, but he did contribute to a book. Its full title is *Pedestrianism; or, an account of the performances of celebrated pedestrians during the last and present century; with a full narrative of Captain Barclay's public and private matches; and an essay on training,* and it's attributed to Walter Thom. Barclay appears as the book's hero rather than author, but he provided a good deal of inside information about himself and about walking in general. The third-person narrative allows him to sing his own praises in a way that would have appeared boastful or arrogant if he'd put his own name to it.

Half the book is an anecdotal history of walking, but the main section describes Barclay's walk, how he looked while he walked. He assumed:

> a sort of lounging gait, without apparently making any extraordinary exertion, scarcely raising his feet more than two or three inches above the ground . . . His style of walking is to bend forward the body, and to throw its weight on the knees . . . Any person who will try this plan will find that his pace will be quickened, at the same time he will walk with more ease to himself, and be better able to endure the fatigue of a long journey, than by walking in a posture perfectly erect, which throws too much of the weight of the body on the ancle-joints (*sic*).

It describes his diet: roasted fowl (hot and cold), strong ale, tea, bread and butter, beef steaks, mutton chops, porter, wine, and 'such vegetables as were in season'. And above all it describes his difficulties and his pain. 'The spasmodic affections in his legs were particularly distressing', we're told. They started on day twelve in his calves, thighs and feet, and got worse until he was in 'great pain' by day twenty. By day thirty-three 'he could not rise up without assistance'. On day thirty-four he couldn't move without crying out. By day thirty-six, says Thom, he was walking so slowly it significantly reduced the amount of time he had to rest; though this is scarcely borne out by evidence in other parts of the book.

A section at the end gives 'box scores' for Barclay's walk, the statistics of his times, speeds, totals, averages, and so on. His first mile, for example, was done in a brisk twelve minutes, and although he gradually slowed down, he was still moving along pretty nicely. On day eighteen he was averaging under seventeen minutes; on day thirty-six, after he'd covered well over eight hundred miles, he was still averaging only a tad over twenty minutes per mile, and his slowest mile in the whole event was only twenty-five minutes. His thousandth mile was walked in just twenty-two minutes, and would have been quicker but there were so many spectators crowding around and cheering him on, he could barely find room to walk.

*

In the interests of research, I decided to do an extended one mile per hour walk. It took place in England, in Suffolk, the same county where Barclay walked his thousand miles, but not in Newmarket, rather in a village called Yoxford, where I used to go to write. Suffolk has the great advantage of being flat.

My emulation of the captain was never going to be absolute. For one thing, I would be doing my walking on public paths and streets, not along a designated track. There would be no cheering crowds, nobody timing me, nobody wishing me well or ill, nobody providing me with mutton chops and porter, nobody betting on my success or failure. Perhaps these things would have spurred me on.

Rather more crucially, I wasn't going to try to walk a thousand miles. I decided to start, with infinite modesty, by doing fifteen miles in fifteen hours. I knew I could walk fifteen miles easily enough. It was spreading those miles out over the day, with all the gaps and the waiting, the stopping and starting; that, I thought, was going to be hard. And I was dead right.

Walking slightly more slowly than the good captain, at more or less three miles per hour, twenty minutes per mile, doing the miles in pairs at the end and beginning of two consecutive hours, I planned to follow a pattern of walking for forty minutes and resting for eighty. That didn't seem too arduous. In fact I thought I could use those rest periods to do something useful, do some writing, read a book, and so on. I was dead wrong about that.

Yoxford is an interesting little village, peaceful, population less than seven hundred. There's a former country house, now a hotel-cum-Malaysian restaurant, called Satis House, where Charles Dickens almost certainly stayed, and he used the name Satis House for Miss Havisham's home in *Great Expectations*. Since Dickens was a manic walker there's every reason to believe he walked in the very places that I did.

Yoxford is also where W. G. Sebald begins one of his cosmically melancholy walks in his book *The Rings of Saturn*. He writes, 'I set out on foot . . . along the old Roman road, into the thinly populated countryside . . . I walked for nearly four hours, and in all that time I saw nothing apart from harvested cornfields stretching away into the distance under a sky heavy with clouds, and dark islands of trees . . . ' I'm pretty sure he's wrong about the Roman road starting at Yoxford. There *is* a good straight Roman road nearby, but it's some way to the west of the village. However, the gloom he describes, the external part anyway, was accurate enough on the day of my walk.

A walk around Yoxford has its historical and literary pleasures, but when you're walking like Captain Barclay, you're not very appreciative of such things. I would set off from the house, walk briskly but aimlessly for a mile, as measured by my GPS, then stop and come right back. This felt peculiar and arhythmic, and I was a little concerned about what the neighbours might think. I didn't want them to think I had 'a screw loose'.

Fortunately I didn't see many neighbours: the cold, damp, rain and occasional snow flurries kept them indoors. I varied my routes as much as I could – to the station and back, round the cricket pitch and the bowling green, and up to the end of the village as far as the closed-down fish-and-chip shop. At one point I found myself at the end of a mile sheltering under the trees in the local graveyard as the sleet lashed down on me, and I heard the sound of a farmer's shotgun being repeatedly fired in the distance, at least I hoped it was the distance. Actually this didn't feel too bad. There's nothing like bleak, adverse conditions for raising a walker's self-esteem.

As it got colder and wetter I walked more quickly, tensed up, head down, shoulders raised, hands shoved into pockets – very much not the Barclay style – and before long I was chilled through and my back was aching, but I carried on doing the miles.

It soon became apparent that my plan of doing anything in the non-walking periods wasn't going to work. It became impossible to think about anything except the next walk. I also discovered that waiting to walk is far more difficult than walking.

I did my fifteen miles in fifteen hours without any physical difficulty, and with some satisfaction, but the real satisfaction came from conquering the difficulties imposed by the frustrating, stop-start pattern. Walking, then stopping, then waiting, making sure each mile was completed inside each designated hour, required a discipline and an attention to detail that was quite at odds with the way I usually walk. In that sense it was some of the hardest walking I'd ever done.

I did a similar walk in midsummer, and it was easier than the one done in winter, but not much. There were pleasures, but they weren't much like the ones that normally go with a good walk, and the fact is, notions of walking for pleasure really didn't mean much to Captain Barclay. For him a walk was all about testing himself, and others, to the limit. He wanted to demonstrate his strength and stamina. He wanted to beat his competitors, though essentially he had none; which is not to say that others haven't emulated him over the years.

About half a century after Barclay's success, an Australian called Allan McKean performed a similar thousand-mile, thousand-hour walk. He did it in late 1858 in Ballarat, in Victoria, then (incredibly) he did it again a few weeks later in Melbourne, ending this second walk in early 1859. The *Melbourne Argus* reported that, 'He completed his thousandth mile (actually his two-thousandth) in fifteen minutes thirty-nine seconds, and appeared to be as little fatigued as when he had accomplished one-half of his allotted distance.'

Perhaps I ought to be doubly impressed by McKean's efforts, and certainly I wouldn't want to belittle them, and yet in the end Captain Barclay remains the man that I, and history, have more respect and affection for. To be the first to do something is inevitably going to be a lot more impressive than to be the first to do it twice.

Most recently it was done again, in 2009, by Richard Dunwoody, the former jockey, now racing tipster, motivational speaker and celebrity ballroom dancer. He did it fairly easily too if the website is to be believed. It surely helped that he was supported by a logistics team, physiotherapists and members of the University of Ulster Sports Studies team. No mutton chops for him either.

He was also (and I'm not sure if this would help or not) accompanied from time to time by 'a host of celebrities from the world of sport and entertainment' (that's the website speaking). These included Jilly Cooper, Lester Piggott, 'Bond girl' Rachel Grant and Sheikh Mohammad bin Rashid Al Maktoum, Ruler of Dubai, who chipped in a 'an extremely generous donation'. It was, of course, a charity fund-raising stunt. Again, there's no reason to deride the achievement, but Dunwoody's walk lacked all the colour, all the singularity, all the *eccentricity* that makes Barclay's so compelling.

*

Nobody as far as I know has repeated the walking feats performed in America by two female walkers, or *pedestriennes* as they were known, feats which strike me in some ways as far more remarkable than anything Barclay, McKean and Dunwoody achieved. In 1879 in Brooklyn, an Englishwoman called Ada Anderson walked two thousand seven hundred quarter-miles in two thousand seven hundred consecutive quarter-hours. Two years later this record was broken by the exotically named Exilda La Chapelle at the Folly Theatre in Chicago, who completed three thousand quarter-miles in three thousand quarter-hours.

Clearly both these women walked considerably shorter distances than Barclay or McKean, but what makes their walks so compelling, and so much more difficult, is the severe reduction in the periods allowed for rest and recovery. These can never have been much more than twenty minutes long. By the end, the poor women must have been hallucinating. The *Washington Post* reported that watching La Chapelle's walk was like watching the Spanish Inquisition. Naturally, there was no shortage of spectators.

Anderson and La Chapelle were members of a small group of professional *pedestriennes*. La Chapelle had turned pro at the age of thirteen. For a brief period in the nineteenth century female walking was a serious sport and a serious business. Large crowds turned out to watch and successful women earned a great deal of money. Even so it was an activity that had something disreputable and *risqué* about it: *pedestriennes* weren't much better than actresses. It was only a passing fad however. It was superseded by the more exciting, and even more *risqué*, sport of female bicycle riding, with some successful female walkers making an easy transition from two feet to two wheels.

*

One of the least likely reasons I can think of for walking is because the President advocates it. In 1962, John F. Kennedy, recently come to office, discovered an executive order issued by Dwight D. Eisenhower in 1956, stating that any self-respecting US marine ought to be able to walk fifty miles in twenty hours. Kennedy reckoned that his marines should certainly be able to do anything Eisenhower's marines could do, and asked his marine commandant to check on this. Kennedy suggested that his White House staff ought to be able to do it too.

This, evidently, was a joke: some of his staff couldn't walk much farther than the water cooler. But, as a publicity stunt, a fifty-mile walk was duly set up for White House staffers. Robert Kennedy, then Attorney General, did the walk wearing Oxfords.

As is the nature with stunts, there were unforeseen consequences. Such was the Kennedy charisma and popularity, fifty-mile walks suddenly became a national craze. A lot of very ordinary, very unfit civilians took it unto their heads to walk fifty miles, often in large groups. Boy Scout troops did it. School groups and seniors did it. An eight-year-old girl called Judy Aylwin failed to do it at the first attempt but succeeded in doing it two weeks later, accompanied by her brother.

The administration was understandably alarmed. A great deal of money and energy was being put into the President's Council on Physical Fitness and Sports, to improve the nation's health, but it was clear that if people who had never walked seriously in their whole lives suddenly got it into their heads to tramp fifty miles the results were likely to be anything but healthful. A campaign was started to distance the White House from this walking madness.

Like most fads, this one, perhaps fortunately, wore off pretty quickly. America returned to its sedentary ways. But not before a man who rejoiced in the name of Jim McNutt, from San Carlos, California, had demonstrated that he could do it faster than anybody else by walking fifty miles in seven hours fifty minutes. He'd have given Barclay a run for his money.

*

One of my very favourite walkers is the traveller and writer Sebastian Snow (1929–2001). He was an Englishman of the old school, droll, debonair, tough as old mahogany. He was an old Etonian, and at Eton (this is almost too good to be true) broke his leg playing football, and thereby avoided National Service: they thought the injury would make him unable to march. Naturally enough he became an adventurer and explorer, and took part in various expeditions, mostly in South America, most of them chaotic. But it was in 1973 that he decided to embark on the greatest adventure of his life, walking the length of the Americas, from Patagonia to Alaska.

In fact he failed. He managed a 'mere' eight thousand seven hundred miles from Tierra del Fuego to the Panama Canal: it took him nineteen months, and although he started on the second leg of the journey, he gave up after a few weeks: he'd had enough. Fellow writer and explorer Eric Newby reckoned that Snow's is one of the longest uninterrupted walks ever accomplished.

Certainly a man by the name of George Meegan has succeeded in walking from Patagonia to Alaska, though I suppose you might quibble about whether or not it was 'interrupted'. It took seven years and he did over-winter with his wife in certain locations. Still his achievement is real enough. He covered nineteen thousand miles, including crossing Canada from east to west, having walked up the Atlantic coast of the United States.

I don't think Meegan would disagree that he's far more of a walker than he is a writer. One of the best episodes in his book *The Longest Walk* is his meeting with Sebastian Snow prior to setting off. They meet in Snow's mother's flat in Devon, and although able to offer plenty of advice and information, Snow can't help himself to a second beer without his mother's permission, a permission she denies. Snow, according to Meegan, was forty-two at the time: my calculations make him a bit older.

Snow was, by any standards, an eccentric, and his prose style does justice to his personality. His adventures, as well as his turns of phrase, are sometimes downright hilarious. In his book *The Rucksack Man* he describes having his toe sucked by a vampire bat, and getting stuck in a sleeping bag, unable to get his hands out to undo the zip. He loses his camera, sends letters home detailing the new kinds of boots he wants sent out to him, and rather less comically he spends much of the trip with his contact lenses stuck in his eyes. In the Peruvian desert a 'young and very animated' Peruvian woman stops her car and decides to chat, complaining that desert driving is very monotonous. 'Desert marching is no sinecure,' Snow replies. The woman offers him a lift but Snow turns it down, as he does every other such offer. This is a walking trip. And that's perhaps his greatest achievement, the extent of his resolve and toughness: being able to pass up a ride, however hard the going gets. His refusal causes endless incomprehension and alarm in the spurned drivers. Some of them think he's mad but in fact he's found a method, and perhaps an ideal, he's got into his stride. 'By some transcendental process,' he writes, 'I seemed to take on the characteristics of a Shire [horse], my head lowered, resolute, I just plunked one foot in front of t'other, mentally munching nothingness.'

*

I don't know if it makes any sense to ask what Snow's reasons were for walking, to analyse whether they were eccentric or conventional. He walked because he wanted to, perhaps because he needed to. He was satisfying an urge, and satisfying urges is hardly eccentric: it's what everybody does all the time, and it's far from selfless.

The closest thing I've discovered to a truly selfless walk (and even here there's a problem) is the one performed by the movie director Werner Herzog in November and December 1974. He heard that Lotte Eisner, the film historian and critic, was in Paris, seriously ill and likely to die. He said to himself this must not be, that German Cinema couldn't do without her, and he set off walking from Munich to Paris, in the depths of winter, 'in full faith believing that she would stay alive if I came on foot'.

His account of that journey appears in a short, brilliant book called, *Of Walking in Ice*, a book so evocative that reading it made by teeth and back ache with cold. For three weeks he trudges through wind, rain, snow, fog, ice, asking himself, 'Why is walking so full of woe?' He sleeps rough in barns and huts, breaks into a holiday home to spend the night, and then into a show home at a caravan dealer's. He experiences pains in his ankle, and 'around the groin'. He gets stopped by police who don't believe his story, and when things get really bad, unlike Sebastian Snow, he does accept a couple of lifts.

Clearly this seems a mad way of trying to keep somebody alive, and Herzog does admit, a little bathetically, 'Besides, I wanted to be alone with myself.' That's the problem I mentioned. But the fact is, the magic worked. Lotte Eisner didn't die. She lived another ten years, until 1983. Wim Wenders' movie *Paris Texas*, released in 1984 (and a movie with a lot of walking in it, but more of that later), is dedicated to her. Walking in order to keep somebody alive, may be eccentric in the extreme, but if it works, then maybe there's nothing eccentric about it whatsoever.

Despite Herzog's reputation for dark obsession and extreme behaviour, he lives in a very pleasant suburban house in the Hollywood Hills, in Wonderland Avenue, admittedly a name associated with murder, drugs and porn star John Holmes, because of the so-called Wonderland Gang. Very possibly it's not his only home, but it's exactly six miles from where I live. I know this because I measured it. I know because I walked it.

This is probably the crassest piece of walking I ever did. I wanted Werner Herzog to say something nice about this book, something that could be emblazoned on the cover. So I walked from my house to his house and back, and I delivered a proof of the book along with a letter of explanation and supplication, in full faith that he'd give me a quote if I came on foot.

By Herzog's standards it was probably a tame walk, but if you're ever looking for risky, perhaps suicidal, walking thrills, you should try slogging up Laurel Canyon Boulevard to get to Wonderland. It's not only that the road is a steep narrow race track with blind bends and no pavements, it's also that nobody ever expects to see a pedestrian there. As I pounded up the tarmac I knew perfectly well that if I got run down and killed nobody would blame the driver. They'd think I was some escaped lunatic who'd wandered into the road.

Worse than that, having slipped the book into Werner Herzog's mailbox, I knew I had to make the journey in reverse. It was no easier. I survived, but it was a horrible experience, admittedly not as horrible as trying to haul a steamship over a mountain, as in *Fitzcarraldo*, but damned hard work for a Wednesday afternoon. This was certainly not a selfless walk, but I thought that maybe the gods of walking would decide I deserved a little something for my efforts. It seems not. The gods of walking are an inscrutable bunch, at least as inscrutable as Mr Herzog. My full faith was not justified. I suspect Werner Herzog thought I wasn't nearly eccentric enough.

5

The Ballard Horizon

I work for three or four hours a day, in the late morning and early afternoon. Then I go out for a walk and come back in time for a large gin and tonic.

J. G. Ballard, 'Writers' Rooms', published in
the *Guardian*, 9 March 2007

The townspeople of Shepperton were hiding in their bedrooms, but at dusk a party of women approached the memorial and began to abuse me.

J. G. Ballard, *The Unlimited Dream Company*

A different day, a different year, a different (though hardly unprecedented) 'endlessly strange' London walking project. I was in London for a couple of weeks and in the name of psychogeography I decided to walk from Will Self's house in Stockwell to Iain Sinclair's house in Hackney. I suppose I was also planning to walk in the name of London literature, urban exploration, and certainly cheap irony. The walk was supposed to be light-footed, witty, absurdist, vaguely subversive. I also thought it might be good to write about.

If Iain Sinclair is the dark magus of walking, Will Self is the snarling, spiky, formerly drug-crazed, baroque-vocabularied, stuntman, fancy walks described in even fancier language. His best, probably unbeatable, walk was (as it were) from London to New York; from his home to Heathrow, then from JFK to his hotel in Manhattan. It was a brilliant idea, and I certainly wish I'd thought of it, and I can see that once you'd thought of it you really might have to do it.

You could argue that Will Self came a little late to the psychogeography party. Some have said that he isn't really a psychogeographer at all, which strikes me as just plain silly. If you want to call yourself a psychogeographer, if you call your newspaper column and your book *Psychogeography*, then hell, a psychogeographer is what you are.

In his airport piece he frets a little, though only a little, about the difference between being a psychogeographer and just some anorak with an interest in 'local history', and he says that 'real, professional local historians view us as insufferably bogus and travelling – if anywhere at all – right up ourselves'. He also raises, or at least I couldn't help thinking about it as I read his book, the inevitable problem lying in wait for the psychogeographer/writer who likes to leave home and get about a bit. Any good long walk in a new place will certainly give a writer material, there's bound to be plenty to see, plenty to think about, but in most cases, inevitably, you're just passing through, skimming the surface. Nobody wants to be thought of as a 'shallow topologist'. Seeing places through new and unfamiliar eyes is all very well, but nobody's going to be impressed by some newbie who walks down Carnaby Street and notes that London no longer swings like a pendulum do. You're in danger of writing Sinclair's dreaded 'reportage'.

My Self–Sinclair pedestrian plan was a simple one, too simple for some psychogeographers, I'm sure. I would invite myself to Will's Self's house, we'd have a cup of tea, talk about walking and psychogeography, *The Society of the Spectacle* and what not, then I'd walk to Iain's Sinclair's place, have another cup of tea and do more of the same. To make life just a little more interesting, I'd take a short detour and go by way of Hercules Road, where William Blake used to live, adding about half a mile to the journey. The entire walk wouldn't be more than six miles. This was never going to be pedestrianism on the grand scale.

Sinclair, of course, I knew a little, and I'd had some contact with Will Self. He and I had been put together by *The Believer* magazine, and we'd conducted an e-mail exchange about walking and writing, walking and fathers, walking and drugs, walking and sex.

Self had turned out not to be the snarling, prickly man of legend, though his vocabulary was suitably esoteric (I learned a new word – verglas). I had been just a little alarmed when he used the phrase 'fellow paedophile' in an e-mail. He meant, obviously, that we both liked walking, but I had the feeling there might be spies and censors lurking deep in my e-mail programme who were not big fans of linguistic playfulness and would call in the sex cops. Call me paranoid if you like. The cops didn't arrive, but my e-mails did go haywire for a couple of days after the exchange.

So I e-mailed both parties, Self and Sinclair, not revealing that I was on a psychogeographic project, simply telling them I'd be in town and suggesting I drop in on them. Iain Sinclair e-mailed back that he'd be away, walking in Berlin, for some of the time I was there, and although he might be around at the weekends, there was a Thames walk he was intending to do one of these weekends and that might occupy him. I should just give him a call when I got in. It sounded casual but not especially hopeful. My e-mail to Will Self produced no response whatsoever: perhaps he was away. Or perhaps they were both trying to avoid me. What then? I could still do the walk, obviously, and if they were really away then I'd just stand in the street and stare at their empty houses. That would be weird, but when you're being psychogeographic, a little weirdness is par for the course.

Eventually I did make successful contact with Sinclair, and

yes he was back from Berlin and he wasn't doing his Thames walk, and yes he'd be happy to have me come round at 4.30 on Monday afternoon. He was being interviewed by a PhD student earlier in the day but by that time he'd be clear. Still nothing from Self.

On the day in question I took the tube to Stockwell, made my way to Will Self's street and found his house; it looked thoroughly unoccupied: blinds were drawn upstairs, wooden internal shutters were closed on the raised ground floor. It seemed he really was away. I felt free to stand and gawp to my heart's content at this substantial, white, stuccoed, bay-fronted house. Some builders working in the street did look at me suspiciously but they weren't the kind of blokes who spoke to strangers and asked what they were up to, and frankly I wasn't inclined to do much lingering. It was just a closed-up house. I started my walk.

Even with the Blakean detour it was a pretty straight shot, mostly north, somewhat east: Stockwell, Lambeth, Waterloo, Southwark, across the Thames via London Bridge, then Shoreditch, Hackney, Albion Square: Sinclair-land. I set off, noticing the kind of things you notice when you're committed to a walk, especially when you know you're going to be writing about it. I observed the Spurgeon Estate right opposite the Self house, a 'good' council estate, its goodness marked by signs all over the place telling you what you weren't allowed to do: park, play ball games, allow your dog to walk on the grass, loiter, climb, etc. I made my way to the Albert Embankment, not the most direct route but it seemed the way to go. Improbably, there were two men in a rubber dinghy rowing on the Thames. There was a woman walking along the street reading an Agatha Christie paperback. I passed the Parliament View Apartments, and wondered whether a view of Parliament is really all that desirable. Is the idea that you can keep an eye on your elected representatives across the water? Good luck.

And then in Hercules Road there was the William Blake Estate, and a plaque on the wall of a block of flats, saying he used to live there or thereabouts, and there were the suitably mythopoeic side streets, Virgil and Centaur, and the Hercules newsagent at the end of the road. Then I was in the foodie wonderland of Borough Market, then into serious tourist territory: Clink Street, and the replica of Drake's *Golden Hinde*.

As I crossed London Bridge, I recalled having walked over the original one, in its new location in Lake Havasu City, in Arizona. It looked pretty damn good and solid, and some- how much less out of place than you might think, given the Arizona Desert and the palm trees surrounding it. Here in London, and just over the bridge, there was a store called Snow and Rock offering a free in-store gait analysis. I did think about going in to get my gait analysed, since it was starting to dawn on me that I'd given myself far too much time for this journey. I hadn't wanted to arrive late, I hadn't wanted to have to hurry, and I'd wanted to leave myself enough time to take a few meanders and detours if they presented themselves, but now I saw I was in danger of arriving at Sinclair's place an hour or two early. I needed to walk more slowly; I needed to dawdle, which I always find much harder than walking fast and purposefully. I stopped for a sandwich, then I walked some more, then I sat and read for a bit in Haggerston Park, walked again, but I was still early enough to take a turn around the small garden in Albion Square, just a few yards from Sinclair's front door.

There was a woman in there with a child in a pram, and we exchanged a few words, agreeing how perfect Albion Square was. There was no denying it. At that moment,

Albion Square seemed as pleasant and nurturing as any place in London. And yet I was feeling dissatisfied. The walk there had been good, a proper London walk, but it hadn't seemed especially serious or important or revelatory. It certainly didn't seem very psychogeographical, whatever the hell that meant. As a walk in itself it was fine but as a walk to *write* about it was lacking. This is a problem that faces the walking writer or the writing walker. In a totally Zen world a perfect walk might well leave you with nothing to say. But for those of us who live in other worlds, a good walk is one about which you can say or write something. I admit this is a dilemma and a paradox, and one that I haven't solved. I went to Iain Sinclair's front door, rang his bell and he let me in.

In other circumstances we might surely have discussed all this, but in the event it was a very relaxed, unintense meeting, tea was drunk, there was talk about where we'd been walking and what we'd been writing, but I really didn't have the heart to bring up Debord and psychogeography and, for whatever reason, neither did he. I admit I was relieved. In fact we spent quite a bit of time talking about J. G. Ballard who'd died since we'd last seen each other.

The influence that Ballard's novels and short stories have had on several generations of English writers needs no further documentation from me. Will Self, Iain Sinclair and I have certainly all been fingered by reviewers as belonging to this group. We've all resisted to a greater or lesser extent, but we're all flattered by the comparison, and we're definitely all great admirers of Ballard. *Crash* was the novel that sent many a young turk running to his keyboard to celebrate the psycho-pathology of the car crash, rampant technology, presidential assassinations, dead movie stars, plastic surgery, perverse sex and so on. Walking, however, is not conspicuously one of Ballard's major themes.

'Not much of a walker, Ballard,' I said.

'No,' Sinclair agreed, 'although . . . '

And he launched into a story about a period in Ballard's life when he was banned from driving for a year. He refused to take public transport and walked wherever he went, but he decided he'd only walk as far as what he calculated to be his 'personal horizon'. He seems to have meant this in an oddly literal sense. He would only walk as far as he could see when he was standing at ground level outside his home, which he reckoned was about three quarters of a mile in all directions. He stuck to the plan for a year and got to know his local area pretty thoroughly; then he got his licence back, started driving again and stopped walking. All this is Sinclair's story, not mine.

In fact I'd been considering going down to look at Ballard's old house in Shepperton. I'd thought it would be a literary pilgrimage rather than a walking one, since I hadn't imagined Shepperton to be very fascinating walking territory. But now I could see possibilities.

Next day off I went, taking the train from Waterloo to Shepperton, a journey of just under an hour that involved passing through places that were somewhat familiar to me: Clapham, Wimbledon, Kingston; then through places with names that sounded like the stuff of suburban sitcom: Fulwell, Sunbury, Upper Halliford and the inevitable Hampton Wick. By this time I'd also remembered a small but significant mention of walking in one of Ballard's short stories, 'The Garden of Time'. The protagonist is one Count Axel. Every evening he leaves the library of his Palladian villa and walks in his garden, sometimes with his wife. On the horizon, he sees an 'immense rabble' advancing towards his estate, threatening to destroy it, him and his wife. Each night he picks a crystal 'time flower' and the rabble is magically driven back beyond the horizon until the next evening when it all happens again. But the garden is dying, the number of flowers is limited, the horde must eventually, inevitably, arrive and succeed in their destruction, which they duly do, and the count and his wife are transformed into garden statues.

It had always reminded me of the Tom Waits lines from 'Way Down In The Hole' that run, 'When you walk in the garden/You gotta watch your back', though I guess Waits is conflating the gardens of Eden and Gethsemane here; whereas Count Axel is very much in his own garden, and he's watching not his back but the horizon.

I think we all have our 'personal horizons'. Even the most footloose of us have boundaries that we're reluctant to walk beyond, and these may be metaphoric as much as geographic. Shepperton had certainly never been on my map. But now that had changed. I thought it would be good to stand more or less where Ballard had once stood, and see for myself just where the Ballardian horizon was located. By his own reckoning it seemed that anywhere I walked within three quarters of a mile of the Ballard house I'd be absolutely certain of walking in his territory and in his footsteps.

*

Shepperton, which appears in the Domesday Book as Scepertone, and for which my spellcheck suggests 'Coppertone', features extensively in Ballard's fiction. When I first read his work I had only the vaguest idea of where and what Shepperton was, though I had heard of the Shepperton movie studios, which promised a certain degree of glamour. From Ballard's own descriptions I also knew the place wasn't far from Heathrow Airport, and there was certainly a time when proximity to international airports could be construed as glamorous, but that was a very long time ago.

Ballard also used Shepperton as a geographical shorthand

for the kind of place where apparently nothing much happens and yet where characters are free to develop all sorts of manias and obsessions. Equally his characters often inhabit landscapes that have been transformed or partially destroyed, dotted with ruins, drained swimming pools, abandoned airfields. Some of this was perhaps a kind of wishful thinking on Ballard's part: come friendly bombs.

His attitude towards the suburbs was paradoxical, 'In a way they're more dangerous places [than cities],' he said in an interview with *Re/Search* magazine, 'you're not going to get mugged walking down the street, but somebody might steal your *soul.* I mean that literally – your will to live.' At first this sounds like the typical scorn that arty, metropolitan types have for bourgeois existence; the difference in Ballard's case was that he spent forty-odd years living resolutely in suburbia, writing, raising his children and (presumably) continually risking the loss of his soul.

I looked at a map to find Ballard's street, and saw immediately that the location was a commuter's dream (although for most of his life Ballard was no commuter), right next to the railway station and easy walking distance from the centre of town. My first impression as I got off the train in Shepperton on the day of my pilgrimage was that the place seemed very much as advertised: quiet, clean, safe, a little dull for sure, the population overwhelmingly, and at this point in history amazingly, white.

I had met Ballard a couple of times but I didn't claim to know him. I had certainly never been invited to his house, although literary fame and literary journalism being as they are, I'd seen magazine photographs of both interior and exterior. I knew, everybody knew, that he lived in an ordinary semi-detached house, and hadn't moved even when the big international movie money came flooding in.

I started to walk along Ballard's street. It was full of sub-stantial, well-kept houses, mostly semis and bungalows, a few detached houses, a bit of mock Tudor, carefully tended gardens, new but unflashy cars parked outside. There was a pub at the end of the street, another halfway along it.

I found Ballard's house easily enough. It looked even more modest than in the published photographs. It was certainly one of the less attractive, less well-tended, less 'modernised' houses in the street. Yes, it was semi-detached, but the gap between it and the unattached house next to it was negligible, no room for a drive or garage; in fact Ballard's car – a twenty-year-old metallic grey Ford Granada – was still parked in the front garden. The car was grubby, a couple of tyres were sagging; presumably it had been there since at least the time of Ballard's death, and perhaps much longer, given that he'd had a long, debilitating illness.

The house was empty and closed up. On the ground floor, long lace curtains were drawn across the bay windows so that gawkers like me couldn't peer in. The spikes of ancient potted palms had pushed up between the curtains and the glass in the windows, looking as though they'd thrived for a time before drying out. It was hard now to tell if they were dead or alive.

It was just about possible to read all this as a kind of Ballard landscape, though only of a minor sort. The house was, at least temporarily, uninhabited, but it was far from abandoned: an estate agent would have salivated at the chance to sell it, 'only needs a little TLC'. The car in the garden was no doubt on its way to becoming a rusted hulk, but that would take decades. It was all very far from being the sort of poetic, metaphoric ruin in which Ballard specialised.

To me, now that I was standing there in front of the

house, the notion of Ballard's personal horizon seemed at best dubious. The territory was flat and low. If I looked straight ahead all I could see were the houses on the other side of the street, a horizon that was no more than a hundred feet away. If I looked behind me I simply stared at Ballard's house. Looking down the street in one direction, I saw the way back to the station, looking in the other I saw the end of the street, which was a dead end. A pub was visible in either direction. Go pick the metaphors out of that one.

At the risk of being a spoilsport, I'd looked into the mathematics of calculating the distance to the horizon. There's a fairly simple way of doing it, accurate enough for general purposes, though genuine mathematicians will spit on it. All you need to know initially is how high your eyes are above sea level, i.e. the distance from your feet to your eyes, plus the 'local elevation' of the place you're standing. Shepperton is 33 feet above sea level, so being generous, and to make life easier, we might estimate Ballard's height as six feet, making 39. We take this figure, multiply it by 1.5, then find the square root of the result, and this gives you the distance in miles to the horizon. So 39 x 1.5 = 58.5; the square root of 58.5 is 7.65. So Ballard's horizon was 7.65 miles away, a good deal more than he calculated. I also tried another calculation. If you can see 7.65 miles in all directions you're seeing an area of 184 square miles (π multiplied by the radius squared). That's quite a lot of territory to get to know pretty thoroughly.

Of course, these are theoretical figures. All manner of things can get between you and your horizon, blocking it, narrowing it, creating obstacles both to seeing and walking. I headed for the dead end of the street, and when I got all the way there I was pleased to find that although this was as far as you could go in a car, a man on foot could pass through a gate on to a footpath and into a lush, green, reedy, willowy area called Splash Meadow. An illustrated sign promised all manner of flora and fauna: kingfishers, damsel flies and yellow flag iris among them. This was all far, far too pleasant and bucolic to have any Ballardian resonance.

Splash Meadow proved to be small, a narrow sliver of land, pressed up alongside a golf course, with the unlikely name of American Golf Sunbury. My hatred of golf knows few bounds. It seems to me that golf isn't merely a good walk spoiled, but rather a good piece of walking territory made inaccessible, annexed by fuckwits in pastel clothing. I like to think Ballard would have shared my unreasonable opinion. I went around a section of the course, and then made sure that I walked across one of the greens, happy to be trespassing but not quite having the nerve to gouge holes in the turf with my boot heels, the way I would really have liked to.

*

I had been dimly aware of a low, roaring sound, too quiet to be disturbing or even identifiable, but now as I walked farther along the path, as the surroundings became greener, wilder, more overgrown, the roar got louder, though not any more identifiable. And then, emerging abruptly, unexpectedly out of the undergrowth was a rising concrete ramp, a rather playful structure that curled and swooped upwards through a full 360 degrees. It looked like a relic rather than a ruin, a redundant structure, something left behind to be over-whelmed by weeds and creepers: OK, things might be thought to be getting just a little Ballardian.

With absolutely no idea where the ramp might lead or why it was even there, I ascended, enjoying the continuous, gently engineered rise. It felt good to walk up it. When I got to the top, the ramp's function became absolutely clear. This was one end of a footbridge that took pedestrians from one side of the M3 to the other, where another, similar circular ramp descended into more wild greenery. Now I could identify the source of the roaring; it was the noise of vehicles belting along the motorway.

I went up to the peak of the bridge and watched the traffic, light and fast moving. In truth it was a little scary up there. The bridge was narrow. The railings were low. The motorway was a long, lethal way down. You didn't have to be a serious agoraphobe, acrophobe or gephyrophobe to feel a shudder creeping up your spine. And I could imagine drivers looking up and seeing this lone figure walking on the bridge and wondering if I was going to throw myself off. What the hell was I doing up there? The answer would have been, just going for a walk, making a literary pilgrimage, extending my horizons. And one thing became very obvious from up there; the horizon suddenly seemed very much farther away than it had been at ground level in Ballard's street. From the bridge you could see for miles.

And I did wonder whether Ballard had actually stood here on this bridge. Surely he must have. It wasn't actually visible from his home, but it was certainly within the theoretical three quarters of a mile. And if he had stood here, then it made his 'personal horizon' even more of a literary conceit. The bridge was about twenty feet high: add that to the previous calculations and the Ballardian horizon was now 9.4 miles away, and actually it looked very much farther.

If my Self–Sinclair walk had lacked resonance, this one seemed too resonant by half. I'm always suspicious of the need to find a perfect moment as a climax to a walk, of attaching deep significance to things that aren't necessarily significant at all, but this seemed genuine enough. My Ballard walk had shown me that the horizon, whether personal or

literal, can be changed dramatically if you're prepared to walk
quite a short distance. It was time to head back into London.

*

When I got back there was an e-mail from Will Self. It read:

> Geoff – Sorry to have missed you. Just back from 3,500
> mile peregrination through France and Italy. Yes, in a car!
> But it felt so goood a form of rubbery adultery. W

6

A Psychogeographer Walks into a Bar: New York, the Shape of the City, Beauty, Order, Convenience

> Provincial American cities evoke in me a terrible feeling
> of desolation as evening falls and the citizenry retires to
> home, hearth, peevish wife and importunate children.
> Whereas in Manhattan at any hour of the night one can
> step into the street and encounter a werewolf or at least a
> derelict who will vomit on one's shoes.
>
> Thomas Berger

Here's Garry Winogrand, walking on the crowded streets of New York in the 1970s, carrying a Leica M4 with a 28mm lens, the leather strap wound tight round his hand, the camera being constantly raised and lowered, to and from his eye, turning his head, refocusing his gaze, looking for visual triggers, for subjects, endlessly, relentlessly pressing the shutter, shooting pictures, sometimes just shooting.

Winogrand walks but not at the same pace as the pedestrians around him, and sometimes he stops completely so that the flow of people splits and eddies past, and sometimes he sees something across the street, and pushes through the crowd, dashes over there, dodging traffic or forcing the traffic to dodge him. Once there he continues taking photographs. You'd think that New York's angry, purposeful walkers would knock him out of the way, walk all over him; but he's found a way to avoid that. Sometimes he smiles and nods at the people he's photographing, offers a word or two, chats, and in the main nobody minds; it's a technique he's developed, a way of presenting himself as just another eccentric on the streets of New York, self-absorbed, obsessive, but essentially harmless; which is not a complete misrepresentation of Winogrand.

And then somebody perceives him as something else. A woman, irate, offended, full of righteous indignation, believes that in photographing her, Winogrand has stolen something from her. 'Hey, you took my picture!' she protests, and Winogrand, in his rough, tough, amused New York voice says, 'Honey, it's *my* picture now.' It's an old story, and one that I very much want to be true.

*

I was in New York, walking up Lower Broadway from Canal Street late one weekday afternoon. The street was as packed as it always is at that time of day, although the pedestrians usually move fast and efficiently. Today, however, the crowd had come to a complete halt. They were watching something, though I couldn't see what, and it was only as I joined the throng that I realised they were watching a burning car. Its engine had caught fire and even though there was a cop in attendance and somebody had used an extinguisher on it, there were still a few flames and a cloud of smoke rising from the engine. The pedestrians were taking a great delight in this and we all stood about, blocking the pavement, making wisecracks, enjoying this impromptu entertainment. A few people were taking photographs. I had my camera with me, and I considered joining in but in the end decided against it.

Suddenly we became aware of an angry voice behind us and somebody started to push through the crowd. I turned to see who was in such a damned hurry and my eyes fell on a very tough looking, achondroplastic dwarf. He was a little over four feet tall, wearing an immaculate three-piece suit and smoking a cigar, and he was seriously pissed off. If you wanted an argument he was more than ready to give you one. The crowd parted and let him through. Now I really thought about taking a picture but the guy looked as though he might try to stick the camera down my throat.

I suppose this was one of those 'only in New York' moments, and while being pushed aside by dwarves isn't an everyday occurrence in lower Manhattan, it nevertheless seemed something perfectly ordinary and unexceptional, just part of the texture of living and walking in New York.

*

There are plenty of people who will tell you that walking in New York is a universally difficult and painful business. They are mostly English people. They cite the lack of flow and rhythm, the stopping and starting as each block presents you with a traffic signal and the instruction to walk or not walk. Of course New York pedestrians try their damnedest not to obey instructions, to walk when they're told not to, but self-preservation demands that once in a while they stop and let the traffic have its way. Walking in New York involves a lot of waiting to walk. It also involves a lot of distraction, there's so much to look at, so many faces and characters, so many things you might think of trying to photograph.

I lived in New York between 1997 and 2003, an interesting time, not least because it saw the removal of the Walk/Don't Walk signs, and the arrival of signs with a red hand for stop and a white walking man for go. The change must have cost millions, and like any good, cynical New Yorker I thought I detected a scam, a pay off. Precisely for whose benefit did the city abandon the English language in favour of this signifier? Who, even in New York, is so illiterate or so foreign as not to be able to recognise the words 'Walk' and 'Don't'?

The city fathers who designed Manhattan's grid pattern of

streets claimed it would bring 'beauty, order and convenience' to the city, and to some practical extent that's true. The pattern does exert control, both on drivers and walkers, and the numerical and occasionally alphabetical arrangement means it's hard to get thoroughly lost in Manhattan. However, within that structure people's eccentricity, waywardness, hostility, madness are free to run wild. Perhaps a more random or 'organic' structure would have created, indeed necessitated, more self-control. I know that's a big perhaps.

*

I first visited New York in the late 1970s when the city's reputation for Darwinian, perhaps Malthusian, selection was all part of its dangerous charm. You had to be 'fit' in certain specific ways. If you couldn't survive, you didn't belong there. If you failed to survive, you didn't deserve to. The locals I knew offered a lot of wisdom on how you should walk the streets in order to remain unmolested. You should stride along, head down, looking purposeful, showing that you were aware of what was going on around you, but also demonstrating that you weren't too interested because there was somewhere really important you had to get to in a hurry. The other part of the equation was that you should never look like the most vulnerable person on the street. The bad guys were cowards: they only went after stragglers. As long as there was somebody near by who looked more like a victim than you did, you were OK, theoretically, comparatively.

It made for a particular and peculiar walking style, alert yet cocooned, and always hoping there was some wimpy college student or feeble old person within striking distance to divert attention from you, from me. It was easy to get this wrong. I did my best but even so I got hassled; not mugged, not robbed, not attacked, not raped, but messed with. Maybe

I was trying too hard, or maybe my attempt to look like a tough guy in a hurry was so unconvincing that it became the very thing that marked me out. In those days I stayed clean and sober as I walked the streets of New York. I would no more have wandered drunkenly through Manhattan than I'd have worn a sign saying, 'Please Kill Me'.

When I started going back to New York in the mid 1990s, and eventually living there, things were very different. For one thing I was older, a little tougher, more substantial. I looked less like prey. But the city had changed far more than I had. It was no longer bankrupt, for example, and there weren't hookers in hot pants on every street corner. And many things about the culture had changed too. In the 1970s if you really wanted drugs or pornography you had to steel yourself and make a trek to Times Square: fans of *nostalgie de la boue* absolutely loved this. However, by the 1990s you could get drugs and pornography just about anywhere. Times Square had to change. People, of course, complained about its Disneyfication, bemoaning the fact that the mean spirit and the dark heart of New York had become soft. Any damn fool could now walk safely in New York, and to New Yorkers that just didn't seem right.

A case can still be made, however, using accident statistics, that walking in New York remains a thrillingly dangerous activity: fifteen thousand pedestrians are injured by cars every year in New York. That's 21 per cent of the nation's accidents, despite the city having only 2.7 per cent of the nation's population. Nearly three quarters of these injuries occur on crossings, and quite a few of them occur while the pedestrian is actually on the pavement. How edgy is that?

In recent years, the injury figures have been dropping a little, but it seems likely that although this must owe something to improved road design and increased public safety awareness, it owes rather more to the fact that people are simply walking less because they're scared of being run down.

Alcohol plays a surprising part in those car/pedestrian injuries – it's not usually the driver who's been drinking. Drunk drivers account for just a few per cent of pedestrian deaths; in forty per cent of the cases the pedestrian has been drinking. It will surprise nobody to learn that considerably more drunken pedestrian deaths occur at night than in the daytime. Careering around New York City at night with a snootful of booze is such a high-risk activity it's surprising that anybody survives.

*

New York was where I learned to drink Martinis. I often thought the Manhattan cocktail would have been a more appropriate choice, given its name, but for me it never addressed the pleasure and pain receptors in the way a Martini did, with its clean, ice-cold gin, its hint of vermouth and dilution, the perfect silver bullet. A Martini felt more like a drug than a drink. It had my name on it. It hit hard: it wasn't for wimps.

After a Martini or two I would happily walk the dark streets of Manhattan feeling a little 'bagged', a bit 'lit up', with a new sense of power and possibility. Certain edges were taken off and certain others (the ones to do with feelings of invulnerability and inflated self-esteem) were sharpened up in their place. It wasn't quite sensory derangement *à la* De Quincy, but it was definitely an altered state and that was good enough. Sometimes it felt like floating as much as walking.

I was two Martinis to the good when I first proposed to the woman who's now my wife, but who was then more or less a complete stranger. We were walking down Crosby

Street, a narrow access street parallel to Lower Broadway, and I had spent a total of one hour in her company. She didn't say no.

Later, once we were an item, there were many nights when we walked through SoHo, where her office was, heading north up Thompson or Sullivan Street, with ahead of us the illuminated Empire State Building and behind us the illuminated Twin Towers, and we said that one of these days we'd have to go up to Windows on the World, the swank bar in the north tower, and have a Martini or two. It never happened. We didn't know there was any reason to rush.

*

I wasn't in New York on 11 September 2001. I was three thousand miles away in England. My wife was three thousand miles away in the opposite direction, visiting her sister in Seattle. After the event I spent some time wondering whether we should consider ourselves lucky, or if we should regret having been absent at such a crucial and calamitous moment in history. There was some guilt too because by then I felt like a New Yorker and it seemed only right that I should have had to go through what other New Yorkers had gone through.

As soon as I could, I got on a plane and went back to New York. Dust and shreds of paper were still falling all over the city, and there was a strange smell in the air that was reported to be the horrifying combination of jet fuel and incinerated human flesh, but in itself really wasn't so bad, quite sweet, like something roasting in honey.

And once I was back in the city, I did what everybody else was doing. I walked to Ground Zero, to see what there was to see. I joined the procession of people a mile or more from the zone, on Lower Broadway, a long stream of walkers that got broader and flowed less freely as it neared its destination. It was a solemn crowd but not a quiet one. This was New York.

I'm told that in the early days people weren't allowed to take photographs of Ground Zero, that anyone seen using a camera had it confiscated. It had never occurred to me to take my own camera along on that day, but already the era of confiscation was over and at least half the crowd was shooting stills or video, though I don't know what it was seeing.

We were kept at bay, behind barriers. The viewpoint we were allowed was a distant one and even the most powerful telephoto lens wouldn't have got you in very close. We could see rubble, a spout of water being hosed from a great height, and we could just about make out the famous twisted, perforated façade, but it wasn't nearly so clear or so dramatic as the pictures we'd seen in the newspapers and on TV.

In the end there was very little to see. As a place of pilgrimage, Ground Zero seemed inadequate. It was a walk without a goal, though not a drift. I had a sense of frustration and deflation. I wanted more from this walk. And I noticed that all around me people were crying, and that seemed incomprehensible at first. There was nothing there to cry about, no relics, no triggers, nothing. I found myself quite unmoved.

And then, up against a barrier that was blocking our way, I saw a member of the National Guard, an older man, fat-faced, densely built, but not looking much like a soldier. A stream of people kept walking up to him and he handed something to each of them, a paper tissue that they could cry into. He did it quietly, undramatically, and the gentleness and dignity of the gesture moved me more than anything else I saw that day. It was as much comfort as anyone could offer, or had any right to receive. The tears started rolling down my own cheeks and I didn't try to stop them.

*

I walked down to Ground Zero again, a little less than a

year later, a week before the one-year anniversary. There
were very few people there at that time, and the site had the
windswept feel of a tourist attraction out of season. There
was even less to see than there had been on that first visit,
but now you could get right up to the wire fence and peer
down into the vast, excavated pit, six storeys deep. It had all
gone. The evidence had all been taken away. You had to be
impressed by the sheer industry and determination that had
been required to clear away all that horror and debris and
chaos.

I went there again a week later, on the anniversary itself,
when the crowds had returned, and only families and VIPs
were allowed anywhere near the pit. The rest of us just milled
about in the surrounding streets. The front page of the *New
York Post* ran a photograph of the standing twin towers with
the headline 'Lest We Forget'. I found myself infuriated,
spitting with rage. What kind of attention-deficient rubes
did they take us for? We were being entreated to remember
something none of us could possibly have forgotten. Did they
think it might somehow have slipped our minds?

*

In Paul Auster's novel *City of Glass*, one of his New York
Trilogy, a detective follows a character called Stillman as he
wanders around Manhattan's Upper West Side. Eventually
the detective realises that these wanderings, when plotted on
a map, have a shape to them and are spelling out the phrase
'Tower of Babel'. In fact, Stillman never does spell out the
last two letters 'EL', which Auster explains for the benefit of
Gentiles is 'the ancient Hebrew for God'.

Stillman's wanderings make for a fine literary conceit, but
even as you read the book, and look at Auster's doodles that
illustrate the walks, you realise that on the ground things
wouldn't be nearly so clear. Walking the shape of an 'O' for

instance is exceptionally difficult on a grid; Auster's badly drawn 'O' could be a badly drawn 'D', and the 'W' in 'tower' is so shapeless it might have been a V or a U, or a roller-coaster, or as the detective says 'a bird of prey perhaps, with its wings spread, hovering aloft in the air'. This is another big perhaps.

The walking of a shape, symbol or word is one of the basic practices of psychogeography, what they call a 'constrained walk', exploring a city on foot while following a restrictive or perverse logic, which might include tossing a coin at each street corner to determine the route, walking so as to avoid all security cameras, walking in a dead straight line without regard to actual geography, and so on. If you were to object that all walks are constrained one way or another, you'd get no argument from me.

Psychogeography had again been on my mind because I was about to attend the Conflux psychogeography festival in Brooklyn. Given my reservations about psychogeography you might find it odd that I'd go to a festival, and frankly so did I. The event was, and I'm quoting now, 'the annual New York City festival where visual and sound artists, writers, urban adventurers, researchers and the public gather for four days to explore the physical and psychological landscape of the city. Say hello to Brooklyn!'

Well, I was happy to do that, and I'd also been spending some time staring at maps of New York, partly inspired by Auster, looking for patterns, hoping that the layout of streets might reveal some symbol or logo that could form the basis of a constrained walk of my own, something I'd do quite independently of the festival. I was hoping to see and then walk the shape of, say, a nuclear-disarmament symbol, a Volkswagen trademark, a meaningful word, maybe a muted post horn. However, the only two shapes I could make out on the streets of New York were the cross and the swastika and I was reluctant to walk either of those. Still, I wasn't worried. I was going to a psychogeographical festival. I'd be inspired: I felt sure some project would present itself.

*

Things were scheduled to start at ten o' clock on Thursday morning at Conflux headquarters in an art gallery in Williamsburg, Brooklyn. I got up in good time to discover that New York was caught in the fierce tail of a hurricane. I had no idea what effect it would have on the festivities. I'd thought I might get to the gallery by walking over the Williamsburg Bridge, but that now seemed impossible. I told myself that walking in the rain had a long, respectable and melancholy history; nevertheless I took the subway from Manhattan.

On the train, with an open mind and a certain unshakeable scepticism, I read about some of the promised highlights such as 'The World is My Studio', in which an artist called Sitka was giving 'a narrated tour in which she talks about everyday objects and spaces as if they were her work, contextualising things like moving cars, people's pets and social gestures as the products of her artistic practice'. Debord calls this 'playfully constructive behaviour'.

There was Paul Harley's 'Pansy Project', in which he revisited 'city streets planting pansies where he has received verbal homophobic abuse. These self-seeding pansies act as a living memorial to this abuse and operate as an antidote to it; each pansy's location is named after the abuse received then posted on his website.' There was a group from England called 'You are here but why?' who were going to comb the streets looking for scrap material from which to build a desk. I admit that the scepticism was getting the upper hand over the open mind.

When I got to the gallery, just a little before ten, it was

closed, and two hassled young women were struggling hope-
lessly with the lock on the gallery door. It looked like they
had enough on their plates without answering questions from
me. There was a café next door where a few would-be psychogeographers were sheltering from the rain and waiting for
something to happen. I joined them.

Only very gradually did it become apparent that the start
had been delayed, not because of some organisational glitch
but by sabotage. The gallery wasn't simply locked; it was
sealed. Someone, a disgruntled artist it was assumed, had
come along in the night with a caulking gun, glued the
gallery door shut, and squirted more of the caulk into the
lock. Then, on the concrete in front of the gallery, he (it was
surely a he) had painted the exhortations, 'Mr Gorbachev,
open this gate! Mr Gorbachev, tear down this wall!'

The gallery walls were not torn down, but a locksmith
duly arrived and opened the door, so that the group of us,
twenty-five or so by now, who'd gathered in the café, were
belatedly able to get into the gallery. Some opening remarks
were made by Christina Ray, the curator of the festival. Over
the years, she said, the festival's events had become more
technologically based and less 'analog'. A lot was happening
on-line, a lot of the psychogeography was virtual. I found
this disappointing. There are few activities more analog than
walking. And she said that whereas in previous years Conflux
had often featured maps to help you find your way around,
this year there would be maps to help you get lost.

I looked out through the window and saw that in front of
the gallery, in the rain, a young woman was sweeping the
pavement. This, I knew, was a walking-art project entitled
'Sweeping (Sidewalk Performances #1)' and the artist was D.
Jean Hester. By her own account:

I will sweep the sidewalks near the gallery . . . sweeping the public sidewalk is an expression of pride in one's place, as well as a gift given to others who use the area. While sweeping and engaged in a 'helpful' activity for the neighbourhood, I may greet people who pass by with a 'Goodmorning!' Will the activity of sweeping make me more approachable, allowing people to interact with me in a less guarded fashion?

I didn't have an absolute answer for her question. True, I did approach her, but the interaction was guarded on both sides. By the time I got out to the street, she'd stopped sweeping. She'd been at it for all of ten minutes, and that was a disappointment. I'd imagined she'd be sweeping throughout the festival, for the whole four days, for a hundred hours or so of continuous, endurance sweeping and walking. But no.

She told me it was really hard to sweep in the rain, what with holding her umbrella and all. I asked her how large an area she was planning to cover, and she said that, given the rain, she was just going to do the small stretch in front of the gallery, but maybe when the rain stopped she'd do the whole block. Again I had been over-ambitious on her behalf. I'd thought she might try to sweep the whole zip code. Then I asked whether she was sweeping the road as well as the sidewalk, since I could see there was a lot of garbage lying there in the street. No, she said, just the sidewalk. We agreed it was good to set yourself limits.

The first event in the gallery was a 'discussion session' with an artist called Sue Huang, about her ongoing project 'Street Cut Ups'. This involved walking the streets, looking for texts on signs, posters, ads, and so on, which she would cut out, take away and then stick together to reveal other, more subversive meanings. It came as no surprise that she claimed to be influenced by the 'cut up' method, and by the Oulipo group, the French experimentalists who specialise in 'constrained writing'. It was more surprising, and disappointing, that her press release referred to one 'William S. Borroughs'.

The 'discussion session' consisted of the artist sitting at a table in the gallery with a laptop in front of her, like a nervous vendor at a trade show, as people milled around her, one of whom would occasionally stop and ask what she was up to. Again I had unreasonable expectations. I'd thought the artist would lead a tour, and we'd walk through the streets of Brooklyn, slashing at posters, snatching words, liberating them, performing a specialised form of anti-logorrhoea, sucking words in rather than squirting them out. But we looked out through the window at the rain, and it became all too clear that nobody was going anywhere. Except me. This session was due to last an hour to be followed by a session with a different artist, which I suspected would be all too similar. I couldn't face that. I left the gallery, went back to Manhattan and kept my powder dry.

*

The next day I was signed up for something called 'Public Parking', a walking tour of certain Brooklyn car parks, organised by the Temporary Travel Office, the brainchild of one Ryan Griffis. I'm a great fan of walking in parking lots, partly because it's a perverse thing to do, but also because it's a small act of reclamation and defiance. Taking a walk, even just a short cut, through a parking lot is a way of saying that this open space, and sometimes it can be the only open space for miles around, isn't the sole province of cars and drivers. And if there's a chance of being run down by cars manoeuvring into or out of parking bays then so be it.

I felt there had to be some ironies in a walking tour of Brooklyn car parks, but I wasn't sure the Temporary Travel

Office's ironic fault line was in the same place as mine. Certainly the professed purpose of the walk was po-faced enough, which didn't mean that it was easy to take it entirely seriously. 'Public Parking,' said the Temporary Tourist Office, 'is an investigation into the realities of utopian thought as materialised in the mundane and pragmatic spaces of parking lots,' and there were references to 'participatory mapping of personal utopias upon the topography of property development'. I tried to remain optimistic.

The tour started at four in the afternoon. It was still raining hard. A dozen or so people packed into the Temporary Travel Office's rented van, dripping and steaming, and for forty-five minutes or so Ryan Griffis, a pleasant, friendly, nervous, enthusiastic man, drove us through Friday-afternoon rush-hour traffic, heading eastward to the first of the parking lots.

As we drove through a Brooklyn of factories, workshops, warehouses and self-storage units, we heard a recorded commentary, interspersed with music, telling us facts and figures about parking. It sounded like urban studies research rather than art, but this suited many of the people in the van, since it appeared there were some genuine parking-lot scholars and enthusiasts on board.

The traffic was terrible, the drive was painfully slow, and the recorded commentary ended long before we arrived at the first lot. This was the Grant Avenue Municipal Parking Lot, adjacent to the Grant Avenue subway stop on the A Line in deepest, eastern Brooklyn. It had been chosen precisely because it was so far from anywhere. It was a nice enough parking lot in its way, spacious, not full, a place you could leave your car without fearing it would be stolen or stripped down. There were helpful signs telling you how to park: at ninety degrees to the retaining wall, and inside the parking bay, and to reverse into the spot so that leaving was made easier. Our van pulled in and parked.

Rain was sluicing down, hard as ever, but some of us, though by no means all, felt a duty to get out of the van and set foot on the lot. But none of us walked very far. We huddled under umbrellas, walked maybe a hundred yards from one corner of the lot to another, making the kind of conversation you might make on a tour of parking lots with people you didn't know.

Then we all returned to the van and drove a very long way back west to see two other lots, one private rather than municipal, and one that was no longer a car-park lot at all but had been 'developed' and was now the construction site for a theatre designed by Frank Gehry. Nobody left the van at these sites, in fact the van didn't even stop. As a professed walking tour it was all a bit of a bust, but we were running late because of the traffic, and by now we were a van full of restless, fidgety, full-bladdered tourists.

As we drove back to the gallery, we lost the traffic and eventually we were passing through an amazing landscape of gorgeous industrial ruin. I had, and still have, only a sketchy idea of exactly where we were, but it was somewhere near the water and in sight of the Williamsburg Bridge, an area of big, blank, formidable buildings interspersed with empty lots. There was nobody walking on the street, and you couldn't have said there was any activity as such, and yet there was evidence of inscrutable things going on: anonymous trucks parked in front of loading bays, dumpsters full of intriguing waste, barred and bolted doors and windows suggesting something precious or forbidden on the other side. I'd have been happy to walk around there on my own, and the next day I tried.

*

The rain had finally stopped and I was returning to Conflux, this time for a lecture by Denis Wood called 'Lynch Debord! About two psychogeographies', but I gave myself a couple of hours to take a walk before it started. Denis Wood is best known as the author of *The Power of Maps*, a book that discusses the ways in which maps serve all kinds of purposes, very few of them having much to do with getting from A to B. Every map, he says, is made in somebody's interest, and that interest is very unlikely to coincide with yours. Given the title of the lecture, I assumed he was, metaphorically, going to string up Debord; and I was looking forward to that.

I walked where previously I'd driven. The ruin was every bit as gorgeous as I wanted it to be, blank scary buildings, wrecked soulful cars, walls and gates so high and fierce that you knew something horrible must be happening on the other side. The most curious thing I saw, by far, was a huge factory, built of red brick, with a sign outside that said, 'If it's made of rubber we make it.' This was good in itself but then I saw the name of the business, and I still have some trouble believing this – it was called the Auster Rubber Co. Inc.; no kin of Paul as far as I knew, but an intriguing coincidence. I walked all the way round the block that contained it, aware that I was tracing a rectangle that couldn't seriously be mistaken for any letter, however misshapen.

*

The Conflux lectures were being held in the back room of a bar, the Lucky Cat. I got there ten minutes before the Denis Wood lecture was due to start and I barely managed to squeeze in. There was standing room only and not much of that, and although I could see someone far away, stationed beside a screen and talking, I couldn't hear anything he said.

This lecturer, it turned out, wasn't Denis Wood, but the guy delivering the previous lecture. There was no sign that this event was about to end, and even when it eventually did, it seemed unlikely that the crowd would clear out and free up any seats. Denis Wood was going to be a hot ticket: if you were in possession of a chair down at the front you weren't going to give it up.

The Lucky Cat was as airless, humid and packed as a New York subway platform in highest summer. Sweat dripped off me and off everyone else. There was a cloying smell of fried food and ketchup in the air. Maybe if I could have got to the bar and bought myself a drink it would have been different, but there was no way I could get through. I thought I might fall down or throw up. And suddenly I realised there was no way in the world I could bear to be in that space for another second, much less to stand there for the amount of time it would take to watch someone deliver a lecture on Debord and psychogeography.

I staggered out to the street. The evening was a warm one, but compared to the bar it offered a blast of cool, bracing air. I stood for a minute or two, watching as more people piled in for the lecture, and at first I thought I should go back in with them and tough it out. And then I thought, no, I didn't have to do that. I didn't have to do that at all. There was no duty, no obligation, nobody checking up on me. I was perfectly free to miss the lecture, to abandon my plan, to walk away; and that's exactly what I did.

And as I went, I realised that walking away is one of life's greatest pleasures, whether it's walking away from a bad job, a bad relationship, a bad educational course or a bad psychogeography festival. There was an extraordinary sunset over Williamsburg that night. The clouds looked like orange lizard skin and there were many people on the street photographing it. The sky was putting on a show to celebrate my decision. I felt fantastic: I'd escaped. I was giddy with relief.

I had no complaints with anyone at Conflux. They were what they were. They did what they did. My needs and expectations weren't their responsibility. I blamed myself. I was too cynical, too unhip, too much of a sour puss, a loner, a solitary walker. And perhaps it's absurd to call yourself a loner and a solitary walker when your chief walking pleasure involves exploring the streets of major metropolitan cities, but that was how I felt about New York, that it was a city crammed with solitary walkers, just like me. I realised I didn't need a guide or a map. I would find my own version of a 'constrained walk'. I'd find my own damn way of walking this city.

*

But first I needed a Martini. I took the subway back to Manhattan and found myself in University Place, near Washington Square, an area where a man might reasonably find a bar to serve him what he needed. It was a busy night, everywhere was crowded, and when I saw a restaurant with a bar that opened right on to the street and an empty bar stool, I went in and sat down. I now saw that I was in an Indian fusion restaurant, not the obvious home of great cocktail making, but I tried to be positive. I asked the girl behind the bar for a Martini and a look of panic flashed across her face. This was her first day, she told me: she'd never made a Martini before. She turned to one of the waitresses for help and her friend talked her through the process. For a first try it really wasn't bad.

I'd picked up a free magazine on the way in, and now I saw there was an ad on the back page showing a map of Manhattan. I looked at it with a certain desperation. I was still feeling the need to do a 'constrained' New York walk. I hoped that some walking route would leap up off the map and demand to be done.

And then – and OK, I'd sunk most of a Martini by then – as I stared at the pattern of streets near to where I was, I quite clearly saw the shape of a Martini glass. Really. A stretch of University Place formed the base of the glass. 8th and 9th Streets heading west formed the uprights of the stem, while Christopher Street and Greenwich Street diverged to form the two sides of the conical bowl. The triangle was completed by Hudson Street, not an absolutely straight line across the top since it contained a slight kink or rise about halfway along, but that was acceptable, and could be thought to resemble the meniscus of liquid that rises above the rim of a truly full Martini glass.

I looked carefully, drew on the map with a pen, emphasising the outline. What else was there to do but walk the streets that represented the shape of the glass, and at certain strategic points around the route find a bar and have another Martini? There was something a bit dumb about it, but it didn't seem a whole lot dumber than some of the things the Conflux crowd had come up with. It featured walking, exploring the city, imposing a shape on the environment, and depending on how many Martinis were drunk, the strong likelihood of sensory derangement. What more could a psychogeographer want?

As a route for a walk, and a bar crawl, it had its attractions. It took me past and/or into some famous watering holes: the Cedar Tavern, home of the fighting Abstract Expressionists and from where Jack Kerouac was supposedly ejected for peeing in an ashtray, the White Horse where Bob Dylan went to hear the Clancy Brothers, the Stonewall, scene of gay resistance, though closed and available for rent when I walked past. And in Greenwich Street I saw, painted on a wall, the outline of a muted post horn: if you're in the right frame of mind a post horn can look a lot like a Martini glass.

But you know what, all in all it was another bust. The overriding problem was that walking the streets gave no sense of following the Martini-glass pattern. Even though I had it clearly enough in my head, on the ground it didn't compute. You'd have had to be a bird or a tracking satellite or a god to see what I was doing down there.

It occurred to me, not exactly for the first time, that psychogeography didn't have much to do with the actual experience of walking. It was a nice idea, a clever idea, an art project, a conceit, but it had very little to do with any real experience of walking. And it confirmed for me, what I'd really known all along, that walking isn't much good as a theoretical experience. You can dress it up any way you like, but walking remains resolutely simple, basic, analog. That's why I love it and love doing it. And in that respect – stay with me on this – it's not entirely unlike a Martini. Sure you can add stuff to Martinis, like chocolate or an olive stuffed with blue cheese or, God forbid, smoked bacon, and similarly you can add various things to your walks, constraints, shapes, notions of the mapping of utopian spaces, but you don't need to. And really, why would you? Why ruin a good drink? Why ruin a good walk?

I abandoned my own constrained walk with almost as much enthusiasm as I'd abandoned the psychogeography festival, but I carried on walking. I walked the dark streets of the city feeling remarkably free; a spring in my step and several much needed Martinis in my bloodstream.

*

I don't doubt that Guy Debord drank a few Martinis. Guy Debord drank everything. He enjoyed the derangement of the senses; he was a man who wasn't afraid to drink and drift. In his memoir *Panegyric*, he writes:

I never for a moment dreamed of concealing this perhaps questionable side of my personality, and it was clearly evident for all those who met me more than once or twice . . . At first, like everyone, I appreciated the effect of mild drunkenness, then very soon I grew to like what lies beyond violent drunkenness, once that stage is past: a terrible magnificent peace . . . Although in the first decades I may have allowed only slight indications to appear once or twice a week, I was in fact continuously drunk for periods of several months.

He must surely have been drunk while conducting some of his psychogeographic drifts. He adds, 'I have wandered extensively in several great European cities, and I appreciated everything that deserved appreciation. The catalogue on this subject could be vast . . . ' He then proceeds to catalogue, not his walks, not things observed, much less unities of ambience, but rather all the booze he'd knocked back, starting with beer – English, Irish, German, Czech, Belgian – then moving on to celebrate the world's wines, spirits, cocktails, punches *et al.*

Debord ended his life in scholarly isolation, living in a cottage in Champot, in the Upper Loire, with his second wife Alice Becker-Ho. The photographs taken of him in the early 1990s show a plump, cheerful man, usually with a drink and a pipe in his hand. He doesn't look like most people's idea of a walker, though we know that walkers come in all shapes and sizes. In any event, as he got older he did far more drinking than walking, and eventually he developed a form of polyneuritis brought on by alcohol. The pain was so intolerable that he committed suicide in 1994 by shooting himself in the heart.

Debord never visited New York, but in his article *Theory*

of the Dérive, he writes: 'Within architecture itself, the taste for dériving tends to promote all sorts of new forms of labyrinths made possible by modern techniques of construction,' and he quotes from an uncited newspaper article, describing a proposed New York apartment block:

> The apartments of the helicoidal building will be shaped like slices of cake. One will be able to enlarge or reduce them by shifting movable partitions. The half-floor gradations avoid limiting the number of rooms, since the tenant can request the use of the adjacent section on either upper or lower levels. With this setup three four-room apartments can be transformed into one twelve-room apartment in less than six hours.

Debord concludes that here, 'One can see the first signs of an opportunity to dérive inside an apartment.'

He was wrong about this too. If he had ever been in one of the minute apartments in which the vast number of New Yorkers actually live he'd have seen just how severely limited are the prospects for the 'at home' drift. In fact, it's always seemed to me that one of the reasons New Yorkers spend so much time walking the streets is precisely because their apartments are so small. They need to get out and walk, to experience the city's 'beauty, order and convenience', so that they don't go completely mad. This may also be the reason why they need to spend so much time in bars.

*

I walked to Ground Zero again the day after I abandoned my psychogeography festival, more or less five years after 9/11. As ever there was nothing much to see, and the crowd was thin, although some work had been done to make the place more tourist-friendly: walkways, notice boards, signage. Still, there was a sense of lost purpose. The pilgrimage element had largely disappeared. You didn't need to join any stream of walkers. Tour buses were pulling up very close; you could hop off, take a quick stroll, take a few photographs, get back on the bus, be able to say you'd seen it. And in order that visitors might have something to look at, a series of large, iconic photographs of the disaster had been mounted on chain-link fences surrounding the site. In the absence of anything more tangible, people were taking photographs of the photographs.

I still go to New York a couple of times a year and I do all the things I did when I lived there, walking and drinking Martinis among them, though I've never been to another psychogeography festival. And sometimes, though I admit not every time, I walk down Lower Broadway to see what there is to be seen at Ground Zero, to see what's left and see what's changed. In one sense there is less and less to see, which is to say that what was there – the wreckage, the hard evidence of anguish and ruin – has gone, and what's there currently is a vast building site that one of these days will be a set of buildings.

The last time I was there, in order to create maximum space on site, the room available for walking had been much diminished, and that which remained had to be shared with huge trucks going to and from the site. This had evidently caused some problems and a number of old guys had been employed to help pedestrians watch their backs. They wore yellow caps and waistcoats with 'Pedestrian Safety' printed on them, and their main job seemed to be to interpose them-selves between trucks and goofy pedestrians.

And I swear I saw and heard this: there was a young woman wandering around looking lost and confused. She didn't know where she was supposed to be going or what she was supposed to be looking at, and finally she said to one of the pedestrian-safety guys, 'Where is the . . . the *thing*?' The old guy turned to her sympathetically, but a big truck roared past at that very moment and I never heard what he said. Nevertheless, she raised the camera to her eye and proceeded to photograph the 'thing' whatever she thought it might be.

It was hard to blame her. Everybody photographs everything these days and New York remains the most visually compelling, if not the most easily photographed, of cities. I take pictures all the time when I'm walking around there, following in the steps of a small army of New York street photographers, and although there's lots of eye-catching stuff it can be enormously difficult to come home with a picture that really captures the sprit and complexity of New York. This, of course, is because I'm not a real photographer.

Still, to photograph on the streets of New York, however amateurishly, is to photograph its people and its walkers. The great New York tradition of street photography includes (I'm not exactly picking names at random here, but I could) Alfred Steiglitz, Berenice Abbott, Paul Strand, Joel Meyerowitz, Lisette Model, Angelo Rizzuto, and so on all the way through to Bruce Gilden. I was in New York to interview him.

*

Gilden specialises in gritty, grainy, black-and-white, flashlit grotesques. He's drawn to people who are troubled and troubling, the ones with noses that jut and droop, mouths that hang slackly open or clench with tension or around fat cigars. He's a fan of bad make-up, bad hair, bad wigs, of clothes that are too big or too small, or out of style, or that were never quite in style in the first place. Sometimes his characters look terrifying, sometimes they look terrified. They may be wild eyed or dead eyed, obese or skeletal, mad or maddening, hyper-aware or utterly oblivious. If he can get a couple of these opposing types in the same frame that's great, but often the frame is so tight it will hold only one person. Gilden operates at close range, Leica in one hand, flashgun in the other. There's nothing discreet or clandestine about the process. He's right in the faces of his subjects. Bruce Gilden and New York were made for each other.

I went to meet him in the offices of the Magnum photo agency. He was sixty-ish, lean, balding, bearded, scruffy in a comfortable way, intense, big-eyed, a serious man who laughs a lot. A part of Gilden conforms to everybody's idea of what a New Yorker should be: motor-mouthed, tough, abrupt yet ultimately warm.

I began with the fairly obvious observation that New York was a city of walkers and that being a street photographer must inevitably involve doing a lot of walking.

'Sure,' he said. 'If you don't walk you're not gonna get the picture.'

That might have been the end of it right there. Fortunately Bruce Gilden is a man who likes to talk.

'My style,' he said, 'is very predatory, like Moriyama had a book called *The Hunter*, years ago, and I was always intrigued by the title. I'm basically shy and also I have a fear factor. I'm a physical guy, I'm quick tempered so what that means is that I'm afraid of violence but also I'm violent. I have a very good sense of where danger is, who can be dangerous. I'm streetwise OK, so having said that, you know when you put your camera up and put it in someone's face and you come from a background like mine there could be fire, so I've learned to have a very good bedside manner.'

I suggested that if you're in the street and you find Bruce Gilden pointing his camera at you, that probably means you're a grotesque. He smiled and didn't deny it.

'People have said that what Bruce does is really easy: he

photographs characters. No. It's not easy. I don't want to be accused of sneaking something. "Hey you, are you taking a picture of me? What are you? A sneak?" But when you use the flash, people know you took a picture. You can't say, "I didn't take a picture." So I'm quite honest usually unless there's really a lot of danger.

'I used to have a schedule. I would go out about two, two-thirty in the afternoon and stay out till it gets almost dark. I'd go on 5th Avenue from 49th Street to 57th, up and down, up and down, up and down, one side of the street too, not the other, the west side. It's quite funny, you know. And Broadway between 43rd and 47th, the west side, it'll be darker on that side of the street. But the problem here for me is that I've been on the street so long, you know, I'm trotting over the same ground. And there aren't so many characters as there used to be.

'I used to work 42nd Street when it was a little bit of a hovel but you had to be careful there, people really didn't want to be photographed. Once I saw these young kids pick-pocketing people, and you know I had my camera and they gave me a little shit, they were maybe thirteen, but they weren't little, and I said to the guy, "Listen, if you don't like it let's go round the corner." That's the way I felt, OK. Because if they respect you they're fine. If they don't respect you they'll shit all over you. And you know I'm not the toughest guy in the world, but I'll stand up for my rights, though there are times when you have to put your tail between your legs and not take that picture. I can be quite ferocious but I'm also not stupid.

'I walk hard in the streets, OK. Even when I'm not taking pictures. I was coming out of the subway the other day and I know when people are jerking with me, and there was this black guy about thirty-five, you know, solid, and he was going to get me, you know, I saw it, so I armed him, you know, with my elbow and he looked at me and said, "What are you doing?" and I said, "Well, you know, I didn't hear you say excuse me," and I guess he knew that I wasn't just going to roll over so he kept going.

'If you walk hard and you're smart then people don't think you're weak. Once you show weakness, weak people take over. This is an active city and you have to be aggressive. I'm not a humanitarian and I don't claim to be. I can be kind but I can also be nasty. So . . . I'm a good friend, I'm not a good enemy.'

This sounded to me like the authentic voice of the New York walker. I thought it might be fun to be Bruce Gilden's friend, but not easy. As I left him I felt invigorated. There was something exciting in the way he described walking in New York as a risky activity, a form of combat, a struggle for dominance, sometimes a contact sport. There was something very familiar and accurate about it too. New York is a city where the people not only enjoy getting in your way as you're walking down the street, they'll actually go out of their way to obstruct your progress. They'll inconvenience themselves for the greater pleasure of inconveniencing you.

But there's a certain kind of hard walker, or perhaps a certain kind of crazy bastard, that people do leave room for. He looks madder and more determined than most, with a walking style that says, 'Get out of my way,' and most people do, because it's also saying more than that. It's saying, 'Fuck you. And if you've got a problem with that, then OK, let's take it round the corner.' If you're looking for an argument in New York, you can find one on every block.

As I walked away from the Magnum offices I started to walk really fast and hard, my idea of the way Bruce Gilden walked: determined, fierce, angry. It was only an act, only a pose that I was trying on for size, but I was serious about it, in some way I meant it, and it worked. It was strange and oddly gratifying because people really did start to move aside for me, to get out of my way. I don't know if they really thought I was a madman looking for trouble, but they were taking no chances and I didn't blame them. On most days I'd have done exactly the same. Most days you steer clear: you look at this nutcase and see what New York has done to him, turned him into a furious walking monster. You have a healthy amount of fear and maybe just a little sympathy. And then on other days you realise that the furious walking monster is you.

What happens when you meet another of your own kind, when a Bruce Gilden walks into another Bruce Gilden, doesn't bear thinking about. You probably wouldn't want to be standing in the street next to it, but it'd be very interesting to see a photograph of it. You just wouldn't want to be the guy taking the picture.

7

Death and Pedestrianism

> I doubt if I possess the temperament which enables
> one to contemplate with equanimity a number of dead
> men promenading in their shrouds.
>
> Sax Rohmer, *The Death Ring of Sneferu*

I was walking in the Wisewood Cemetery, in Sheffield, a place I'd walked many times before. It's rather a lovely spot, very green, set on high ground above the city, with a gentle downward slope, and there's an openness and sometimes a windblown, hazy bleakness that's very appropriate for a cemetery. I wasn't just out for a stroll, I was looking for two graves: those of my parents and grandparents. I was having trouble finding them, and of course I was feeling guilty about it. A more dutiful and regular visitor would have been able to go right to them.

In my defence I could say that although nothing changes about the location of the graves themselves, quite a lot changes around them. Once they were easy to find, they were the newest ones, set at the very edge of the rows of graves. But more graves appear all the time, so my parents and grandparents are surrounded by more and more new arrivals. No longer at the edge, they seem ever more lost in the crowd.

I told myself that a certain amount of searching, exploring, walking among the other graves, was appropriate, maybe even necessary. Some visitors, I always see them whenever I'm there, just drive right up to the graveside. Perhaps they visit more often than I do, but you know, rolling up in your Ford

Escort and hopping out to leave a bunch of petrol-station flowers never strikes me as all that respectful. At the very least you should park your damn car and walk to the grave.

As I searched that day I realised that I'd done a surprising amount of walking in graveyards. If I'm out walking and see a churchyard or cemetery up ahead, I always go in and walk around. Of course in general it's not a very purposeful kind of walking. I read the names and dates, calculate the ages, chart my own age against those of the deceased, saying to myself, 'What a shame, cut off in his prime,' or 'Ah well, she had a good innings.' Funny how notions of 'prime' and 'good innings' change as I get older. And I'll admit to a certain amount of meaningless *Schadenfreude*: yes, I lived longer than she did, I outlived all those guys over there.

Reading a gravestone is often a matter of trying to decode clues. In the Wisewood Cemetery, for instance, there's a black marble headstone with an image of a Jaguar (the car not the animal) etched into it. And I've often wondered what the story is. The deceased was an enthusiast, no doubt. But did he own a Jag or a lot of Jags, or did he just aspire to owning one. Was he maybe a Jaguar dealer? Could he conceivably have died at the wheel of a Jaguar?

And just occasionally you see the grave of somebody famous. Wisewood Cemetery contains only one such grave, and the fame involved is limited. Steve Clark, who was guitarist with Def Leppard, is buried there. Herewith a Def Leppard lyric from 'Pour Some Sugar On Me': 'Step inside, walk this way, You and me, babe, Hey, hey!'

Clark had one of those miserable rock deaths: a guy who loved to play guitar and loved to drink, initially in that order but then the order was reversed. He became unreliable, was given a six-month 'leave of absence' and a while later was found dead of anti-depressants, painkillers and alcohol.

The gravestone has a not-quite-in-proportion image of Clark etched into it, hair long, shirt baggy, guitar slung low across his thighs. Compared to those of the serious rock martyrs (Hendrix, Morrison, Elvis), Clark's grave probably doesn't get visited all that much, but enough people come to leave flowers, bits of jewellery, pieces of handmade amateur art. And you have to believe that the fans who visit Steve Clark's grave are more committed. They're making a small pilgrimage, not just visiting a tourist site.

Eventually I found the family graves I was looking for, paid my respects, and afterwards walked a long route around the cemetery. And I realised, and it came as a surprise, though I suppose a part of me had known it all along, that this was the kind of thing I used to do with my father. He was a man of unspecific religious inclination, he certainly never went to church services, but if we were out walking and we happened to pass a church we'd always go into the graveyard and walk around in a respectful way, though I can't remember us ever going inside the church. Some of this coincided with the time I was studying basic history of architecture at school and as we walked around I'd identify lancet windows, flying buttresses, nodding ogee arches and whatnot. This never impressed my dad as much as I thought it should.

I realised that I've continued this graveyard tradition, and although I don't 'collect' famous graves it struck me that I'd made walking expeditions to quite a few final resting places of the famous: Little John's grave, in the Peak District, Laurence Sterne's in Coxwold, Yorkshire, D. H. Lawrence's in Taos, New Mexico. In Los Angeles I've visited the two famous cemeteries, Hollywood Forever and Forest Lawn, the latter satirised by Evelyn Waugh in *The Loved One*. He writes of 'golden gates and floodlit temples', which actually understates things a little. These places are indeed tourist attractions, the graves of hundreds of major and minor celebrities, along with thousands of just plain folk. Hollywood Forever houses Fay Wray, Rudolph Valentino, Tyrone Power. Forest Lawn is now a chain; the Hollywood Hills branch is home to Betty Davis, Humphrey Bogart and latterly Michael Jackson.

There was however one grave, actually a tomb, that I'd been intending to visit for decades and had never made it. It belonged to Sir Richard Francis Burton and his wife Isabel, that's Burton the greatest of all nineteenth-century English explorers of Africa and Asia, an Orientalist, soldier, linguist, and the first non-Muslim Westerner to visit Mecca. Walnut juice and circumcision were involved. A prolific writer, an anthropologist and a 'sexologist' before the term was invented, he is perhaps best known today for his translations of *The Kama Sutra, The Perfumed Garden* and *The Arabian Nights.*

The Burton tomb is in the churchyard of St Mary Magdalen's Catholic Church, in North Worple Way, Mortlake. It appears in all those books of London curiosities and eccentricities, understandably so, since it's a stone mausoleum in the shape of a tent. It's sometimes referred to as a Bedouin or Arabic tent but in fact it's a full-size replica of one that Burton had specially made when he and Isabel travelled to Syria. Burton could stand up in it, and he was five foot eleven. In the pictures I'd seen, the tomb looked bizarre, as kitsch and excessive as anything you could find in a Hollywood cemetery. Whether it would appear that way in reality remained to be seen.

I decided to walk there from Hammersmith. It was mid-August, and warm enough, but the sky and the river were slate grey. I walked over Hammersmith Bridge, through Barnes, past Barnes Pond complete with ducklings, past the former homes of Gustav Holst and Ninette de Valois (blue plaques told me this) and eventually down Tinderbox Alley to North Worple Way. There were other ways to get there but I really wanted to be able to say I'd walked down Tinderbox Alley. And then, once in North Worple Way I got lost, a situation made more complicated because at first I didn't realise it.

Right away I saw a signpost directing me to St Mary's Church and I imagined this must be for the benefit of visitors who came to pay homage to Sir Richard Burton. Things seemed even more promising when I found the churchyard and saw a sign that said 'Entrance to Labyrinth'. This was great stuff. It seemed I'd stumbled across some mystical nexus of Burtonian walking, exploration and myth.

In fact, the labyrinth was a disappointment, a small circuit mowed into the long grass in a corner of the churchyard, marked with stones and bits of tree branch, and when I picked up the leaflet telling me how to use the labyrinth, the nexus started to seem a bit threadbare. 'Share in a dance with others,' it said. 'Look up on the way out, returning to the world with the joy of Resurrection – and a new step, with plenty of skips in it!' The leaflet also suggested I address an 'important question' while in the labyrinth, and the question I was having trouble answering right then was where exactly Sir Richard Burton's tomb was located. The churchyard was divided into several parts, but none of them was large, and a full-size stone tent isn't the sort of thing you can miss. And then I realised I was in the churchyard of St Mary the Virgin, a name and a concept rather different from the St Mary Magdalene I was looking for. I went in search of the other Mary.

I retraced my steps. It was easy to see how I'd missed the other church. St Mary Magdalen was part of a cluster of buildings, including a school and convent, with a high wall and gatehouse. To get to the graveyard you had to pass through a courtyard and a doorway that would deter the casual passer-by. I was not deterred. Once in the churchyard there was absolutely no missing the Burton tomb.

Burton's niece Georgiana Stisted (who wrote a biography of Burton, intended 'for the masses as well as for the classes') described the churchyard as a 'shabby sectarian cemetery', which seems unnecessarily harsh. It was certainly small and hemmed in by terraced houses just the other side of the churchyard wall, but as a final resting place it seemed perfectly good, and genuinely peaceful. I was there forty-five minutes or so and there were no other visitors.

Perhaps the Burton tomb deters as many as it attracts. It was certainly the star turn, and perhaps it overpowers the humbler, smaller graves around it. But seeing it for the first time with my own eyes, it didn't seem so bizarre or kitsch after all. It seemed odd and perhaps excessive, but there was nothing ludicrous or laughable about it. It really was a remarkable thing, beautifully well-made, the sandstone really did look like fabric, hanging in very convincing folds. Isabel claimed it was so realistic people sometimes asked why she didn't remove the canvas so the coffin could be seen.

The tomb had some Islamic touches, stars and crescents, in addition to the more obvious Christian symbol of a crucifix mounted high on the tent's pinnacle. There was a book carved into the stone, with the dates of Richard and Isabel's deaths, and there was also a stone slab on the front with a poem by Justin Huntly McCarthy that refers to Burton as 'last and noblest of the errant knights', which seemed a forgivable exaggeration.

But most extraordinary of all, the tomb had a window in the back. You could climb up a ladder set in the ground behind it, peer down through a sheet of plate glass and see the coffins of husband and wife set side by side, with plenty of room between them; his made of steel, hers of mahogany. There were also various items of funereal bric-à-brac: crucifixes, lamps, religious paintings, camel bells. Some of this was hard to see since the glass was dirty on the inside. I couldn't imagine how anybody would ever be able to clean it.

Isabel was quite a piece of work, a woman who got her own way. Right before he died, Burton apparently said to her that he wished they could 'lie side by side in a tent' for eternity, and it's a pretty fair bet that he was imagining a flimsy, canvas construction in some sandy, windswept desert place, something that would soon be lost to the elements. It seems unlikely that he had in mind a stone confection in a churchyard in Mortlake, but these things are hard to organise when you're dead. Isabel also claimed that Burton had made a last-minute conversion to Catholicism, which seems just preposterous.

Burton's desire for a modest grave seems very appealing, very modern. There was little that was modest about his life, and perhaps that's why he felt no need for posthumous grandeur. His wife obviously felt differently, and in a way I'm glad she did what she did, glad that the Burton tomb exists and that I finally got to see it. It's a genuine curiosity, perhaps a folly, an extraordinary and eccentric monument to an extraordinary and eccentric man, and also an odd and flamboyant (and far from selfless) proof of a wife's love.

*

I realised that I've been an admirer and reader of Burton for a very long time, certainly since my schooldays. It will give you some idea of the deranged atmosphere of my all-boys grammar school if I tell you that Burton's translation of *The Perfumed Garden* was passed around as a hot book. I know we were particularly intrigued by the chapter 'Sundry Names Given to the Sexual Organs of Women'. I can't pretend to have kept the details in my memory all these years but turning to it now I find it contains this rather amazing classification: '*El tseguil* (The importunate) – This is the vulva which is never tired of taking in the member. This latter might pass a hundred nights with it, and walk in a hundred times every night, still that vulva would not be sated . . . Luckily it is a rarity.'

Using 'walk' as a synonym or euphemism for having sex also strikes me as a rarity, although I know it does have some currency as a synonym or euphemism for masturbation, from the song in the old Yellow Pages ads, 'Let your fingers do the walking.' As a linguist and sexologist, Burton would surely have been fascinated by that.

Burton certainly did a lot of walking in the course of his expeditions, though I doubt that he'd have thought of himself as a great walker. Often it was necessary as part of a journey, but Burton was committed to the end, not the means. He took those forms of transport that got him where he wanted to go: camels, horses, boats were used as available. He walked when he had to and when he could. At one point in his expedition with Speke to find the source of the Nile, he was so sick with malaria he couldn't take a step without being supported, but still he walked. In his account of the expedition he tells the story of one of their guides who had to loiter behind, 'because his slave girl was too footsore to walk. When tired of waiting he cut off her head for fear lest she should become gratis another man's property.'

Burton's visit to Mecca certainly involved plenty of walking, following in the footsteps of Mohammad, walking seven times around the Kaaba, the cube-shaped shrine in the centre of the Great Mosque. Pilgrims are required to walk the first three circuits quickly, the last four slowly, because that's the way Mohammad did it, and as they walk, they must try to touch the sacred Black Stone, part of the Kaaba, on each circuit.

Burton walked the walk, spending a good many hours with the other walking pilgrims at the Great Mosque. There was much cursing and pushing, he reports, especially when he monopolised the Black Stone and went to elaborate lengths to measure the dimensions of the Kaaba, and try to determine what it was made of: aerolite, he thought. At last he emerged 'thoroughly worn out, with scorched feet and a burning head – both extremities, it must be remembered, were bare'.

After Mecca he visited the even more impenetrable city of Harar, in Abyssinian Somaliland. One of his local contacts told him, 'I would as soon walk into a crocodile's mouth as set foot in the city.' The expedition was a disaster and Burton was lucky to escape with his life: others were less lucky. Burton survived to write a book about the experience called *First Footsteps in East Africa.*

Burton sometimes walked for pleasure too. He first encountered his wife Isabel while walking on the ramparts of Boulogne. She was attracted to the 'vision of my waking brain', but it wasn't till they met later in London while walking in 'the Botanical Gardens', presumably Kew, that things moved on. At their second botanical-garden meeting she came upon Burton as he was writing poetry, and after a brief conversation he asked her to marry him. She replied, 'I would rather have a crust and a tent with you than be queen of all the world.' This meant yes. They walked together – sometimes metaphorically, often literally – for the rest of their lives. In Damascus, they walked all the time, their favourite route taking them up a steep hillside, high enough to look down on the entire city.

Burton also walked with others. When he was in São Paolo, he befriended a man called John James Ambertin and they often walked together in the 'butterfly-haunted forests'. In Edinburgh he regularly walked along Princes Street and up Arthur's Seat, accompanied by Lady Stisted and her daughters, one of whom was later so rude about the churchyard in Mortlake.

Towards the end of his life, posted to Trieste and in poor physical shape, Burton still walked for two hours a day with Dr Grenfell Baker, his physician and regular companion, discussing plans for the publication of a new book to be called *The Scented Garden*, a much revised version of the previously published *The Perfumed Garden*.

On the very last day of his life, Burton and Dr Baker were setting off on their walk when Burton spotted a robin drowning in the fountain in his own garden. Baker rescued it, and Burton opened his coat and 'warmed the bird at his breast' as he carried it into the house where he entrusted it to a porter. We don't know whether or not the bird survived, but Burton did not. He went to bed complaining a little of gout, and died in the course of the night.

For well over a century Isabel has been castigated for burning the manuscript of *The Scented Garden*, along with Burton's papers and journals, accused of acting out of prudishness and the misguided desire to protect her husband's reputation. A strand of current scholarship forgives her, on the grounds that she was in part following Burton's instructions, and in part trying to stop his works falling into the hands of unscrupulous publishers. Either way, the unpublished works are gone and the tomb remains.

*

Walking, like reading, like researching, can never be completely aimless. There may be no predetermined goal but you have to choose one path rather than another, you take your bearings from time to time, you're inevitably heading somewhere whether you know it or not: sooner or later serendipity takes over. And so I can't absolutely tell you when or why I started reading Sax Rohmer, but as soon as I did, I realised that he too was a fan of Sir Richard Burton.

I suspect rather few people read Rohmer any more (although naturally there's a website, rather a good one), but just about everybody knows the name of his creation, Fu Manchu, the evil Chinese genius, scourge of the white races, privy to all the secret places of London, and so on. For a period in the 1920s and 1930s, Fu Manchu made Rohmer one of the most popular and successful writers in the world.

The name Sax Rohmer was invented. In an interview in the New Yorker in 1947 he explained that 'sax' means blade in 'ancient Saxon', and the surname was simply intended to give the impression of one who roamed the world. Born in 1883, he had started humbly enough in Birmingham as Arthur Henry Sarsfield Ward, and moved to London to become a jobbing journalist. One of his assignments involved spending time in London's Chinatown, then located in Limehouse, to bring back a story about Chinese criminality: drugs, gambling, prostitution, all the vices of the Orient brought to England. Whether Rohmer really spent much time among serious criminals is doubtful, but he certainly spent time in Limehouse, wandering the streets, getting to know the area and some of its people, and he was enough of a pro, or maybe hack, to bring back the story he was sent to find. He also found inspiration for Fu Manchu.

These days, Rohmer's depictions of the yellow peril come over not just as politically incorrect but downright laughable. If you wanted to defend him (and essentially it's a fool's game) you might say that however crassly he depicted the

Chinese, Fu Manchu was a genius, honourable in the way
that supervillains can be, and always the smartest guy in the
room. I can see that this won't cut much ice with post-
colonial sensibilities.

Rohmer's association with Limehouse hardly makes him
an Orientalist the way Burton was; what links that two men
is that Sir Richard Burton's influence appears, in one form
or another, in a surprising amount of Rohmer's fiction. For
one thing there's a recurring character in the Fu Manchu
novels called Sir Lionel Barton.

> Long ago we had placed the name of Sir Lionel Barton
> upon the list of those whose lives stood between Fu
> Manchu and the attainment of his end. Orientalist and
> explorer, the fearless traveller who first had penetrated to
> Lhassa, who thrice, as a pilgrim, had entered forbidden
> Mecca, he now had turned his attention again to Tibet –
> thereby signing his own death-warrant.

This is from *The Mysterious Dr Fu Manchu* (1913). And in
the *Quest of the Sacred Slipper*, one of Rohmer's non-Fu
Manchu novels, a scene takes place in 'the lofty apartment in
the British Antiquarian Museum known as the Burton Room
(by reason of the fact that a fine painting of Sir Richard
Burton faces you as you enter).

Then there's a nice moment in *The Yellow Claw* (again,
not a Fu Manchu novel) when the snooty guests at a private
view are dumbfounded by a painting called *Our Lady of the
Poppies*, depicting a female nude in a bizarre chamber carved
from black rock and decked out with gold pillars. The guests
wonder whether the chamber exists in real life, and one of
them, a Mr Gianapolis, offers the opinion, ' "In Smyrna you
may see such rooms; possibly in Port Said – certainly in
Cairo. In Constantinople – yes! But perhaps in Paris; and –

who knows? – Sir Richard Burton explored Mecca, but who has explored London?" '

Rohmer also published a collection of short stories, *Tales of Secret Egypt*, written in imitation of Burton's translation of *The Arabian Nights*. So let's accept that Rohmer admired and was fascinated by Burton. His assertion that certain things in London might be every bit as mysterious as those found in the most distant, exotic parts of the globe, appeals to the modern urban explorer as much as to the reader of ripping yarns.

In fact, quite a few of Rohmer's characters are avid London walkers. Helen Cumberly, one of those impressed by *Our Lady of the Poppies*, says, ' "I want to be home early, so if I leave you at about ten o'clock I can walk to Palace Mansions. No! you need not come with me; I enjoy a lonely walk through the streets of London in the evening." '

And here is Dr Petrie, Nayland Smith's sidekick in *The Hand of Fu Manchu*:

> There is a distinct pleasure to be derived from a solitary walk through London, in the small hours of an April morning, provided one is so situated as to be capable of enjoying it. To appreciate the solitude and mystery of the sleeping city, a certain sense of prosperity – a knowledge that one is immune from the necessity of being abroad at that hour – is requisite. The tramp, the night policeman and the coffee-stall keeper know more of London by night than most people – but of the romance of the dark hours they know little. Romance succumbs before necessity.

Here Rohmer seems to be channelling the Dickens of 'Night Walks': stealing from the best.

Success allowed Rohmer and his wife Elizabeth (they met while out walking on Clapham Common) to travel extensively outside England. These trips weren't expeditions in Burton's sense but they were more than tourism, and Rohmer used them for research: three trips to Egypt, one to Haiti to investigate voodoo, sojourns in Baden-Baden, where he and Elizabeth 'went almost daily for long walks in the aptly-named Black Forest ... Here, as in Egypt, he rubbed shoulders with pagan deities and myths older than Christianity.' The quotation is from *Master of Villainy: A Biography of Sax Rohmer*, attributed to Cay Van Ash and Elizabeth Sax Rohmer, though Rohmer wrote parts of the book himself.

Rohmer also went to New York where he befriended Harry Houdini and had the terrifying experience of crossing the road with him, walking through busy traffic, against the lights, in Times Square, 'missing fast-moving cars by fractions of an inch, diving behind others, pausing momentarily, dodging forward again, finally reaching the opposite side of the street in perfect safety'. Rohmer compared it to the Japanese art of ninjutsu.

*

I decided to visit Sax Rohmer's grave. It's located in St Mary's Catholic Cemetery in Kensal Green in north-west London, another sectarian place. It's right next to, but separate from, the bigger, much better known, Kensal Green Cemetery, final resting place of Charles Babbage, Harold Pinter, and the ashes of Freddie Mercury. St Mary's boasts a less glittery, more eccentric crew: Louis Wain, Mary Seacole and Marcus Garvey among them.

I expected it would be a challenge to find Sax Rohmer's grave, one of one hundred and sixty-five thousand spread over twenty-nine acres. I guessed it would take quite a bit of searching, quite a lot of walking up and down between the rows of graves, but that was fine: I liked walking in graveyards.

St Mary's Cemetery was the classic model of what a good old-fashioned graveyard should be like. There were a few isolated mausoleums, some bigger and grander than Burton's in Mortlake, though none as singular. However, in the main, the place was absolutely crammed with much smaller graves, packed side by side, shoulder to shoulder, as though jostling for space, topped with statuary, crosses, suffering Christs, angels, broken pillars with ivy carved in them.

The impression of disorder was reinforced by the ground itself. The earth was soft, mossy, undulating and all the graves had shifted slightly so they no longer lay perfectly flat, with the result that their headstones and statues weren't truly vertical, they were all leaning but in different directions and at different angles from each other. Yes, it looked somewhat like a city, but not a city of neatly regimented buildings, rather something ramshackle and improvised, hastily constructed, not quite plumb, a shanty town to be explored. I began my search, though I was far less alone than I'd been in Mortlake. There was evidently a well-established short cut through the cemetery, and mothers and children passed through from time to time. There was a man cutting the grass. He had a big blue van belonging to a landscaping company called City Escapes: an improbable name for a firm tending graveyards, it seemed to me.

Even within the cemetery there was further segregation, or at least demarcation. The Devlins, Murphys and Morans clustered together at some remove from the Sorentinos, Espositos and even Ferraris, though the Italians had spiffier graves, decorated with religious mosaics and photographs of the loved ones. I was enjoying my walk.

Then, more by luck than anything else, I found Sax Rohmer's grave. It had been surprisingly easy, hadn't taken more than fifteen minutes. It was in a more open, treeless

area of the cemetery, close to one of the boundary walls that
was topped with barbed wire. The nearby graves were not at
all fancy, and neither was Rohmer's: it consisted of a simple,
and rather modern-looking, black-marble headstone.

In fact Rohmer got third billing on the headstone, after his
mother Margaret Mary Furey and his father William Ward,
though above his wife, who survived him by twenty years. He
had also reverted to the name Arthur Henry Sarsfield Ward,
though the headstone added the line 'best known to his
countless readers as Sax Rohmer'. These words along with
all the names and dates were gilded, and a candle, roses and
a lancet window were etched into the black surface of the
marble.

I felt what? Disappointed? No, that didn't seem right or
appropriate. How could I have complaints about a grave's
modesty? I was all for modesty. But as the object of a quest,
as a journey's end, the Sax Rohmer grave seemed a little too
slight. I didn't want a full blown Burtonesque desert tent,
but I did wish there had been something more special about
Rohmer's grave. I didn't want grandeur necessarily, but I'd
have liked some singularity. If you were going to etch some
imagery into a headstone, why wouldn't you choose something more appropriate, more literary, a book perhaps, or
something with a hint of the Orient or the desert? Even in
the Wisewood Cemetery in Sheffield, Steve Clark and the
Jaguar man had managed that; though my parents and
grandparents, it must be said, had not.

                                    *

The world is full of walkers whose paths never quite cross.
Times and places fail to coincide. Routes that intersect in
geographical space are separated by decades, even centuries
of historical time. Rohmer was seven years old (and still
calling himself Arthur Ward) when the seventy-year-old

Burton died. When Rohmer died, aged seventy-six, I was just six. There was no way in the world any of us could have met and discovered ourselves to be fellow travellers, much less fellow walkers. But I think we all have one thing in common: we all liked walking in graveyards, and we all in our different ways walked in graveyards in Cairo.

Burton, naturally, got there first. He spent several months in Cairo, in 1851, preparing for his trip to Mecca. As well as viewing the pyramids, and observing that they'd been 'remarkably well sketched', he and a companion, Shaykh Mohammad, would often walk into the wilderness outside Cairo, into the Mokattam Hills to visit al-Qarafa (literally, the cemetery), a four-mile-long series of graveyards, a necropolis that had existed since the seventh century. Currently it is, in part, a squatters' colony where the homeless live among and inside the tombs and mausoleums of their dead ancestors, and sometimes among and inside the tombs and mausoleums of complete strangers.

Sax Rohmer evidently also visited al-Qarafa, since he wrote in his novel *The Return of Fu Manchu*:

> The muffled drumming of sleepless London seemed very remote from us, as side by side we crept up the narrow path to the studio. This was a starry but moonless night, and the little dingy white building with a solitary tree peeping, in silhouette, above the glazed roof bore an odd resemblance to one of those tombs which form a city of the dead so near to the city of feverish life on the slopes of the Mokattam Hills.

I've been to Cairo just once, a long time ago, and my memories are patchy. I was trying to be something more than a tourist, and generally failing. Of course the pyramids had to be seen, but it was hard to see them without being mauled by gangs of 'guides'. I was also trying to do some walking, and in order to rid myself of my would-be escorts, I simply turned my back on them, and on the pyramids too, and started walking into the desert. Various small boys seemed to think I'd gone mad. They yelled and pestered and pointed urgently in the direction they thought I should be going. But when I carried on walking they left me alone – there was nothing for them out there in the desert, least of all other tourists to guide. For me there was peace, space, emptiness, isolation, and the pleasure of walking.

Yet despite what the kids thought, I wasn't completely insane. I wasn't going just to wander off into the void. After I'd walked in a more or less straight line for what I considered a good distance, I changed my route and walked in a big curve that took me back towards civilisation, ancient and modern. I only had a vague sense of where I was going, but it's hard to get lost when you have the pyramids as a landmark, and there was no need to head back too directly. I walked along the top of a hillside, part rock, part sand, and found myself in a cemetery. I was drawn to it as always. It was small, neat, well kept, surrounded by a low stone wall that separated it from the rest of the desert.

There were no headstones but there were large, flat slabs of concrete with white painted stones set in them as markers. And along one edge of the slabs there were deep, square, man-size holes that somebody could climb down to get underground, where the bodies were. It really did look as though, if you were truly desperate, you might go down the holes for shelter. You might even live there, though it wouldn't be much of a life.

OK, this wasn't the same city of the dead that Burton and Rohmer walked in, but for my purposes it was near enough. I tell myself that a man is free to choose his own

fellow travellers and kindred spirits. You don't need to be
absolutely literal about it. When you walk, you always walk
in other people's footsteps, sometimes these are real, sometimes metaphoric, sometimes imaginary, sometimes wishful;
never, you hope, are they fake.

*

Not long after I visited the graves of Burton and Rohmer,
I went back to the Hollywood Forever cemetery in Los
Angeles. I wanted to check the feeling I'd had that Burton's
tomb would fit here perfectly. But when I first went into
the cemetery and started walking along the neat pathways,
between luxurious stretches of green lawn, I thought that
perhaps I'd misremembered the place. Yes, there were a few
extremely grand graves, some big, elaborate mausoleums, but
there were plenty of those in England. And in any case
the cemetery contained many ordinary graves too. I thought
maybe Hollywood Forever wasn't really so wild and kitsch
after all. And then a peacock walked across my path. And
then another. There was quite a flock of them scattered about
the place. They really weren't the kind of thing you'd find in
an English cemetery.

Presently I came across a new monument, one that had
arrived since my last visit, a piece of funeral statuary, a
memorial to Johnny Ramone; or more precisely a statue *of*
Johnny Ramone. Not for him a simple marble headstone or
one etched with his image, not even a large tomb, this was a
larger than life-size effigy: pageboy haircut, leather jacket,
Mosrite guitar, all cast in bronze, the Johnny Ramone guitar
pose frozen in time. I'd say the guitar is held a little higher
than Johnny wore it in life, but that may be because the
bronze ends at mid-thigh as the legs disappear into a large
chunk of granite. Toto, I said to myself, I've a feeling we're
not in Kensal Green, not even Mortlake, any more. I also

thought of some Ramones lyrics: 'I don't wanna walk around with you, I don't wanna walk around with you, I don't wanna walk around with you, So why you wanna walk around with me?'

Finally I also thought of the Henry James short story 'Ghostly Rental', which features a young divinity student, who describes himself as a 'methodical pedestrian', and is extremely fond of walking in graveyards. On one of his trips he meets a strange old man who says, 'Walking, yes. Take all your exercise now. Someday you will have to settle down in a graveyard in a fixed position.' That really isn't why I walk in graveyards; but it would surely be reason enough.

8

As I Tripped Out One Morning: Music, Movement, Movies

They tell me, 'Son, we want you, be elusive, but don't walk far . . . '
David Bowie, 'We Are The Dead'

A question: How many roads must a man walk down before you call him a man? It's a good question, and who better to ask it than Bob Dylan, who devoted a whole episode of his radio show to the topic of walking. His recitation of 'She walks in beauty, like the night' is not to be missed. I was asking it myself while in Manhattan, walking along Madison Avenue where it crosses 135th Street. I had been following a songline. I was investigating the way in which certain songs can act as self-guided walking tours.

Bruce Chatwin, one of the great 'sacramental walkers' (his term), describes the songlines in his book of the same name. They are part of the belief system of the Australian Aboriginals, who of necessity were walkers since they never invented the wheel or domesticated a rideable animal. They believed the world was sung into being by ancient spirits, consequently if you knew enough songs you would know the whole world. Chatwin writes, 'A song . . . was both map and direction finder. Providing you knew the song, you could always find your way across country.' I wanted to see if something similar might work in New York City.

I had a song in my head: Kirsty MacColl's rendition of 'Walking Down Madison', words by MacColl, music by Johnny Marr, a couple of British musicians who spent plenty of time in America. It's one of those songs ('Streets Of London' is probably the most famous example of the genre) that catalogues the horrors of the big city: in the McColl song, it's homelessness, poverty, knife attacks and hypothermia. She rhymes Madison with gun, fun, bums, nuns and 'philosophising some', which neatly lays out the territory she's dealing with.

Whether people who live in large cities actually need any musical reminder of the horrors of the urban environment is debatable, but this song is better than many. It says that a single street, or Avenue in this case, can connect high and low, rich and poor, the hopeful and the hopeless. The distance, physical and metaphoric, between the penthouse and the basement is 'not that far', with sharks in the penthouse and rats in the basement. It isn't a subtle song.

I sang the song to myself as a soundtrack for one hundred and ten blocks of the Avenue, from Madison Square Park where it starts, up to where it becomes the on ramp of the Madison Avenue Bridge. True, I was walking up rather than down, which was not precisely what the song describes, but it seemed more interesting to walk from an area I knew to one that I didn't. By the time I got to the end, through Spanish Harlem, then East Harlem, I'd be in completely unfamiliar territory.

The song is political in its way, and since Madison Avenue is the home of the New York advertising industry, political targets are comfortably at hand, but advertising isn't mentioned in the song, and perhaps that would have been too easy. I, for one, didn't know there was any such thing as the Madison Avenue Advertising Walk of Fame. It runs along Madison from 42nd to 49th Streets. There's a plaque set right there in the sidewalk to prove it; it reads, all in capitals, and the dots are theirs not mine, 'In recognition of the contributions of advertising to pop culture and its most enduring and beloved icons and slogans . . . the American Association of Advertising Agencies dedicates the Madison Avenue Advertising Walk of Fame as a permanent tribute to the most creative of all industries . . . advertising.'

Evidence of this creativity was available right there. Famous American advertising icons and slogans, beloved no doubt, had been printed on banners that were hanging from the lamp posts. Some of these were less than wholly familiar to an Englishman. Certainly I had heard the slogans 'A mind is a terrible thing to waste' and 'Sometimes you feel like a nut sometimes you don't', but the AFLAC duck (mascot of an insurance company) and Juan Valdez (fictional spokesman for the National Federation of Coffee Growers of Columbia) were new ones on me.

It was no surprise that the home of American advertising was pretty swank, but around about 60th Street things became even swanker, with shops selling designer clothes and high-end luxury goods, elegant restaurants, a store with a chrome ejector seat in the window, a chauffeur-driven, pink Rolls-Royce waiting at the curb. But it wasn't so swank that a few blocks later it couldn't accommodate a young black man standing on the corner saying repeatedly to passers-by, 'Help me out, please,' and then to himself, 'Let it go.'

Then at about 100th Street things changed with a bang. There were medical buildings, some project tower blocks, a lot more life, more people walking, street traders, crowds on the sidewalk, and of course it became a good deal less white. In a schoolyard at 104th Street a lone white teenager was sitting on a wall by the chain-link fence, trying not to look nervous, and failing. He wasn't within a hundred yards of any other kid in the schoolyard, none of whom shared his skin colour. If this were a movie you knew he'd integrate and ingratiate himself in some novel manner, as it was it looked like he was just sitting there praying for his school-days to be over.

At 117th Street a group of forlorn but surprisingly good-natured people was blocking the sidewalk, among them one man on crutches, one woman in a wheelchair and a black kid who was saying loudly to nobody in particular, certainly not to me, 'Gimme a bottle of Cleeko, eighty dollars, I'm ready to go.' I don't think he seriously thought anybody was going to give him anything.

When I got to about 120th Street and Marcus Garvey Park, still called Mount Morris Park on the map I had with me, I was reminded of another song, Joe South's 'Walk A Mile In My Shoes'. The fact is, walking a single mile in anybody's shoes isn't so very hard. You could walk that distance in shoes that really didn't fit you at all. Walking a mile, even several miles, in the boots I was wearing that day, my own boots, was perfectly fine. They were pain-free and totally comfortable for about four and half miles, but then they started to feel really quite uncomfortable, and after about five miles they became absolutely excruciating.

Suddenly I felt a terrible twinge and wrench in my right little toe. It felt as though all the skin had been abruptly ripped away from it in one sharp slice. I limped into the park, found a bench, took off my boot and sock, and saw that yes, all the skin had indeed been abruptly ripped away in one sharp slice. It hurt and it didn't look pretty.

I thought about ending my walk, and hobbling to the 125th Street subway station. I'd already walked over a hundred blocks; there'd be no great shame in retiring injured. But I looked around the park at all the people who were hanging about there. They all looked as though they had a lot of troubles, and although I didn't presume to guess what those troubles were, I thought they were probably all a whole lot worse than a toe with the skin stripped off. I sat for a while but then I put my boot back on and decided that – like Felix in a different song – I would keep on walking.

*

Given people's capacity to write songs about anything whatsoever, it's hardly surprising that there are countless songs about walking. The earliest form I know is the *chanson d'aventure*, devised by the Provençal troubadours in the twelfth century. Traditionally these songs often begin with the line 'As I walked out one morning', and they go on to describe a troubling or surprising meeting or some unusual sight encountered: compare and contrast with Bob Dylan when he goes out 'to smell the air around Tom Paine' in the song 'Tom Paine' on John Wesley Harding.

There's evidently something contradictory here. The moment you use those opening words, the listener knows something surprising is about to happen, which means that it's not really so surprising after all; which is an issue at the very heart of the idea of 'going for a walk'. We may not want our walks to be 'adventures' in the most extreme sense: we can do without pirates, gun play, caverns measureless to man, but we do hope to see something new on our walks, even in the most familiar surroundings.

'Walking out' in the troubadours' sense sounds like an everyday activity, something close to home, not necessarily part of some great thousand-mile journey, and the implication is that adventures and wonders are to be found wherever we are, if not in our own backyard, then within walking distance of it.

The trope 'as I walked out one morning' is curiously close to the traditional blues opening line 'I woke up this morning'. And if you're trying to write a simple blues lyric it's very tempting to rhyme blues with shoes, and before you even know it, you're writing a song about walking.

Robert Johnson didn't resist the temptation and wrote 'Walkin' Blues'. Johnson's words aren't easy to understand at the best of times, but to my ears he seems to be singing,

I woke – up this mornin' – feelin' 'round for my shoes
I know by that I got them old walkin' blues.

He has the walking blues because his 'little Bernice' has gone. She's walked out on him, and rather than stay at home moping, he's hitting the road again on foot. A whole bunch of fellow blues walkers, including Bonnie Raitt, Eric Clapton and the Grateful Dead have followed in Johnson's footsteps and done cover versions.

Johnson's plan to hit the road might not solve all his problems. In another of his songs, 'Stop Breaking Down', he says that every time he walks down the street some pretty mama starts 'breaking down' with him, and he wishes she'd stop.

Johnson, like most blues players, frequently uses the rhythm known as the 'blues shuffle', the very basic 'dum da dum da, dum da dum da' pattern at the heart of the classic twelve-bar blues. It's always struck me as a misnomer. The blues shuffle sounds more sprightly and purposeful than I expect a shuffle to be, especially if it's combined with a 'walking bass' line.

The walking bass isn't confined to the blues, it's in all kinds of pop and jazz music. With one note for every beat of a four/four bar, it's certainly a rhythm you can walk to, as opposed to, say, the three/four time of the waltz that makes you want to dance, or Stravinsky's polyrhythms that might make you want to celebrate the rite of spring. Karlheinz Stockhausen claimed to hear the march of the jackboot in any recognisable time signature.

Walking bass has something in common with 'stride

piano', the style of jazz playing where the player's left hand 'strides' up and down the piano, alternating bass lines and chords. Some of these lines may 'walk' regularly at the pace of a basic beat, but this being jazz, there'll be arpeggios, syncopation and the introduction of mixed time signatures. You might be able to walk to this but you'd look darned odd.

One of the greatest stride pianists is Fats Domino, a man who's written at least three songs with the word walking in the title. The best known of them, called simply 'I'm Walking', was, according to legend, written after his car broke down and a fan saw him making his way on foot to the nearest garage and yelled, 'Look, it's Fats Domino walking!' Fats went home and turned his misfortune into a song; or so the story goes.

In song, as in life, there are a lot of people who'd much rather be riding than walking. And you might think that country and western music, with its fondness for pickup trucks and eighteen-wheelers, would find walking a particular humiliation, but it appears not. Here walking is often synonymous with honesty and plain dealing, whether it's Faron Young's 'Walk Tall' or Johnny Cash's 'I Walk The Line'.

Rodney Cowell sings a song called 'I Walk The Line (Revisited)', which is about the joys of hearing Johnny Cash sing 'I Walk The Line' on the radio, but it's a car radio and Crowell is driving in his '49 Ford, an irony the song seems not to notice. But it wouldn't be country music at all if there wasn't some mawkish sentiment also attached to walking, as in Wayne Newton's 'Daddy Don't Walk So Fast', which is what the kid says as his daddy abandons him and walks away.

Some people reckon that Patsy Cline's 'Walking After

Midnight', written by Alan Black and Don Hecht, is a great song of female independence and empowerment, but it strikes me as deeply problematic. On the surface it appears to be about a female protagonist who has, we don't know how, lost her lover, and so she wanders the streets, after midnight, looking for him. Why she chooses this method and this time of night is left for the listener to guess, but earlier, more prudish sensibilities than ours couldn't imagine what any woman could be doing in the streets after midnight unless she'd become a hooker, a streetwalker. Another possibility might be that having been abandoned, she's simply lost her wits, *à la* Ophelia, and is walking around in a daze, looking for love in all the wrong places, though this doesn't seem remotely empowered.

When men sing 'Walking After Midnight', as they often do, the streetwalker possibility seems much more likely. The guy searches the night for his lost love, trying to save her from a life of vice. Of course you could conceivably reverse the sexes in this scenario too: the woman's searching the streets because she thinks the guy's become a rent boy, but this is probably trying too hard.

Sexual role reversal plays a part in another great walking song, 'These Boots Are Made For Walkin' '. As sung by Nancy Sinatra, this does indeed sound like a song of empowerment. She's walking over the guy and striding on to freedom. When you hear the original male version, as sung by the song's composer, Lee Hazelwood, it becomes a particularly nasty piece of vindictive masculine domination. Hazelwood, it always seemed, was perfectly happy with that interpretation.

You might think that walking is in itself too tame a subject for the full-on, balls-out, hard-rock song, and writers of rock songs seem to agree. Not wishing to appear pedestrian, they envisage fancy or extreme walking that takes place in unusual or downright impossible circumstances: on the moon (the Police), on thin ice (Elvis Costello and Yoko Ono), through walls (Steve Hackett), on locusts (John Cale), on broken glass (Annie Lennox), on sunshine (Katrina and the Waves) and, a particularly obscure favourite of mine, through syrup, in a song by Ned's Atomic Dustbin.

The rockingest song with the word walking in its title and lyrics, is surely Aerosmith's 'Walk This Way'. Supposedly it was inspired by the movie *Young Frankenstein*, in which Marty Feldman, as Igor, invites visitors to the castle to 'walk this way', which they do by copying his shambling, hump-backed gait. In the context of the movie it's very funny, the silliness of the pun only adding to the comedy. In the Aero-smith song the pun has pretty much disappeared. Here it's a song about being sexually initiated at the hands of a cheerleader, and the lyrics don't repay a very close reading, but the gist of it is that the girl is telling the guy to follow her round the back of the bleachers, not to imitate her cheerleader moves. Either way, it doesn't sound like a very long or challenging walk.

The fact that Run-DMC joined Aerosmith for a fantastic hit version of 'Walk This Way' is enough to make us realise that rappers can be walkers too, oh not very far or very fast, that would scuff up their immaculate sneakers, but when-ever you have a lot of pimps you're likely to have a lot of people doing Tom Wolfe's 'pimp roll'. There's Snoop Dogg, 'walking down the street, smoking, smoking, sipping on gin and juice', Cypress Hill's 'Stoned Is The Way Of The Walk', Lil' Wayne's 'Walk It Off' and Xzibit's, 'Get Your Walk On'.

The walk Xzibit is referring to here is the Crip Walk, originally part of Los Angeles gang culture. Back in the day, Crips would make heel-and-toe or V-shaped movements with their feet to spell out letters and words on the ground, often after they'd committed a crime. One word they tended to spell out was Blood, the name of their gang rivals, and then they'd 'erase' the word by scrubbing their feet all over it. This does sound wonderfully baroque. It's not a walk that would get you from A to B, but it was certainly a walk that could get you into a lot of trouble if you did it in front of the wrong people: Crips believed it was for Crips only. But eventually it became mainstream. Ice-T Crip-walked on TV, and since then all and sundry have been doing it. You can find tutorial videos on YouTube, a lot of dance moves have been added, and it's now often known as Clown Walking. It's also been said that it looks like doing hopscotch on crack.

*

References to walking are more at home in the apparently safer territory of the show tune and the standard. Walking here tends to be an innocent activity from an earlier, gentler, less sexualised age. And so we have songs like 'Walking My Baby Back Home', 'Walking In A Winter Wonderland' and, of course, 'You'll Never Walk Alone'.

The oddest walking-related show tune I know is Irving Berlin's 'My Walking Stick' of 1938, written for the movie *Alexander's Ragtime Band,* which is about how very attached the protagonist is to his walking stick. I say 'he' because it's quite evidently a man's song even though, in the movie, it's sung by Ethel Merman, who performs it as a male impersonator. The lyrics say you can take his hat, his tie, his spats, and he can get by just fine, but take away his walking stick (which for the sake of a rhyme sometimes becomes a cane) and he'll go insane. If he's down lovers' lane and he's caught, then without it, he's nought. It was a different age. The song makes a lot more sense in a Louis Armstrong version.

*

In October 1938, *The Times* of London ran a leader headline that read, 'While dictators rage and statesmen talk, all Europe dances – to the Lambeth Walk.' It was referring to a song of that name from the hit stage show *Me and My Girl*, book and lyrics by Douglas Furber and L. Arthur Rose and music by Noel Gay.

To be fair, the Lambeth Walk is as much a dance as it is a way of walking, a jaunty strut that involves linked arms and raised knees, and the occasional shout, 'Oi.' Traditionally it's being done by lovable, heart-of-gold, salt-of-the-earth Londoners. As the song says, 'Any time you're Lambeth way, any evening any day, you'll find them all doin' the Lambeth Walk.' The song rapidly became a hit and a political cause. King George VI and Queen Elizabeth went to see the show and loved it, and the song was even popular with some people in Germany, so popular that Noel Gay was asked to sign a document declaring that he had no Jewish blood in him. He declined. In 1939 this led to the Lambeth Walk being denounced by the Nazi Party as 'Jewish mischief and animalistic hopping', though to a rational person it looks like neither of these things. In due course, in 1941, a short English newsreel propaganda film appeared which went by various names including *Lambeth Walk – Nazi Style*. It filched footage from Leni Riefenstahl's *Triumph of the Will* and edited it so that Hitler and his troops appeared to be doing their own ridiculous, militarist version of the Lambeth Walk. The film's provenance is mysterious, but it's most convincingly credited to Charles A. Ridley, though that's a name that's otherwise disappeared from film history. It's said that Goebbels was so infuriated when he saw the film that he ran out of the room literally kicking and screaming.

Lambeth Walk is the name of a street as well as a song, and I went there, following another songline.

'Everything's free and easy
Do as you darn well pleasey.
Why don't you make your way there,
Go there, stay there?'

I could think of several reasons. No doubt lovable, heart-of-gold, salt-of-the-earth Londoners still live in the area, but none of them was in evidence on the day I went walking there. In fact there were few people on the street at all.

Lambeth Walk was not thriving, and it seemed to be in trouble. There was a building called 'Denby Court', a block of sheltered housing. But the people in Denby Court weren't just sheltered, they were incarcerated, behind walls, bars and metal fences, protected by metal spikes and closed-circuit TV cameras. The need for so much protection suggested that the inhabitants were permanently under siege, living in constant terror. What monsters walked this street?

On the day I was there, there didn't seem to be much to fear, unless you count the kid on a bike who did an aggressive wheelie a couple of feet in front of me, as if to say . . . well, I'm not sure what . . . that a kid on a bike owns these mean streets, that I was obviously a stranger there and that I'd better watch myself, that I must be a sucker to be walking rather than riding a bike? . . . who knows, but he was definitely making a statement.

Perhaps he thought I had no reason to be there, and in a way he was right. There was nothing to see or do or buy. The Lambeth Walk Carpet Shop was boarded up, as was Lambeth Walk Seafoods and its sign had been smashed to pieces. Something called CORAS, the Columbian Refugee Association, seemed still to be in business, even though it was closed and there was a serious-looking metal blind rolled down over the front. Something called 'Joy's Mini Market's' (*sic*) was open for business, and a black woman, possibly Joy, was sitting on a box outside. I wasn't going to do anything so crass as to ask her about the dance but I did try to make eye contact, and she was having none of it.

In fact, Lambeth Walk has some history of economic failure. In the nineteenth century there were two wells there, one called Nearer, one called Farther, trying to sell water for its medicinal properties. The wells didn't last long and there was now no sign they'd ever been there. Finally, I came to a bleak little courtyard where the owners of a couple of market stalls were just closing up for the day; one had been selling household products in industrial-sized packs, the other selling toys. And painted on the wall above them, high enough to deter all but the most determined taggers, was a faded mural showing a jolly man and woman with knees raised, arms linked, doing, there was no doubt about it, the Lambeth Walk.

*

It might have been tempting, on these songline walks of mine, to wear a personal stereo and have the relevant song playing as I walked. For several reasons, I didn't. One was simply the issue of irritation: to have the same song playing over and over again might have driven me nuts. More crucially, as I walked I didn't want to be insulated from the sounds of the environment. The things you hear when you walk are every bit as important as the things you see, or for that matter touch, taste and smell. There's also the safety issue. I wanted to be able to hear the approaching car, the ominous footsteps, the people yelling at me. Perhaps I was being old fashioned.

There's at least one generation, probably several, who can't imagine what it's like not to have music that's portable and always available via the Walkman and its various higher tech developments through to the iPod, known in some quarters as the 'isolation Pod'. The name Walkman is one of those not quite English words belonging to some global tongue, devised by the people at Sony, who first marketed the personal stereo in 1979 in Japan. Toshiba had a rival product called the Walky. Walkman strikes me as a very unsexy word, and you'd think Sony might have called it the Runman or the Jogman, but the early versions were so sensitive that if you ran or jogged, or even walked too quickly, the playing mechanism faltered.

At the risk of sounding like old man Methuselah, not only can I remember a time before the personal stereo, I can remember the first one I ever saw. It was in London, and it was in 1979, before the Walkman went on sale in England. I was working in a bookshop, and was behind the counter with a couple of other assistants who were big music fans, when a young Japanese man came into the store wearing a Walkman. It was as strange as seeing somebody with a jetpack on his shoulders. We had a halting conversation in which we tried to ask him what the Walkman was like. We couldn't believe that the sound quality was any good, and the Japanese man very definitely wasn't going to offer his earpieces for us to try. We didn't blame him. We didn't expect it, any more than we'd have expected him to offer us the use of his jetpack.

At least one of us said it would never catch on. Although it was easy enough to see the advantages of being able to take your music with you anywhere, the notion that life required a personalised, pre-recorded soundtrack was a new and an unexplored one. We had no idea of the extent to which the personal stereo would subsequently be used to provide 'background music', to be a form of editing, something filmic, a way of combining sound and vision, manipulating what you see and hear, to make yourself believe you're living in a movie.

Absurd and unlikely juxtapositions are par for the course. They're expected and welcomed. By now we know that any sound and any image can be put together to create some sort of meaning. If you're walking, wandering lonely as a cloud, you might think that one of Erik Satie's 'Gymnopédies' would be just the job, but if your iPod randomly selects some Napalm Death, then that will create its own oblique and ironic resonances too. These may be random, but they will not be meaningless. The mind will make sense of them. This is something we've all learned from watching so many movies.

Erik Satie, incidentally, as well as being a composer, pianist, Rosicrucian and master ironist, was also a fine, determined, obsessive walker. Every day he left his home in the suburb of Arcueil and walked to his studio in the centre of Paris, then at night he walked back again. It was a substantial journey, six miles in each direction, and some of it was potentially dangerous: Satie carried a hammer for protection.

Guillaume Apollinaire tells us that Satie did a lot of composing on his nocturnal homeward walks. He would create music in his head, then stop from time to time under a convenient streetlamp and write it down in a notebook. His productivity was greatly reduced during World War I when so many Parisian streetlamps were turned off. It's easy enough to believe that you hear the regular, repeated rhythm of the human footfall in much of Satie's work. He also said, 'Before I compose a piece, I walk around it several times, accompanied by myself.'

There is one cinematic moment, where Satie's music is forever welded to an image of walking, and that is in the Hal Ashby/Jerzy Kosinski movie *Being There*. It's the last scene, when the hero, Chance the gardener, played by Peter Sellers, walks on water, across a lake, to the accompaniment of a version of Satie's 'Gnossiennes'. The movie credits say 'Rearranged by Johnny Mandel', though surely 'arranged' would have been enough.

The scene was a spur-of-the-moment invention. The script they were shooting ended with Peter Sellers and Shirley Maclaine simply meeting each other while walking in the woods. Compared with seeing the hero walking on water, this was obviously tame stuff. Ashby found walking on water was a surprisingly easy movie effect to pull off. All you need is a certain kind of mobile platform that can be found at an airport, you sink it just below the surface of the water so that it can't be seen, and then any actor can take a short straight walk along it and appear to be doing some miraculous aquatic pedestrianism. In *Being There*, the narrowness of the track also allowed Sellers to poke an umbrella into the water just a few inches away from his feet and have it sink deep below the surface, giving the impression there was no platform at all.

Sellers insisted he was an actor who had no 'true self'. He disappeared into his roles and became invisible. There is, therefore, no such thing as a 'Peter Sellers' walk. Certain other actors are far more inclined to have a trademark stride. A few who immediately spring to mind are Charlie Chaplin, Groucho Marx, Pee-wee Herman, Arnold Schwarzenegger and John Wayne. All of these might be construed as comical to a degree: by the time a walking style has become recognisable it has also become absurd. It also seems to be a particularly male trait. The only genuinely distinctive 'female walk' I can think of is Marilyn Monroe's stylised wiggle. Sometimes this is attributed to her weak ankles, but that sounds like an explanation for something that needs no explaining.

I'm one of those people who find Charlie Chaplin largely

unwatchable these days, and his walk is certainly part of what I can't bear, its cuteness, its *faux* humility, its feverish attempt at ingratiation. If this sounds like too contemporary an opinion, Wyndham Lewis felt much the same about Chaplin back in 1928. His novel *The Childermass* is set in the afterlife, a world overseen by a character known as The Bailiff who sometimes appears in the form of Chaplin. Characters in the afterlife are then forced to perform routines from Chaplin movies: it isn't hell exactly, but it's near enough. For Lewis this represents all that's wrong with popular culture: it's become no more than repetition and imitation at the expense of authenticity.

Certainly Chaplin is anything but inimitable. It's said he based his onscreen walk on that of a real tramp, a man rejoicing in the name of Rummy Binks, who held the horses outside (and presumably drank inside) a pub called the Queen's Head in Lambeth, belonging to Chaplin's uncle. There's also a story, maybe an urban myth, that Chaplin once entered a Charlie Chaplin lookalike contest, and lost. One version has him saying to a reporter that he was tempted to give the contestants lessons in 'the Chaplin walk, out of pity as well as the desire to see the thing done correctly'.

By the time of his movie *Limelight* (1952), Chaplin had transferred some of his concerns about walking on to another character. Chaplin takes the part of Calvero, a fading comedian; Claire Bloom plays Terry, a ballerina suffering from hysterical paralysis. There's nothing physically wrong with her, but she can't walk. It comes as no surprise to anybody when, late in the movie, she finds her feet again and yells, 'Calvero! I'm walking! I'm walking!' One must have a heart of stone to watch this scene without hooting in derision.

The main thing that makes *Limelight* endurable is the brief presence of Buster Keaton. Now there's a man who knew how to walk across the screen (as well as fall, tumble, slide, leap, swing, etc). In *Limelight* he plays another fading old comedian, and one who gets far, far less screen time than Chaplin. The two of them perform a creaky musical routine: Keaton on piano, Chaplin on violin. The act is filmed very straight, very deadpan. There's a long period at the start of the scene (two minutes or so out of a total of seven) where Keaton fumbles with his sheet music while Chaplin shows off a series of 'funny walks' based around the idea of having one leg shorter than the other. These are skilfully done as far as they go, but they point up a fundamental difference between the two comedians. Keaton could be funny when he walked, but he didn't do funny walks.

For Keaton, as with any good actor, the walk was not a trademark but a part of characterisation. In *Sherlock Junior*, for instance, he plays a would-be detective following a suspect by walking about a foot behind him, their strides interlocking. More typically Keaton's gait is a combination of the stoic, the hesitant, the noble. He walks on, not in expectation of joy or success, certainly not in expectation of being loved like Chaplin's 'little fellow', and yet for all the abuse and misfortune that the universe heaps on him, Keaton's walk remains brave and optimistic.

It appears that Keaton believed he owed a great deal to Felix. According to Mark Newgarden (an illustrator and animator, who got it straight from the mouth of Otto Meisner, Felix's creator) there was a time in the 1920s when Keaton paid the producer of the Felix cartoons (Pat Sullivan) so that he could use an approximation of Felix's walk: that backwards and forwards pace, head down, arms clenched behind the back. Newgarden, and indeed I, find it amazing that Keaton thought he needed to protect himself by making such a payment. What court would ever have found Keaton guilty of stealing a walk from a cartoon animal? Still, these were Keaton's golden years; perhaps he had enough money and he thought it was a good investment, to spend a little then and head off even the slightest possibility of legal trouble.

The song 'Felix Kept On Walking' has some seriously extraordinary lyrics:

> Felix kept on walking, kept on walking still,
> Now poor Auntie Eva has a full-grown 'beaver'.
> On the tiles he went last night,
> Those tabby cats to thrill,
> Met a Frenchy cat named Lou,
> She said, 'Do you parley vous?'
> He said, 'Yes, but not with you,' and kept on walking still.

Like Felix, Keaton did indeed kept on walking, through TV specials, commercials, industrial-training films and, in 1965, *How to Stuff a Wild Bikini*, followed, in 1966, by Samuel Beckett's *Film*. Imagine the horror of Chaplin mawkishly puttering his way through the same catalogue of parts.

*

Moviemakers may in general be happier depicting the rapid motion of actors: dancing, running, diving, swinging from jungle creepers, jumping off buildings, but there's no shortage of great movie walking: Errol Flynn as Jim Corbett in *Gentleman Jim*, walking through the packed streets of New York City and using his fancy footwork to avoid bumping into passers-by, for example, and Fred Astaire walking down the Champs Elysées in *Funny Face*; because Astaire is Astaire even his walking looks like dancing. The characters in Luis Buñuel's *The Discreet Charm of the Bourgeoisie* repeatedly find themselves transported from their bourgeois homes to a country road which they walk along briskly, though without any obvious purpose, dressed for a dinner party rather than a country walk. And remember Michael Douglas as the crazed, disgruntled defence engineer in *Falling Down*? You know the guy's insane because he abandons his car and walks all the way across Los Angeles for his daughter's birthday.

Usually there'll be music on the soundtracks to go along with any walking scenes. Some arrangements will be more appropriate and thought out than others. However, there are certain movies where music and walking fuse together in a magically cinematic way. Admittedly, some of these fusions may take place in the brain as much as in the movie itself. I often think of Dustin Hoffman's walk as Ratzo Rizzo in *Midnight Cowboy* (a real limp: he put a stone in his shoe so that he wouldn't have to 'act'), and I hear the song 'Everybody's Talking At Me' even though I know that's the music that plays when he's on the bus rather than on foot.

And of course I think of John Travolta, as Tony Manero, strutting his way through *Saturday Night Fever* while the Bee Gees sing, 'You can tell by the way I use my walk I'm a woman's man, no time to talk.' But the scene I often remember best is from the ludicrous sequel, *Staying Alive*, where the conversation goes, 'You know what I wanna do?' 'What?' 'Strut.' And Travolta goes striding off across the Brooklyn Bridge, or is it the Verrazano Narrows?

All this, I know, is just scratching the celluloid. However, when I began writing this book I had no doubt about what I thought was the perfect coming together of music, walking and film: the opening scene from Wim Wenders' *Paris, Texas*. The camera, up in a helicopter, makes a long swoop across the pale, jagged Texas desert, and finally rises over a long, sharp, horizontal ridge to reveal Harry Dean Stanton, playing the part of Travis, in a suit, tie and baseball cap, walking along, floppy and swift moving, in the middle of the harshest of landscapes, not on any recognisable track, coming from nowhere, going nowhere.

The accompanying music has a perfection about it. The scene, in fact the whole movie, is unimaginable without Ry Cooder's slide-guitar-driven score, based on Blind Willie Johnson's 'Dark was the Night', which in turn was based on a nineteenth-century hymn. It's 'mood music' all right, but it's hard to define the mood. It's deeply ambiguous – desert music, with a floating, swaying, self-renewing sadness. You wouldn't necessarily think of it as music to accompany walking, though it does have a forward movement, a restlessness, a rise and fall, tension and release, as it struggles with and then descends into melancholy. It's a cinematic moment that could make you fall in love with a director, an actor, a musician, a cinematographer, a desert. It's a perfect start to a movie, a huge visual statement that asks an even bigger question. It's a moment so strong and enigmatic that the rest of the film sometimes seems to exist simply in order to explain and justify that image.

The scene had long been etched firmly in my mind, and there was another scene, or at least a shot, that I remembered. Still quite early in the movie, Travis is trying to escape from the brother who has come to 'rescue' him, and he begins to walk along an endless, dead-straight railroad track into an empty, pale-blue, featureless, desert landscape.

I decided I'd better see the movie again. These two scenes were there, much as I remembered them, but there were a couple of other walking scenes I'd forgotten about. One has Travis walking across a freeway bridge where he encounters a madman screaming at the traffic below. He gives the screaming man a sympathetic pat on the back as he walks by. The other scene shows Travis trying to make amends to the son he abandoned four years earlier: the boy is now eight. Travis asks his brother's maid how he should walk in order to look like a 'rich father'. She tells him he must walk with his head up, his body stiff, and with dignity. We can see that Travis isn't quite able to pull this off, but he and the maid are happy enough with the effect. He then meets his son after school and they walk home together, but instead of sharing the same sidewalk, they walk along on opposite sides of the street, doing little comic walking routines for each other's amusement. It's a scene of enormous warmth and charm. It's hard to think of Harry Dean Stanton as a purveyor of silly walks (he's as far from being a John Cleese as I can imagine), and that's precisely why these walks work so well, because they belong to the character rather than the actor.

But then that's pretty much it for walking in the movie. Sure, people walk across rooms and across parking lots, but there are no more genuine walking scenes. *Paris, Texas* turns into what it was threatening to be all along; a road movie. Travis buys a 1959 Ford Ranchero, and father and son drive off in search of mom, played by Nastassja Kinski. They find her, mother and son reunite, and Travis, knowing that he's the problem rather than the solution, drives off with an ambiguous smile on his face. The film has become a Sam Shepard story of love, loss, alienation, and manly men driving alone in pickup trucks; which is to say it has become rather unsurprising.

Within the scheme of the film Travis has redeemed himself. He's become part of something. In the beginning he was a lost, crazy man, walking alone through the Texas desert. In the end he's a sane man, integrated, driving along highways in his impossibly cool, twenty-five-year-old classic Ranchero. There is a moral here that I'm not very comfortable with.

Naturally one has sympathy for Travis. We don't want him to be a lonely, miserable outsider, and yet I can't see why a man driving along in a Ranchero is necessarily any better off than a man walking alone in the desert. It would have been crass for the end of the movie to have him returning to the desert on foot, yet the vision of the smiling man driving his pickup into the American night feels like too easy a resolution.

And now there was something about one of those earlier scenes that worried me too. In the beginning Travis walks in straight lines, without regard for topography or established paths. He doesn't walk down any actual roads. When his brother sees him walking along the railroad track he stops him, peers into the distance, in the direction Travis is heading, and says, 'What's out there? There's nothing out there.' It rings hollow, because there *is* something out there and maybe it's something that can be better found on foot than in a pickup truck.

So what's the answer to the question; how many roads must a man walk down before you call him a man? The answer surely has to be none. A man's still a man even if he walks down no roads at all. It's just that he's likely to be more interesting company if he's walked and sung his way down a few more than that, and if he doesn't rely too much on his pickup truck.

*

Meanwhile, back on Madison Avenue, since I didn't intend to walk across Madison Avenue Bridge I was at journey's end, and I headed west along 135th Street towards the subway station. For most of the time I'd been in East Harlem I hadn't been absolutely the only white man on the street. There had been one or two others along the way. But now as I walked along 135th Street I was certainly the only one, and apparently a rarity, rare enough for someone to shout out in my direction for the benefit of the guys he was with, 'White man! White man!' I wished he hadn't, for all sorts of reasons. He wasn't, I'm pretty sure, saying, 'Hail, fellow, well met. Welcome to the neighbourhood.' He was saying it more in the tone of someone who'd seen some exotic or threatened species, the way you might have called out, 'Look, a spotted owl!' though no doubt there was some disconnect between what he said and what he meant. In fact, I don't really know what he meant and I certainly didn't know how to respond. 'Why yes, you're right. I *am* a white man, aren't I?' In the event I simply pretended not to hear.

I had some of that feeling of being in a movie, oh not an especially original one, you know the kind where the white guy strolls into the wrong part of town and terrible things happen to him. I was also reminded of a couplet from Kirsty MacColl's song,

When you get to the corner don't look at those freaks,
Keep your head down low and stay quick on your feet,
                                                    oh yeah.

I don't know that the guy yelling at me was a freak, but I did keep my head down and continued walking at a brisk New York pace, all the way to the subway entrance. And as I walked I was reminded of one last song, Lou Reed's 'Waiting For The Man', which asks another question, 'Hey, white boy, what you doing up town?' 'Walking a songline,' wasn't the answer that anybody in Harlem would have expected or, I'm sure, accepted.

Some Desert Walkers, Walking in and out of Nature, with and without God, with and without Water

The desert is where God is and man is not.

Frank Lloyd Wright, freely translating
Balzac's 'A Passion in the Desert'

I don't know much about gods, but it seems they like their believers to do a lot of walking. Equally, a lot of people are very keen to walk with God; a surprising number are confident they already do.

In 341 AD, St Anthony, an Anchorite, one of the Desert Fathers, sometimes known as Saint Anthony of the Desert, aged ninety, had a vision that told him Paul the Hermit, the very first Desert Father, was 'near by', living in a cave in a different part of the Egyptian desert. Prayer walking was part of the Desert Fathers' creed. They walked as they prayed, prayed as they walked. Anthony started walking to find Paul, although he had no idea where he actually was. Fortunately, according to St Jerome, who is the only source for these events, a visionary centaur appeared to Anthony and pointed him in the right direction. Having walked through the desert for three days, he found Paul the Hermit, aged one hundred and thirteen, weak and close to death.

The two saints spent the night in prayer and next morning, knowing he was about to die, Paul asked Anthony to walk back to the monastery from which he'd come, to pick up a robe that had belonged to Athanasius the Great and to bring it to him. Paul wanted to be buried in the robe.

Anthony did what was asked of him: walked for three days back to his monastery, picked up the robe, and began the journey back to Paul's cave. On the third day of this walk, i.e. his ninth consecutive day of desert walking, Anthony had a vision of angels and prophets ascending to heaven with Paul the Hermit among them, a clear sign that Paul was already dead. And so it proved.

Finding Paul's body in the desert cave, Anthony wrapped it in the holy robe as preparation for burial, but found he was too weak to dig the grave. Two lions then came running out of the desert, knelt beside the body of Paul the Hermit, roared in lamentation, and dug a grave with their paws before disappearing into the desert again.

It's strange just how visionary you can get when you're ninety years old and have been walking in the desert for nine consecutive days.

*

I was in Death Valley, in the Mojave Desert, early one November. I was there to do some walking, and I'd gone to the general store in Furnace Creek, bought some supplies and was sitting on a bench outside, sipping a can of fizzy drink before setting off again.

One of the guys who worked in the store, a large, heavy, slow-moving man, strolled by and gruffly said to me, 'So where you from?'

I said, 'London.'

'London,' he repeated. 'So how do you like walking in my desert? I bet you think it's all a big nothing.'

Few things could have been further from what I actually thought about the desert, which I wasn't much inclined to think of as 'his' or anyone else's, but in an attempt to keep things simple and casual I said, 'I really love the desert.'

The man grunted and softened a little, then told me that he was originally from the LA area, actually Pasadena, but he'd had to get out. 'If you walk on concrete for too long you start to think like a predator,' he said. I thought this was a great line, but then he added, ' 'Cause everybody wants something from you,' which I thought rather spoiled the effect, because I really didn't see why having people want something from you would turn you into a predator.

The less simple and casual thing I might have said to him was, first, that I don't think the desert is a big nothing at all, that only an idiot could think that; I actually think it's a beautiful, intense, profoundly moving 'something'. And then I'd have said that although by far the majority of my walking has been done in cities, and continues to be, I've also walked in a lot of places that are not cities. I've done my time walking in the great outdoors (not that cities are 'indoors' exactly), and by and large these outdoor excursions were big nothings. The desert however is something else. And if I'd been feeling really forthright I might have said that although by and large I don't understand spiritual and religious longings, much less spiritual and religious certainties, some-times when I'm walking in the desert, there are moments, just moments, when I have some vague sense of over-arching well-being, something that might conceivably be what serious religious believers mean when they talk about revelation and transcendence. At the same time I'd be very reluctant to say I know with any certainty what the words 'revelation' and 'transcendence' actually mean.

*

By and large I have some problems with 'walking in nature'. I have trouble with the phrase and the people who use it, as much as with the activity itself. It's a form of words that comes weighted down with all kinds of meanings, values and assumptions, most of which I don't accept, much less share.

I've been trying to find where the phrase 'walking in nature' came from, without much success. I'm guessing its first use must have been an ancient one, but it's the hi-jacking of it by what I might as well call New Agers that I find so pernicious. A quick browse among New Age sources will soon have you screaming for mercy as you're told that nature is an unalloyed source of goodness, purity, benign intention, spiritual insight, higher consciousness and (oh, spare me) healing.

Here's a blogger and writer who calls himself the Mindful Hiker (his real name's Stephen Altschuler):

> Walking is not anything separate from life. It is integral to life, especially walking in nature. Yesterday, I encountered a rattlesnake on the trail – came quite close to it – and I marvelled at its wildness, the ferocity of its rattle as I almost stepped on it. It was the first time, in all my wild hiking, I'd ever seen a rattlesnake in the wild. The snake was large but what I will remember most over the years was that rattle. What a wild noise! What a warning to stay clear. It was completely real, that rattle – a true expression of the rattlesnake being itself.

Here's Linda Leonard PhD, a Jungian analyst who writes self-help books with a spiritual bent:

> I find nature so nourishing. I love to hike, especially in the mountains. When I'm walking in nature, I feel in awe of the wonder of creation. Nature is full of surprises, always changing, and we must change with it. In nature, the soul is renewed and called to open and grow.

You want to be called upon to open and grow? Go take a

walk through the Isle of Dogs on a Saturday afternoon when Millwall are playing, lady. You'll see nature red in tooth and claw right there.

And here's a sculptor called Bernard Perroud:

> Walking in nature is like wandering over a lover's body. All the senses (including the subtlest ones) fully awakened, we look for these shelters of blissful and regenerative rest. For these places to generate the creative impetus, we need to leave the world of thoughts. The womb of a woman is the ideal (security) shelter. Walking in nature, the shadowy places attract us. A hollow in the ground, the shade of a tree with its comfortable roots, a cave, a stone jutting out, a hollow tree.

OK, I realise that mocking the jejune philosophising of New Agers is like dynamiting New Agers in a barrel, but that doesn't mean it's not worth doing. I don't doubt that the Mindful Hiker *et al.* are sincere and well intentioned, but they seem incapable of having two consecutive, logical thoughts. More crucially their ramblings raise the question of which bit of nature it is that they've been walking in. Frozen wastes? Disease-ridden jungle? Malarial swamp? Flood plains and tornado alleys? Or just the local wildlife sanctuary.

And here is Garrison Keillor, not a man I take to be much of a New Ager, in a piece from one of his syndicated columns entitled *Take a Hike. It'll Do You Good.* He passes an evangelist in the street while walking in Manhattan and reflects:

> I'd like to stop and chat with him – he is the Lord's foot soldier – but he has his work to do and I have mine. Mine is to wander, which is what a writer does. When you walk in the open, exposed to beauty and grandeur and our

common mortality, no words can quite suffice, but one must keep trying. It's a good life in a paradise of a world.

This might be secularism posing as old-time religion, but actually I suspect it's the opposite. Walking, nature, spirituality – they make a powerful, and potentially very specious, trinity. It's hard to know exactly who's to blame for this, perhaps people who've misread their nature poets, who think Wordsworth's 'Daffodils' is actually about daffodils, who think that a stroll around Windermere will automatically stimulate intimations of immortality.

So many people who want to walk in nature want to walk in a very specific version of it. You might argue they want to walk through a white, middle-class, middle-aged version of it, though I think that's a different argument. What I'm sure of is that they want to walk in *managed* nature, which is probably just as well, since nothing else is currently available to us. At this point in history every environment, for better or worse, is a man-made environment. Those places that are of 'outstanding natural beauty' are not pristine, much less untouched, rather they've been managed in very specific ways to create very specific effects and to give the walker a very specific experience. Wandering lonely as a cloud doesn't seem much of an option in today's Lake District

You might think it would be different in America, the spaces are certainly wider and wilder, the population is spread more thinly. But it's a highly mobile population that prides itself on its get up and go. If a place has been declared worth seeing, if a trail has been declared worth walking, then the chances are there'll be people there seeing it and walking through it. There is, of course, the argument that it's people who need managing, not nature itself.

Death Valley, for example, which is certainly one of the

wildest places on earth, is managed by a company called
Xanterra Parks & Resorts, who get their name, they say, from
Samuel Coleridge's Xanadu in the poem 'Kubla Khan'. And
yes, Coleridge's Xanadu is 'a savage place', though one without car parks and air-conditioned accommodation, I think.
And when Xanterra also tell you they're 'proud stewards of
the park', you may well find yourself wailing, though not
necessarily for a demon lover.

Left to its own devices nature just might not be the
educative, compassionate, nurturing place that some would
like it to be, in fact insist that it always is. There's a smug-
ness as well as a narrowness in this notion of nature, but
that's as nothing compared with the self-aggrandisement
that goes along with it. What I think the 'walking in nature'
brigade are up to is trying to assert their moral and spiritual
superiority, first over those who don't go walking at all, and
then over people (like me) who walk for our own, less lofty,
though equally valid reasons. I might go for a walk – an
ordinary, secular activity – but these other guys go *walking
in nature* and they have a deeply spiritual experience merely
by putting one foot in front of another. My way of walking,
in Oxford Street, on Southend Pier, by the Regent's Canal,
even in the desert, is obviously not good enough. Walking
in nature, *wanting* to walk in nature, elevates these good
people in ways that I can only imagine, or at least only read
about in their ramblings.

*

A description of nature that makes much more sense to me
than anything the New Agers can come up with is to be
found in a book called *The Desert* written by the naturalist
and art critic John C. Van Dyke in 1901. There's serious
doubt these days about whether Van Dyke was really the
intrepid desert explorer he made himself out to be, but his

observations certainly ring true. He writes:

> And yet in the fullness of time Nature designs that this
> waste and all of earth with it shall perish. Individual, type,
> and species, all shall pass away; and the globe itself become
> as desert sand, blown hither and yon through space. She
> cares nothing for the individual man or bird or beast; can
> it be thought that she cares any more for the individual
> world?

Is that a religious thought or an anti-religious thought? Is
it some notion of being at one? It's pretty much my version
of nature he's describing there: rough, scary, sometimes
beautiful, but always utterly indifferent. In the face of this, a
walk seems like exactly what it is; something but not much,
certainly not a means of salvation. It may be pleasurable and
worth doing, it may stop you getting depressed, but in the
end it's just a walk. Why would you want it to be more?

*

The fact is, I lack the spiritual gene. It wasn't always this
way. I think perhaps I used to have it, or at least wanted to
have it. There was a time when I read Julian of Norwich,
St John of the Cross, *The Cloud of Unknowing*, 'Four
Quartets', and thought I understood their mysticism, and
perhaps mysticism in general. I pondered St John of the
Cross's opinion on walking: 'If a man wishes to be sure of
the road he treads on, he must close his eyes and walk in the
dark.' I used to think I knew what a long dark night of the
soul was. I used to force myself to believe I experienced
moments in and out of time. Now I know I was wrong. It
appears the gene was recessive, and it has duly receded. Now
I think I was deceiving myself.

Since I was born and brought up in England, it was a long
time before I ever set foot in a desert, though I was familiar

enough with the concept. I'd seen it on screen: in Road-runner cartoons, in cowboy movies, in Russ Meyer's *Faster, Pussycat! Kill! Kill!*, as any other-worldly landscape in any number of cheap science-fiction movies, and in a few very expensive ones too. The initial appeal was primarily visual. The desert appears in so many movies because it looks so good.

On the other hand, it never looked like a place you could actually go walking. It seemed too mythic, indeed too other-worldly, for that. When I eventually discovered you could drive a car out into the American desert, park at the side of a dirt road and walk off into the distance, that was quite a moment, quite a realisation, though not precisely a revelation; and I've been doing it regularly ever since.

Of course I realise that I'm not walking into uncharted or untrodden territory. The American deserts exist in their current form because of various legal, political and com-mercial decisions. It isn't, in any sense, untamed nature. But there are parts of it where you really can go and be alone for hours and walk for miles and be totally, spectacularly alone. Compared with an afternoon hiking the overcrowded paths of the Lake District, it's a distinctly wild ride.

I know that some people find the desert frightening: all that space, all that isolation, all the terrible things that can happen to you. And, of course, I realise that terrible things really can and do happen out there, from dying of thirst or falling and breaking something to encountering Mansonite cults, but that's part of what I like about it. Charles Manson at his trial: 'I am the biggest beast walking the face of the earth.' Charles Manson at his 1992 parole hearing: 'But there's a line that man walks. All men walk a line. And I walk that line in prison.'

You have to be on your mettle when you're walking in the

desert, you have to take charge of yourself, you have to know what you're doing. And to an extent the desert helps you. It sharpens up the senses, makes you more aware and more self-aware. I've never felt lonely in the desert.

Do I at any time feel 'at one with nature' when I'm in the desert? Do I have visions or revelations? Do I walk with a higher power? Do I walk with God. The simple answer is no. A slightly more complex answer is: I don't even know what you're talking about.

*

I've only ever been really lost in the desert once and, of course, once might have been enough. Ultimately it lacked drama, because I lived, and because it was brief, certainly no more than a couple of hours, but it was a long couple of hours, and for all I knew they could have been close to my last.

It was in Western Australia, about twenty-two miles outside the mining town of Kalgoorlie. I was with my girlfriend and we'd just picked up a Land Cruiser in which we planned to do some not too serious off-roading, and some walking. But that was ahead of us. On the afternoon in question we were making a minor foray into the desert, to get the lie of the land and the feel of the vehicle.

We drove out to a ghost town called Kanowna, which even by ghost-town standards was a big let-down. There really was nothing worth seeing. There had once been twelve thousand people to be found there, along with their churches, hotels, breweries and a railway station, but there was no sign of habitation now, and although a few signposts had been put up indicating where a post office and court-house had once been, they weren't marking anything other than a few bits of rubble and piles of ancient tin cans. Tin cans can last a very, very long time in the desert.

Somewhat disappointed, we parked the Land Cruiser and

got out. We didn't bother to take water or even sunhats with us. There seemed to be no need. We weren't doing anything so definite as 'going for a walk'. We were just pottering about. We investigated some old tailings dumps, peered into a lethal-looking open mine shaft. If we walked more than a mile I'd be surprised.

Before long we decided to head back to the Land Cruiser. After we'd walked for a while in what we felt sure was the right direction, we realised we were mistaken. We walked some more but we didn't arrive at the vehicle. In fact, now that we looked around us more carefully, we realised the Land Cruiser was nowhere to be seen. That didn't seem right: it scarcely seemed possible. We set off in another likely-looking direction, and that didn't take us to the Land Cruiser either. Above all, it seemed plain odd and incomprehensible, comical in its way, but it was frightening too, and we realised it was perfectly possible that both our attempts to get back to the vehicle might in fact have taken us farther away.

We felt like idiots. If we'd been heading out to do some serious desert walking we'd have done all the right things: studied maps, carried a good supply of water, brought a GPS, a compass. As it was, we had nothing. It seemed absurd that we could get lost in territory like this. It was a tame, flat, unexceptional, unthreatening bit of desert, but that was a large part of the problem. It was a landscape without landmarks, and certainly without any high place you might climb up to in order to get your bearings. This terrain was featureless, with every bush and rock looking very much like every other bush and rock. Then we started to notice a lot of stripped animal bones lying on the ground, and we saw a skull, the kind you get in Roadrunner cartoons, that opens its jaws and says, 'You'll be sorry.' We realised just how bad and serious our situation was.

To cut a short story even shorter, we did, of course, eventually find our way back to the Land Cruiser. It had everything to do with good luck, nothing at all to do with good judgement, and I know that the story might very easily have turned out quite differently and that I'd be in no position to write it.

We wandered aimlessly for what seemed an age, but which, as I say, was only a couple of hours, and suddenly we spotted the open mine shaft we'd previously walked past. From there we were able to find our way back to the Land Cruiser. End of story. In some ways it was an anticlimax, though not an unwelcome one. It taught me that simply walking off into the desert is a very stupid thing to do, but perhaps that's something I shouldn't have needed to learn. Walking lost in the desert was an entirely unspiritual experience. It did not make me feel at one with anything, least of all nature.

*

I think that many of the Death Valley 49ers would have said the same. Death Valley 49ers (that's of 1849) are the Mojave Desert's most famous lost pioneers. Although they too were without compass and GPS, they did have a map, one that promised a short cut through the desert, via the Walker Pass, taking five hundred miles off their journey from Salt Lake City to California, where the Gold Rush was in full swing. The words 'I know a short cut' should strike fear into the heart of any long-distance walker.

The 49ers started out as part of an expedition led by Captain Jefferson Hunt, under the auspices of the Mojave San Joaquin Company, known as the Mojave Sand Walking Company, a name that gives me pleasure every time I think of it, although this started out as a wagon train rather than a walking expedition.

Hunt's progress was too slow for some, and there were various splits and regroupings, some temporary, some permanent, before a faction known as the Bennett-Arcane party, following the dubious short-cut map, at last found themselves lost, stranded, exhausted and helpless in the heart of what is now called Death Valley.

Two of the younger, fitter men – William Manly and John Rogers – decided they would simply walk out of the valley on foot, cross the Panamint Mountains, get help and return to rescue the survivors, if any. This, incredibly, they did, although Manley confessed in print that it at least crossed his mind never to return at all.

Manly and Rogers walked two hundred and fifty miles from Death Valley to the San Fernando Valley, where they obtained supplies, along with two horses and a mule. They were intending to ride at least part of the way back, but both horses died *en route* so it turned into another walking expedition. Then, later, once they'd saved the people left behind, they all had to walk the route out yet again.

Manly eventually wrote his account of events in a book called *Death Valley in '49*. It's the story of his life as well as the story of the 49ers, and part of it reads like a primer on the pains of walking and a catalogue of adverse walking conditions. He writes:

> Walking began to get pretty tiresome. Great blisters would come on our feet, and, tender as they were, it was a great relief to take off our boots and go barefoot for a while when the ground was favourable . . . This valley was very sandy and hard to walk over . . . All the way had been hill and very tiresome walking . . . At times we walked in the bed of the stream in order to make more headway, but my lameness increased and we had to go very slow indeed.

Manly himself makes very little mention of God in his book, or the Almighty's role in his enforced walking, though he does describe the desert as the 'most God-forsaken country in the world'. Others make more of it, speaking of 'God's purpose' in imposing such an ordeal on them. Manley is at best sceptical.

Undoubtedly walking may be represented as a form of divine punishment, as the variations on the story of the Wandering Jew indicate. Although he was supposedly present at the crucifixion, the Wandering Jew doesn't appear in the Bible, and seems to have been an invention of the thirteenth century, though refined and made more widely significant in the seventeenth thanks to a series of pamphlets published in Germany from 1602 onwards.

He goes by many names, Buttadeus, Ahaseurus and Isaac Lacqudem among them, and is variously a shoemaker or Pontius Pilate's doorman. What is central to the myth is his mocking of Christ. He sees Jesus carrying the cross and taunts him for walking too slowly. Jesus certainly received worse insults, but on this occasion he did not turn the other cheek. He condemned the Jew to walk the earth until the time of the Second Coming.

There is some resemblance here to Cain, the fratricide, to whom God says, 'a fugitive and a vagabond shalt thou be in the earth.' This isn't quite the same as condemning him to 'walk the earth', but both fugitives and vagabonds no doubt end up doing a fair amount of walking.

There's also a resemblance to Jules Winnfield, played by Samuel L. Jackson in Quentin Tarantino's *Pulp Fiction*, who says: 'Basically I'm just gonna walk the earth. You know, like Caine in *Kung Fu* – walk from place to place, meet people, get in adventures.' It must have been such a delight for Tarantino, as he wrote the script, to invoke the biblical

Cain and then immediately ditch him in favour of David Carradine's TV character from *Kung Fu*.

An Armenian bishop visiting England in 1228 not only asserted that the Wandering Jew was still alive and walking, but that he'd actually met him. This was good news for Christians. To have someone around who'd been an eye-witness at the crucifixion would be a great help in proving the historical basis of Christianity. But it was also a myth that had its uses for Jews. The Wandering Jew dramatised and personified the diaspora, while also emphasising the anti-Semitism and downright vindictiveness of certain Christians, and of the Christian God.

The story of the Wandering Jew is also a very rich and inventive myth about the nature of punishment. The sinner is punished not only by enforced walking, but by joyless immortality. He must walk for ever but he isn't going anywhere. There's no destination, no journey's end, no pleasure along the way. He is walking with no purpose, just killing time that ultimately can't be killed. He must exist in a state of constant fatigue, never experiencing rest, nor even the possibility of rest. He approaches an exhaustion that will never arrive, because if it did then he would stop walking, and the divine power will not allow that.

Following the sighting by the thirteenth-century bishop, the Wandering Jew was spotted all over Europe throughout the seventeenth and eighteenth centuries, and at least once in the nineteenth century in the United States. According to Alex Bein in *The Jewish Question: Biography of a World Problem*, the Wandering Jew was last seen in America in 1868: 'The *Desert News* reported on Sept. 23, 1868 that he [the Wandering Jew] had visited a Mormon named O'Grady.' His passage to the United States raises all manner of literalist questions. Assuming he travelled by boat, did he have to spend the entire voyage walking relentlessly around the deck? Wouldn't that cause some concern among his fellow passengers? Would he bother to explain himself?

An Italian folktale, known as 'Malchus at the Column', is a variant on the story of the Wandering Jew. It devises an even worse and more inventive punishment. Malchus, by this legend, was one of the Jews responsible for the crucifixion of Jesus, and although all the others were forgiven, Malchus remained unforgivable because he'd physically struck the Virgin Mary. Consequently he was confined inside a mountain, chained to a column and forced to walk endlessly around it until the end of the world.

As the story 'opens' Malchus has been walking in circles for so long that his footsteps have dug a circular trench in the earth, so deep that only his head appears above ground level. When the path is trodden lower still and his head finally disappears, the world will indeed come to an end and he'll be sent to a place that God has prepared for him. I can't decide whether this would be an incentive to walk more quickly, dig the trench deeper as quickly as possible and get it over with, or whether you'd try to delay things, fearing that God has some even worse fate in store.

These stories seem to involve a myth more ancient than Christianity, more the stuff of Sisyphus or Tantalus. The notion of a punishment without limit, or motion without hope of rest, is truly horrifying; we do want our walking to take us somewhere: we want it to have an end.

*

The connection between spirituality and walking extends far beyond Western and Abrahamic traditions. Taoism, for example, employs various walking meditations that function as exercise, spiritual practice, and ultimately as martial arts. The best known is Baguazhang, which is based on the I

Ching and essentially involves walking in circles, sometimes known as 'Turning the Circle'. The technique is four thousand years old and is based on the Taoist principles of seeking stillness in motion. It's a way of walking that doesn't (in the practical sense) take you anywhere, although as a martial art it does enable the initiate to walk in such a way that he can defend himself against attackers coming at him from eight different directions.

In the middle of the twentieth century a Chinese woman, and Taoist, called Guo Lin developed something known as Walking Qigong or Guolin Qigong, Qigong being the ancient Chinese art of balancing and strengthening the 'life force'. Walking was her version of it, and she used it as a cure for cancer.

Guo Lin had had several bouts of cancer over more than a decade, along with the surgical procedures to 'cure' her, but finally in 1964 doctors declared that the cancer had won, and Guo Lin was given six months to live. Being full of fight, and perhaps thinking she had nothing to lose, relying on instinct, trial and error, and consulting some texts that had been left to her by her grandfather, a Taoist monk, she developed a method that worked for her. There were bending and stretching exercises, the control of breathing and the massaging of acupressure points, but the cornerstone was walking for two hours a day. At the end of her allotted six months the cancer had gone.

By the 1970s Guo Lin was a living, walking, legend, travelling around China spreading the word, teaching her technique in classrooms that sometimes contained four hundred eager learners. She continued in this way, revered and idolised, until her death in 1984.

There has so far been no large-scale scientific investigation of Guolin Qigong, either inside or outside China. However, the anecdotal evidence is impressive enough to lead millions of people, by no means all of them in China, to practice it every day to prevent rather than to cure cancer.

Posited explanations for how or why Guo Lin's method works are unlikely to convince non-believers. One theory is that it simply increases oxygen supply, and this kills cancer cells, which seems just absurd. Another suggestion is that it is balancing the yin and the yang, which is, of course, what all Chinese medicine professes to do. Still, if you had cancer and were able to exercise and walk for two hours a day (hardly a given for most cancer patients), why wouldn't you try it? Nowhere can I find any evidence that Taoism ever uses walking as a punishment.

Walking meditations are also employed in Buddhism, sometimes called meditation in action. Walking is one of the four asanas, or postures, in which the Buddha is depicted. The one practising Buddhist I know tells me he finds walking meditation much easier than sitting meditation because the mind doesn't drift so much when you walk. Walking forces concentration. You become aware of your body, your breathing, the light, the air and so on: this all helps to create – he says – Mindfulness.

He also tells me that the Buddha encouraged something called the Development of Loving-kindness Meditation. While walking, whether in the town or the countryside, in or out of nature, ancient Buddhists would try to exude benevolence. In the towns this went out to their fellow man, in the countryside it went out to wild animals and was considered a very good way to avoid being attacked by snakes.

*

And so we come to Islam; the only religion I'm aware of that insists its adherents must undertake an arduous walk in the desert. All Muslims are implored to make a journey to Mecca, to participate in the hajj. These pilgrims are not required to walk all the way there (though a few do), but they do have to do some walking once they arrive.

Among other rituals, they are required to follow in the footsteps of Mohammad, just like Sir Richard Burton did, making seven counter-clockwise circumambulations of the Kaaba, the cube-shaped shrine inside the Great Mosque. In fact, Burton was surprised that the walking was counter-clockwise. As an old India hand, he was familiar with the Hindu Pradakshina, the clockwise walking performed in Hindu temples around the sanctum sanctorum.

There is currently a quota system in place in Mecca: only two million Muslims per year are allowed to perform the hajj – many more would do it if they could – but that still represents a staggering number of people crammed into the Great Mosque, walking at different speeds, all trying to touch the Black Stone. It sounds like a recipe for pedestrian chaos rather than spiritual harmony, but for obvious reasons I have no personal experience of it.

Someone who has is Ziauddin Sardar, a contemporary Muslim academic and journalist, who has completed hajj five times. He reports that things are getting worse all the time. When pilgrims arrive at the Great Mosque, he says, they encounter the mutawwa, the Saudi religious police. You know that's not going to be good. To keep the walkers moving, the mutawwa hit them with long sticks. Sardar writes, 'Pilgrims performing the tawaf or praying by the Kaaba are constantly hit on the head and asked to move, and not infrequently beaten and "shooed" as though they were cattle.' He also knows there are 'unreported numbers' of pedestrians on their way to the Great Mosque who suffocate, are crushed underfoot or die of heatstroke. Personally I find it hard to see the spiritual dimension in this kind of walking, but then I do, of course, lack the spiritual gene. And I'm an infidel.

*

I used to be far more of a snob about desert walking than I am now. I could do without the spiritual uplift, I could do without feeling at one, but I did want serious isolation. I wanted millions of acres of untrodden, untouched and un-inhabited desert. If there was a trail or a ranger station or an information board or if I met another walker, I thought this was a terrible defilement, and that my desert walking experience was being spoiled.

Well, that was precious and stupid of me, and I've lightened up a lot, for a number of reasons. First, because I've realised there aren't millions of acres of untrodden, untouched and uninhibited desert available. They may be uninhabited but they're very definitely not untouched or untrodden. Secondly, because once you accept that nature is still going to be managed, then you realise that marked trails, ranger stations and information boards can be useful, might even in certain circumstances save your life.

The problem of meeting other people in the desert remains ultimately unresolvable. I tell myself that if I meet other people walking in the desert they're likely to be, if not exactly kindred souls, at least people who share my interest, people who will most likely want to be left alone, but this isn't always the case.

My best strategy for avoiding other people is simply to walk in the less dramatic parts of the desert. If you go wandering around some fabulous, celebrated desert attraction, White Sands or Zabriskie Point or Monument Valley (and I have walked in those places), well of course you're going to run into crowds of tourists. But if you go walking in, let's say, the Big Morongo Canyon Preserve (if you don't know where that is, then so much the better), you'll certainly find some information boards, some designated trails and even a public toilet, but on most days you can be pretty sure of being the only person walking there. A desert walk, I have gradually realised, doesn't have to involve rolling sand-dunes, fields of cacti, Joshua Trees, breathtaking gorges, rattlesnakes and so forth.

*

The desert, naturally, as St Anthony proved, is a place of mirages, of Fata Morgana. The desert walker 'sees' all manner of things that may or may not be there, figures seen through a heat haze, appearing to move relentlessly towards you but never quite arriving, or large expanses of sparkling, glittering water that turn out to be nothing but sand.

There are, however, some places where the water turns out not to be a mirage after all. Badwater in Death Valley is one of these. Badwater is a long, wide, salt flat, that stretches to the distant blue mountains several miles away. At two hundred and eighty feet below sea level it's the lowest point in the western hemisphere. When I first visited Badwater, a decade and a half ago, you could pull off the road, park on the hard shoulder, and go wandering across the scorched, salted surface. But few people did. Now there's a big, freshly tarmacked car park, so everybody who drives by thinks there must be something really worth seeing out there, and so masses of people park and walk. This is what Edward Abbey called 'industrial tourism'.

Sometimes, especially in the winter, there's water lying on the flat, low, desert bed, standing perfectly, eerily still, reflecting the mountains and the sky like a mirror. From a distance you can't possibly guess how deep the water is – it's easy to imagine it as very deep indeed – but in fact large stretches are at most a couple of inches deep.

In these conditions hundreds of people walk out from the parking lot, across the salt bed, drawn into the emptiness, looking like true believers, like pilgrims, like earthlings going out to meet the mother ship. But since there is no mother ship, no place of worship, nothing to believe in, they just go and investigate the water, discover how shallow and smooth it is, then walk a few yards into it and have their picture taken.

Abul Hasan al-Shadhili, a thirteenth-century Sufi master, claimed that with a bit of practice and spiritual enlightenment, any damn fool, could walk on water. But he said they shouldn't, it was vulgar and distracting. He wanted to make the point that Jesus was a bit of a show-off. And certainly at Badwater, hundreds of people appear to go walking on water. It's playful, good natured, and as far as I can see, not remotely sacrilegious, but it wouldn't mean nearly as much if we weren't all familiar with Jesus's biblical example.

Whenever I've been there I've found it impossible to avoid singing that line from Leonard Cohen's 'Suzanne', 'Jesus was a sailor when he walked upon the water.' This is nonsense, right? If there was ever a moment when Jesus *wasn't* a sailor it was precisely when he walked on the Sea of Galilee: when he was completely, absolutely a pedestrian.

I also found myself thinking about a line from Jack Kerouac, a born Catholic turned self-invented Buddhist, and a man who certainly did some walking in nature, though as far as I can tell he never used the term. He had the spiritual gene in spades but he thought spirituality was a serious undertaking, that enlightenment wasn't something you could turn on like a tap. That was one of the reasons he had serious doubts about LSD, because it seemed to offer an instant religious experience. He thought this was a cheat. For my money he summed it up perfectly when he said, 'Walking on water wasn't built in a day.'

10

Walking Home

> I cannot walk through the suburbs in the solitude of the
> night without thinking that the night pleases us because
> it suppresses idle details, just as our memory does.
>
> Jorge Luis Borges

My mother always said, in what might at first sound like an
approving way, that as a baby I'd been very eager to walk, and
had started early. That means I must have been at it before I
was a year old: the average baby starts walking between twelve
and fourteen months. Then, in a less approving way, my
mother would add that perhaps I'd walked *too* early, while the
bones in my legs were still soft, and that's why I'd developed
bow legs. I'm not sure that I actually have bow legs, but if I
do, then the bowing is so slight that nobody except my mother
has ever remarked on it. Welcome to my childhood. As I got
older and snarkier I always said I started walking early because
I was so eager to get away from home.

I was born on the kitchen table of my grandparents' house,
literally in a dead-end street, in Sheffield, in a tough, poor,
lively, working-class suburb called Hillsborough. The majority
of the family lived within walking distance of each other. For
that matter, they lived within walking distance of everything
they needed: shops, pubs, dog track, football ground, betting
shop, church. The steel factories my uncles worked in were
equally nearby. Everybody walked everywhere. Everything you
could want was right there, unless you happened to want
something else.

My parents and I lived in my grandparents' house until I

was about four years old; when we moved we got a council house, and after some hopping around we ended up in a place called Longley. We'd only gone a few miles, and we went back to Hillsborough at least once a week, but it was spoken of as though we'd moved to the outer fringes of the twilight zone.

Longley was regarded as one of the 'good' council estates. 'Good' meant low on crime, not bad schools, not too many problem families, though these things are comparative and the gradations were very fine. We certainly had a violent, drunken neighbour, and he was largely the reason my parents scrabbled to get the money together to buy their own house and move out of the area. But that took some time. I was well into my adolescence before they joined the propertied classes. Longley Estate was the place I grew up and the place I knew best. I'd walked all its streets, but it was a very long time, nearly three decades, before I set foot there again.

*

Certain ironists like to say that Sheffield is just like Rome, since it's built on seven hills. There, of course, the resemblance ends. And Roman citizens never had to cope with Sheffield winters: long, hard, with plenty of snow. Because I'd got into the 'good school' over the other side of the city I had to take two bus rides to get there, one downhill from home into the centre of town, then a second one uphill to where the school was.

When the snow fell, buses could get down the hills all right, but not up. It wasn't unusual to find yourself stranded in the city centre, surrounded by hills that buses couldn't get up. Sometimes, in the morning, you had to walk to school from the city centre. Sometimes, in the afternoon, you had to walk home from the city centre. Sometimes you ended up doing both. It would have been sensible to wear wellingtons for these walking expeditions, but I didn't, and neither did anybody else. Wellington-wearers were mocked as sissies. We wore ordinary shoes, and often we slipped, and sometimes we even fell down, and yes, there was something sissy-ish about falling down, but not nearly as sissy-ish as walking in wellingtons.

Of course this wasn't the kind of thing you could really explain to your mother, but even so I complained to my mother about the misery and downright unfairness of living in a city built on seven hills. She was sympathetic to a degree, but she suggested I should be like Felix, and 'keep on walking'. At the time I had no idea what she was talking about.

These days there's a persuasive local theory that the hills of Sheffield are what keep the old folk there alive and in good health. All over the city, little old men and women struggle to walk up insanely steep hills, often weighed down by heavy shopping, and they struggle and stop for breath every now and again, but they keep going. They keep on walking.

*

There were many things my family didn't do very well, and holidays was the worst. Both my parents seemed to believe in holidays, seemed to think they were a good thing. They wanted to go away somewhere, and yet there was never anywhere they particularly wanted to go or anything they particularly wanted to do when they got there. We went to the seaside, because that's where people of my parents' class and age went.

In *The Kingdom by the Sea*, Paul Theroux says that wherever you are in England you're never more than sixty-five miles from the sea. This only goes to prove that Paul Theroux never started any of his travels from Sheffield, but I suppose we already knew that. The closest seaside to Sheffield is east through Lincolnshire to Skegness, Cleethorpes, Bridlington. These names carry with them a grey, sodden melancholy. It seemed that all our days out in that direction involved sitting in the car, hoping the rain would stop so that at least we could get out and have a quick walk on the beach. Our hopes were often dashed. We generally had better luck over the other side of the Pennines in Blackpool. Sometimes we went on a day trip, but there were several occasions when we went for a whole week.

My mother always complained that there was nothing to *do* on holiday in Blackpool, that all people did all day was 'mooch around', by which she meant walk up and down all day. She had a point. The boarding houses we stayed in had a ridiculous and strictly enforced rule that 'guests' had to be out of the premises from ten in the morning till five in the evening. You were paying for bed, breakfast and an evening meal, nothing else. That was a lot of time to stay outside. Both Blackpool beach and the Irish Sea that it backed on to were often too cold and bleak to engage with, but it had a six-mile-long promenade: the Prom. That was where you spent the day mooching.

Along the Prom there were fairground rides, amusement arcades, bingo halls, souvenir shops and stalls selling fish and chips and sticks of rock candy, and there was Blackpool Tower, of course; but we never went to these places. My parents weren't inherently mean people, but I think they regarded these things as a frivolous and needless expense. Going to the seaside was holiday enough. Why gild the lily? Instead of being entertained, we joined all the other moochers, walking up and down the Prom, all day long, dragging their kids behind them, not looking as though they were having the slightest bit of fun. The Nicholson family fitted right in.

I can't swear that we really walked the full length of the Prom in both directions every day, but it certainly felt like it. Even though there was public transport, and even though we weren't really going anywhere, my dad insisted we go there on foot. I used to complain about having to walk so far, and of course my dad laughed at me, said these distances were nothing. Today I wonder if he was enjoying himself or whether he was punishing himself, or punishing my mother and me, or whether he was simply doing his best and really didn't know how to take or share pleasure.

*

The problem of what to do as a family was never solved. After my father died I did my best to be a good son to my widowed mother. I was living in London at the time and she would come to stay and I'd try to entertain her. It was never easy. There was still never anything she wanted to do, and my attempts to second guess were hopeless. When I suggested once that we might have a walk round the London Zoo she reacted as though I'd suggested she might like to watch the floor show in a brothel. And so we did nothing much, just wandered round London's shops and streets. We covered miles, and she never complained, but I always had the terrible feeling that I was extending an unhappy family tradition.

I've been back to Blackpool a few times as an adult, and never done much more than walk along the Prom, because I still don't really know what else to do there. Working-class roots are so much less fun than you want them to be. I always arrive thinking I'll enjoy the gritty vulgarity and energy, and I do for a couple of hours, and then after I've walked up and down for a while the melancholy starts to seep into me.

Of course it's a fine line between melancholy and misery. In general, I really enjoy walking out of season by the sea, in the cold, in the grey of winter. There's something very satisfying about being alert and active in an environment that's so dead and devoid of people. Whether I could convey any of this pleasure to a sulky, unwilling child, I rather doubt.

*

My dad wasn't good at teaching me things. I was a slow learner and he was short of patience. When his first attempts to teach me to how to operate, for instance, a yoyo, a tenon saw or, eventually, a motor car didn't bring instant results there generally wasn't a second attempt. He had fixed ideas about how things should be done, including walking.

I was happy to amble along, slouching, hands in pockets, in a sloppy, uncoordinated way, which I think is normal for kids. In the course of writing this book I've spent some time watching children walk and they're all over the place, no rhythm, no balance, no sense of purpose. Maybe it's because they don't have anywhere to go.

My dad pointed out that if you swung your arms you made much better progress. Your arms acted like pendulums carrying you inexorably forward. I could see he was right. I tried it. It worked. This was one of the few things I did manage to pick up at the first attempt. My father wasn't nearly as pleased as I'd have liked him to be.

There was nothing pretentious or aspirational about my father. In fact, it always seemed to me he put far too much energy into insisting on how ordinary he was. Nevertheless, he displayed a curiously aristocratic belief that the rules applying to other people didn't apply to him. So when we were out walking, which is what we did on many Sunday mornings, and saw signs that said 'Private. Keep out. No trespassing.', they made no impression on my father. As far he was concerned these notices were intended only for others.

It might have been nice to think my father was a socialist firebrand who refused to obey the rules imposed upon him by the landowning classes. Indeed, around Sheffield, in the Peak District, there was a good, bolshie local tradition of walking where you weren't supposed to walk: political walking. In 1932, five hundred or so walkers performed a famous and symbolic 'mass trespass' on Kinder Scout, trying to assert the right to walk across private open land that was used only twelve days a year for grouse shooting. There were clashes with police and gamekeepers, some fights, some arrests, some vicious sentencing, but eventually, many years later, a 'right to roam' was established. It was, and still is, regarded as a mighty triumph for the working classes of northern England. The car park at Kinder Scout has an elaborate celebratory plaque. My father, however, didn't quite belong to this tradition. He wasn't defiant, nor was he oblivious, but it was as though he believed that the makers of 'No trespassing' signs would surely regard him as a special case.

And so one Sunday morning, when I was about ten years old and we found ourselves tramping along a woodland path, on the outskirts of Sheffield, my father was unfazed when we were confronted by a 'Keep out' sign. Naturally he ignored it and we kept on walking. We hadn't gone more than twenty or thirty steps when we came up against a large man sitting on the back of a large horse, and the man was furious. He was evidently the landowner and the one responsible for putting up the sign. There was a good deal of 'What the bloody hell do you think you're doing on my land? Can't you read?' and so on. He was pompous, fleshy, tweedy. He did have a sort of authority about him, perhaps because he was on horseback, but that didn't prevent him from appearing ridiculous.

If it had been up to me, then or now, I'd simply have lied

to the man, said that I hadn't seen the sign, apologised and retreated, but my dad didn't quite do that. He didn't deny that he'd read the sign but he wasn't apologetic. He gently said that surely no reasonable person could object to a man and his son taking a walk through the woods on a Sunday morning, even if the woods belonged to them.

My dad was so reasonable and so utterly ingenuous that the man, though still angry, was taken aback. He'd been ready for a confrontation, raised voices, an escalating argument, but my father's suggestion that he might have put up the sign without really meaning it, left him flabbergasted. The best he could do was say, 'How would you like it if I came and rode my horse through your garden?'

My father appeared to be giving the matter serious thought, then said, 'Well, I take your point.'

I didn't take any such point. Something was stirring in my bosom. Let him bring his horse to our garden, I thought. There'd just about be enough room for the horse to stand up, and his presence would surely have caused a gathering of local toughs and hooligans who, in my imagination at least, would have expressed their class hatred, abused the man and probably stolen his horse.

No son likes to see his father defeated, and this was certainly an argument my father couldn't have won, but I thought he'd gained a sort of victory by refusing to argue at all. We turned and walked back the way we'd come, rather slowly and over-casually. I took some comfort in thinking that even though we'd been told off, we had at least successfully trespassed on the pompous ass's land. We'd also succeeded in making him hugely angry. My father wasn't comforted at all by this, and he continued to be genuinely amazed that anyone could be so unreasonable as not to want him on their land.

*

When I was in my early teens I was one of a small group of boys from my grammar school who met up in the centre of Sheffield one evening to see our first X-rated film, having told our parents that we were going to each other's houses. X-rated films could be surprisingly gentle back then, and the one we'd chosen to see was *The Graduate*. I'm amazed now to discover that the movie was released in 1967, and I'm sure we saw it during its first run, but that would mean we were all about fourteen years old, which seems unlikely. Maybe we waited for the second run. In any case, we felt quite grown up, and certainly tried to look it as we bought our tickets at the box office, which we did without any trouble.

The Graduate was far too sophisticated and restrained for our boyish tastes and we were severely disappointed by its lack of lewdness. It also finished surprisingly early and we boys all went our separate ways, but going straight home and arriving back so soon would have made my parents suspicious. So I dawdled, eventually caught a bus back to the Longley Estate, and got off a couple of stops too early, so I could walk part of the way home and kill more time. Wandering the streets at night seemed to be a perfectly safe thing for a boy to do, largely because there was nobody else on the streets at all.

The houses on the estate were small and tightly packed together; there were lights on inside and I remember I could hear televisions. There was a sense of quiet order. The whole area seemed to be dozing, and my presence felt sneaky and intrusive, like I was staring at someone while they were asleep.

I walked all around what I considered to be 'my' neighbourhood. I walked along all the streets that I knew, past the school, the park, the few shops, and the four patches of greenery in front of them, known, incomprehensibly, as 'the Plantation', and also along one or two streets that I didn't know so well. I felt thoroughly, wonderfully detached, an unseen and unknown outsider. You might have thought there was something voyeuristic about it, although there was nothing much to see.

In fact, it was all very dull. I had the sense, one that I'd had before but never quite thought through, that nothing interesting had ever happened in these streets, and that nothing ever would. This was a depressing prospect. I walked until I'd had exhausted all the possibilities of the neighbourhood, then I went home. As I walked into the house, after having had what I would later come to think of as a seminal moment, and having thought I'd walked for a very long time, my mother simply said, 'You're back early.'

I don't mean to keep banging on about Jack Kerouac, but years after that night, I found this passage in *Dharma Bums* that absolutely knocked me sideways:

> Walk some night on a suburban street and pass house after house on both sides of the same street each with the lamplight of the living-room shining golden, and inside the little blue square of the television, each living family riveting its attention on probably one show; nobody talking; silence in the yards; dogs barking at you because you pass on human feet instead of wheels.

That was my life he was describing, although I hadn't seen any little blue television squares on my walk: ours was a neighbourhood where people kept their curtains tightly closed at night.

*

When, years after the event, I tried to tell my friend Steve about the way I'd felt that night, he joked that I was lucky not to have been arrested, but that was never likely to be a problem. The streets were as free of police as they were of criminals.

Steve was (and is) my oldest friend; we started school together when we were both six years old. My first memories of him were of a smiling little kid who'd fallen in the schoolyard and broken his arm. Then later, the very day the cast came off, he'd fallen and broken it again. Steve was my only remaining contact with Sheffield and as near as I'd got to a family; not as near as all that.

He was also a reminder of who and what I might have been. He'd been smart enough to go to college for four years and get a degree, but then he'd come right back, got a job in local government, married and had kids. He still had ambitions that he sometimes talked about, to travel, to take his guitar playing more seriously, to write poetry or novels, but none of this ever came to anything.

Steve was also the man with whom I'd got a criminal record. We'd been hitchhiking from Sheffield to London, when we were students, and after a bad lift and some bad decisions, we found ourselves stranded on the motorway. We walked gingerly along the edge, knowing we shouldn't be there, well aware that it was against the law, and we were spotted by motorway police, picked up and eventually charged with being 'a pedestrian on a motorway'. As far as either of us can tell this act of criminality hasn't blighted our subsequent lives.

*

I decided to go back to Sheffield for a long weekend of walking around the places I walked as I was growing up, and it was natural for me to stay with Steve and his wife Julia. Natural, too, that I should invite Steve to come walking with me. He reckoned he could only do some of it. These days he was suffering with his back, which sometimes made walking too difficult and painful. He said he'd do what he could. On that basis he didn't come with me when I did my first walk around Hillsborough.

The Saturday afternoons of my childhood were always spent at my grandma's house. My mother and I were deposited there while my father went off and did fatherly things. I didn't much want to be there, trapped in my grandmother's living-room while she and my mother discussed the latest family gossip, and eventually a time came when I was eleven years old and it was reckoned that even though I was still too young to be left alone in my parents' house, I was old enough to wander the streets of Hillsborough.

My mother always told me to go to the park at the end of my grandmother's street, but the park seemed to offer less than the scruffy but busy shops in the neighbourhood. There was a single shopping street though it had two names, changing halfway along from Langsett Road to Middlewood Road. It ran to the park at one end and to a former barracks at the other. My great-grandfather had been stationed at the barracks, which was the only reason the family had ended up in Hillsborough.

The shops along the street weren't places an eleven-year-old could easily browse, a Woolworths being the most kid friendly; I remember there being more pork butchers than you'd imagine any community would need, one of them called F. Funk, a name that didn't seem so very odd at the time but certainly does now. Leaving aside more modern notions of 'funkiness', it seemed strange that such an obviously German name wasn't regarded with more suspicion in recently post-war Sheffield.

There was also a shop that made fresh crumpets on the premises and there was some pleasure to be had from staring through the window and watching the crumpets come to life and rise and bubble before your eyes on a hot plate. Even so, this didn't really add up to an afternoon's entertainment.

So I entertained myself: in a way that seemed perfectly natural to me then but which now seems just a bit weird. There were two automobile showrooms in the street, one at either end. The one up by the park specialised in the NSU Prinz, a small, humpy, rear-engined German car, not quite serious-looking, quaint rather than exotic, but a fascinating curiosity. The ones I liked best were finished in a glossy lacquered red that made them look like giant toys.

The dealer at the other end sold American cars: Nash Ramblers, mostly station wagons. Even at the time it did seem a little unlikely that anyone would be trying to sell Nash Ramblers in a working-class enclave in Sheffield: today it seems utterly inconceivable. Who would ever have bought one? I liked them a lot and I always looked out for them, but I don't remember ever seeing one on the road. How would you get spare parts? Which local Sheffield mechanic would be prepared to work on a car like that?

In fact, there are times now when I wonder if it was some sort of deep-cover CIA operation, that the Nash Ramblers were only there because of the NSU presence at the other end of the street. If those Germans thought they could sell weird cars in Sheffield, then they'd have to compete with American know-how.

That's a recent thought. Back then it seemed that these competing enterprises had been put there for my delight, and the two showrooms became the two poles of my Saturday-afternoon walking. I would walk to the Prinz showroom and stand in front of it for quite a long time, rapt, quietly excited, looking at the bright, shiny, unfamiliar cars; then I'd walk the length of the street to the Rambler showroom, and do the same thing there; then I'd walk back to the other, then back again, and so on until the afternoon was used up.

*

It was a rainy Saturday afternoon when I went back to explore Hillsborough. In the intervening years the name Hillsborough had become infamous, not as the name of a district, but as the name of the Sheffield Wednesday soccer ground where the 'Hillsborough disaster', or sometimes 'Hillsborough tragedy', took place on 15 April 1989. It was the occasion of a sold-out cup match between Nottingham Forest and Liverpool, and thousands of fans crowded into a limited standing area that was simply too small to accommodate them. As people packed in from the rear, those at the front were crushed. Ninety-six people died, and some of them died standing up, unable to fall to the ground because of the density of the crowd; hundreds more were injured.

There had been a period of my life, right before I discovered a profound need for girls, literature and rock music, when I used to spend Saturday afternoons watching Sheffield Wednesday. At the time I probably thought it was better than bouncing between two car showrooms; now I'm not so sure. I do remember there was something appealing about being part of a crowd; in those days, pre safety regulations, Hillsborough would sometimes hold fifty-two thousand football fans, most of them standing up. And when the match was over, everybody streamed out together, the crowd moving as a single entity. You had no choice but to walk in the same direction as all the tens of thousands of others. There was something in that shared purpose, especially if Wednesday had won, but you were always aware that one slip and you could be on the ground, under the crowd's feet and nobody would be likely to help you up. They probably wouldn't even know you were there.

The Liverpool fans are famous for singing the song 'You'll Never Walk Alone', a song of Christian, or at least spiritual, comfort when sung in the musical *Carousel*, to console a woman whose husband's been killed in a botched robbery. When it's sung by football fans it strikes me as rather less consoling, but we know that sports fans are a sentimental lot.

That rainy afternoon in Hillsborough I began to walk the length of the shopping street. It was cold and miserable, but my curiosity drove me on. It would have been amazing to find there were two car showrooms still in business, and I was not amazed. The NSU dealership was now called Meade House, belonging to something called the Sheffield City Council's Children and Young Peoples' (that apostrophe is all theirs) Directorate Social Care Services. The showroom windows through which I'd once gazed at NSU Prinzes were gone, and blank, insubstantial, cream-coloured walls had been built in their place. The effect was bleak and characterless, and I could only guess at what terrible good works were planned and executed there.

Naturally the Rambler showroom wasn't there either. Even the building that had housed it had gone and there was now a bus station in its place. And so again I walked between these two poles: between the bus station and the outpost of the Young Peoples' Directorate. I checked my GPS, to see how far apart the twin poles of my childhood actually were. I knew that my eleven-year-old's horizons weren't very wide, but even so I was surprised to discover just how narrow they were. The distance between the two showrooms had been scarcely more than a quarter of a mile.

There was a lot about Hillsborough and its atmosphere that had stayed much the same. The shops were still the same kind of shops, even if they offered goods and services that hadn't been available when I was a boy, such as New Age crystals, though the place wasn't actually open, and there was the Hollywood Nail Bar, 'American Style' it claimed. But others, like the newsagent's and the bookie's and the shop selling gas fires didn't seem to have changed at all. They may not have been the same companies in business all these years, but the new versions were direct equivalents of the ones they'd replaced.

The pubs weren't much different either. When I was growing up, the name Shakespeare had been spoken daily by some family members, since the Shakespeare was the name of one of the local pubs they went to. It had now changed its name to the Shakey, but it looked as unwelcoming to me now as it had back then.

And there was still an excess of pork butchers, including Funk's. In business since 1890 it said on the canopy outside, and clearly not about to give up now. There was a line of people queuing to buy hot pork sandwiches, served with apple sauce, stuffing and crackling. I joined the queue and got served, but eating a hot pork sandwich in the street in the rain, with stuffing and apple sauce running down your chin, seemed just too difficult. I headed for the park where I hoped to find a bit of shelter. I was prepared for Hillsborough Park to be much smaller than I remembered it too, but in fact it seemed bigger, with its athletics track and a boating lake and a public library in one corner, the one I used to go to.

But right there, next to the library, were a wall and a gateway that were completely unfamiliar, yet very enticing. I stepped through the gateway and found myself in a very different world from the rough and tumble of the rest of Hillsborough. I saw before me a classic walled garden, something that could have belonged to an English country house or a stately home, decked out with bowers and trellises, raised beds and benches. And I sat with a bit of greenery overhead keeping the rain off, and ate my pork sandwich, and I felt quite disorientated.

I don't know that my eleven-year-old self would have appreciated a classic English walled garden but my contemporary self found it a wonder, an oasis of calm and elegance and (let's face it) thoroughly non-working-class virtues. And there was nobody there but me. Maybe that was because of the rain, but I suspected not. The people who enjoyed the Shakey and the pork butchers and the betting shops probably weren't the people who appreciated classic English walled gardens.

I finished my sandwich, left the garden and walked into the main area of the park through an arched metal gateway. Looking back I saw some words, a motto, worked into the wrought iron. The words said, 'You'll never walk alone', as sung by Liverpool supporters: this gateway was in memory of the dead football fans.

*

Next morning Steve and I set off to explore our old stomping ground – the Longley Estate. I admit I was wary of going back. There was a theory, not mine, that people like my parents, like me, like Steve, were no longer to be found in council housing. Yes, the council estates had once been full of decent, honest, hard-working people, but they'd all moved on and moved up, the way my parents had, bought their own house, moved into some version of the middle class, and those left behind were the scroungers, the criminals, the crack heads and crack whores and whatnot.

Steve broadly supported this view. His parents, who'd stayed on the estate much longer than mine, had finally tired of all the crime, the graffiti, the vandalism, the drugs and the rumours of drugs, and had fled to live in a mobile-home park twenty miles away in Worksop.

However, on the ground, there wasn't much to support the 'left behind' theory. Longley looked very much indeed as

I remembered it. Apart from a few style changes, some new-fangled front doors and double-glazed windows, and some cars of a later date, a time traveller from the 1960s wouldn't have seen anything to surprise him.

We walked past my parents' old house, the centre of a block of three, very traditional, red brick and slate, with a door right in the middle, windows arranged symmetrically on either side, a real children's-drawing idea of what a house should be. It seemed familiar, far more than I expected it to, given that I hadn't been there for thirty years or so, and yet there was no great pang of nostalgia. I well remembered what it had felt like to live here, to have walked around this area, to have been bored and restless and wanting to get out. Neither I, nor the place, had changed so very much.

And on the surface that applied to the whole neighbour-hood. Steve and I walked, and looked, and noted what had changed but also how much had stayed the same. As in Hills-borough, the shops were a pretty good indicator. There was a hair salon, and although it was offering Power-Tan Sunbeds, which was surely a recent development, it looked much like the hair salon my mother had gone to. The same could be said for the corner shop my mother patronised. There was also a thoroughly old-fashioned-looking place called 'Sew Craft, Cross-Stitch and Wool' which seemed to be thriving.

From time to time we did see tough-looking young men with tough-looking young dogs, the international signifier of the demand for 'respect'. First there were three spindly lads in baseball caps, walking or being walked by some sort of customised, slavering bull terrier. Then there was a family group, young dad and mum, two small kids and an Akita, the Japanese fighting dog, as big as a pony. Then we saw a pair of squat, pierced, tattooed heavies, their style somewhat reminiscent of heavy metal fans cum apocalypse survivors, with cans of beer and a dog on a leash that if I didn't know better I would have thought was a dingo. How we respected them. Perhaps if we'd walked farther we'd have seen dog lovers with their jackals, their timber wolves. Our respect would have known no limits.

Steve and I both recalled being menaced by local dogs, but we reckoned the hounds we were looking at now were far more vicious, and that their owners were also that much more vicious than the bullies we'd encountered. It might almost have made us nostalgic. Then we found ourselves talking about child abuse. I realised, not for the first time, that when we were kids, the estate was quite a hotbed of grown men doing, or attempting to do, dodgy things to little boys. Any lad walking on his own was fair game. Our school friend Brian had had his leg stroked by a man in the local Essoldo. We all knew that was wrong, even if we didn't really know why, but that still didn't stop us, Brian included, finding it absolutely hilarious.

Walking home from the library, I'd once met a man who claimed to be a doctor. He had a black bag and a stethoscope visible in his pocket, and he just possibly may really have been a doctor, but he stopped me and talked to me in a way that now raises suspicion. He asked me what school I went to and what my favourite subjects were. He claimed to know a couple of my teachers, and perhaps he did. What was so seductive was the way he talked to me as though I were an adult. That was incredibly flattering, so much so that I mentioned it rather proudly to my dad when I got home. I could immediately see I'd told him something that would have been better left untold. He said I should be careful walking on my own, but I had no idea what there was to be careful about.

The real prize, however, went to our friend Rob who told

me about something odd that had happened to him in Longley Park. He'd met a man who'd invited him into the public lavatory and taught him how to masturbate. Rob hadn't been a complete novice, but was glad of some extra instruction, and even passed on a few tips to me, but he still felt there was something puzzling about the episode, and I shared his puzzlement, but puzzlement's all it was. Neither of us saw anything frightening or dangerous or wrong in what had happened. Clearly no violence had been used. We did think it was a bit weird, but then so many things that adults did seemed a bit weird. I haven't seen Rob in decades and from time to time over the years I've wondered if he continued to shrug off the episode with such equanimity.

My walk with Steve took us into Longley Park, and we saw that the public toilet where Rob was violated and educated had been demolished, and yet the footprint of the building was still absolutely clear. The grass all around it was green and healthy, but the flat rectangle of earth where the toilet had once been was a damp, muddy, grassless rectangle. We were careful not to see anything too symbolic in this.

*

The day after Steve and I explored the Longley Estate, I took a walk by myself, a necessary walk but not one that I was looking forward to, and not once I wanted to do with anybody else. I'd decided I would walk up what in my mind had become 'the hill that killed my mother'.

My mother had long had a heart condition, a damaged valve caused by a childhood bout of rheumatic fever. By the time I was a teenager she was suffering from shortness of breath and having trouble walking far, and by the time I was in college she could barely walk up a flight of stairs. Then she had an operation to replace the defective valve and was fine for the next decade; and then she was increasingly less fine until she had another operation to replace the replacement, and she was fine again; as far as we knew.

She'd been out to Sunday lunch with my uncle. It was a regular thing. He was the one with the car, who picked her up and drove her to and from their favourite restaurant on the other side of the city. But this time, while they were having lunch, they and the whole of Sheffield were caught out by a sudden, fierce, unexpected blizzard. Snow fell thickly on the city's seven hills. The roads weren't gritted or salted and there was no way my uncle could drive her back to her house: his car simply wouldn't make it up the hills; that old problem. He took her as far as he could, which was not really very far, just to the bottom of a hill called Gleadless Road, a horribly steep road at the best of times, one that demands you drive up it in second gear, a road that buses and trucks struggle to negotiate even in good weather. It wasn't a road that anybody, least of all my mother, would ever choose to walk up, and definitely not while the snow was falling, but in this situation she had no option, or at least thought she hadn't.

She made it to the top, I was never quite sure how. When she told me about it later I was horrified, and we discussed what else she might have done: knocked on doors until she found someone who'd offer her shelter, but that still wouldn't have got her home; called the police, but it didn't seem likely they'd have been willing to provide a chauffeur service for her; called an ambulance and told them about her weak heart, well just maybe. But she was far too proud to do any of these things. She didn't want to present herself as a cripple. She also wanted to get home. Walking was the most straightforward way of doing it. In the end we agreed that anyone would probably have done the same, but then 'anyone' wasn't necessarily a sixty-nine-year-old with a heart condition.

'It damn near killed me,' she said.

Well, it did and it didn't. It didn't destroy her there and then but it definitely didn't make her stronger. Over the next few months it became clear, and clearer still given subsequent events, that this enforced hill climb in the snow had done some new damage to my mother's heart. The replaced valve appeared to be leaking, and there wasn't enough blood or oxygen flowing through my mother's veins. She couldn't get around as well as she once had: walking and breathing were becoming a problem again. This in itself wasn't a great shock. It would have happened anyway. We knew the valves were only good for a decade or so, and although something obviously needed to be done, there didn't seem any great urgency. My mother wasn't going to insist on heart surgery unless and until it was necessary.

My mother died a short while later, quickly it appears, and although there must have been some pain, it couldn't have been prolonged. She died trying to get up from the armchair in her living room. She never quite made it. She got halfway, struggled, and fell back awkwardly, half in the chair, half against the radiator, where she was found the next morning by a neighbour.

I wasn't there when she died, and I'm told it would have done no good if I, or anyone else, had been in the same room at the time. There was nothing anybody could have done. The doctors told me this sort of thing sometimes just happens. Damaged hearts like my mother's sometimes simply stop working. So, to be absolutely correct, the walk up Gleadless Road hadn't in itself killed my mother, but the sudden over-exertion had been enough to wear out a vital part of her system.

I was about five thousand miles away from Sheffield at the time of her death, wandering and walking through the deserts of Arizona. You might imagine you'd feel some psychic twinge, receive some supernatural message of disconnection when your mother dies, but I got nothing. I flew home a week or so later, with no reason to think that my mother wasn't alive, and found a phone message from my uncle, which was odd, and if you thought about it, only likely to mean one thing, but even so it took me some time to put two and two together.

I tried to think where I'd been at the time of my mother's death. I worked out that I was in a motel on the outskirts of Tucson, my morning, my mother's evening, and I would have been planning the details of a day in the Organ Pipe National Monument in the Sonoran Desert, which is truly a strange and wonderful place to walk.

Now, a good decade after my mother's death, I was going to walk up Gleadless Road, the hill that killed my mother. I left Steve's house and made my way to the bottom of the hill and from that vantage point it didn't look so steep after all. I thought that perhaps my mother, and my memory, had exaggerated things, maybe the hill wasn't so scary, maybe it hadn't affected her so badly after all. I began my walk.

There was a pavement on either side of the road and I tried to think which one my mother would have chosen to walk up. To the left of the road was a wooded area and a flat, open grassy expanse. On the other side were rows of houses that ran across the hillside at right angles from the road. This was the Gleadless Valley Estate, a council estate that had won all sorts of architectural awards from people who didn't live in council estates. I felt pretty sure my mother would have chosen this more built-up side. The houses provided a little protection, some shelter from the wind and snow, and in places there were steps and a handrail. If you were making your way up here in a blizzard you'd surely have been grateful for those things.

As I went on, I soon realised that the hill was every bit as steep as I'd previously thought. It was a cool day and I was only wearing a light jacket, but before I was barely halfway up the road I was panting like a hog. I was impressed that my mother had made it at all. By the time I got to the top, which was still some way from where my mother actually lived (she'd have had another thirty minutes' walk before she got home), I was in absolute awe of her determination and tenacity, amazed that she'd had the strength and the legs and the guts to keep going. What a strong, brave, game old lady she'd been. It even occurred to me as I laboured upwards, feeling my temperature and heartbeat rise, the blood rushing into my face, sweat breaking out on my forehead, that the god of ironic deaths might find it amusing to strike me down with a heart attack right there and then as I walked in my mother's footsteps. He didn't. Evidently he's biding his time.

At the top of the hill I stopped. There was no need to do the whole of my mother's route. I turned around and went down again, walking back this time through part of the Gleadless Valley Estate. It looked rougher than Longley, despite its awards. There were more graffiti, more broken and barred windows, more litter, some smashed bottles here and there.

When I got back to the house, Steve asked me how my walk was.

'It damn near killed me,' I said, and he probably thought I was joking.

11

Perfect and Imperfect Walks, Last Walks,
the Walks We Didn't Take

> Life is a maze in which we take the wrong turn
> before we have learned to walk.
>
> Cyril Connolly, *The Unquiet Grave*

If you have some reputation as a walker, and certainly if you've written on the subject, people tend to ask you to recommend a walk for them. This is tricky stuff, far trickier than recommending a book or a movie. If you get halfway through Cormac McCarthy's *The Road* (whether the book or the movie) and decide to give up, then nothing much is lost. You shut the book or turn off the DVD and there you are right in your own living-room. If you get fed up halfway through one of my recommended walks through Death Valley or post-industrial Brooklyn, you may have more of a problem. So I'm reluctant to make recommendations. Even when people ask me to give details of my favourite walk or even, God help me, my idea of the perfect walk, I tend to go completely blank. I'm not even sure there really is such a thing as a perfect walk, certainly not in the way that there's a perfect storm or a perfect wave. But I'm absolutely certain that one man's idea of a perfect walk may be another man's idea of perfect hell.

*

I imagine that being the first person ever to set foot on some piece of terra incognita would have a kind of perfection about it. Inevitably, it's an option that's denied to the vast majority of us – walking in fresh snow or on fresh sand is as close as most of us will ever get – and perhaps we're lucky, since, perfect or not, a great deal of bitterness and conflict can come out of these kind of first steps.

Matthew A. Henson is now widely considered to be the first non-indigenous man ever to set foot on the North Pole. In 1909, he was part of an expedition led by Commander Robert Peary. This was Peary's eighth attempt and along the way he fell ill and became unable to walk. As they neared their goal Henson was regularly sent ahead on foot as a scout while Peary continued on a dog sled, tended by four 'Esquimau' guides. Given this state of affairs, Peary wasn't ever going to be the first man to walk on, much less walk to, the North Pole.

Finding the exact location of the Pole wasn't a straight-forward task, and Henson overshot by a couple of miles, then had to walk back to the right spot, where, by his account, he found his own footprints. In other words he'd walked on the Pole before he even knew it. Thus, by definition, he was literally the first to have walked there. The others soon joined him.

The expedition was a success but Peary wanted to claim all the credit for himself, and, just as important, he wanted Henson to have none. Henson writes, 'From the time we knew we were at the Pole, Commander Peary scarcely spoke to me.'

I have just the very slightest sympathy with Peary. Henson was a great man to have with you, no doubt, but he didn't dream up the expedition, didn't organise it, finance it, didn't lead it. Whether Peary was justified in regarding Henson as at best an employee, and probably more as a servant, is another matter. A little magnanimity might have gone a long way. Instead he expressed rage, only compounded when Henson wrote his own account of events in his book *A Negro Explorer at the North Pole.* Yes, the first non-indigenous man to set foot on the North Pole was a black American, and only long after the event did he receive his due. It wasn't until 1944 that Congress gave him a duplicate of the silver medal they'd awarded to Peary decades earlier. The four Eskimos remain undecorated.

Recently the author Robert Bryce has claimed that nobody on the Peary expedition got within a hundred miles of the Pole. He has, unsurprisingly, been denounced in certain quarters as a racist.

*   *   *

Things were less racially charged at the South Pole, if only because the notion of a racially integrated expedition was unimaginable to its explorers. A Frenchman, Jules Sébastien César Dumont d'Urville, was first man to set foot on Antarctica, and Roald Amundsen, a Norwegian, was the first man to walk to the South Pole, shortly followed, though not literally, by our own Robert Falcon Scott.

Amundsen's description of walking across an area he named the Devil's Ballroom gives some idea of his chilly Scandinavian stoicism. 'Our walk across this frozen lake was not pleasant. The ground under our feet was evidently hollow, and it sounded as if we were walking on empty barrels. First a man fell through, then a couple of dogs; but they got up again all right.' Insouciance is certainly part of the perfect walk, I think.

However, when it comes to chilly reserve, along with nobility, self-sacrifice and British understatement, none can beat Captain Lawrence 'Titus' Oates of Scott's expedition. Oates, suffering from frostbite, and realising that he was a burden that threatened his comrades' prospect of survival, walked out of the tent and to his death in the Antarctic blizzard on 17 March 1912, having said to Scott and the others, 'I am just going outside and may be some time.'

There is a kind of perfection about this walk, however you look at it.

*

There seems to have been little insouciance or selflessness when it came to the first moon walk; I mean the literal sort, not the Michael Jackson version. The original plan for the Apollo 11 mission had Buzz Aldrin down to be the first man to walk on the moon, but Neil Armstrong, as team leader, changed that plan so that he himself could be first. Aldrin was understandably furious, so much so that he refused to take any pictures of Armstrong walking on the moon: a gloriously petty revenge. This moon-walking disappointment is sometimes offered as an explanation for Aldrin's descent into depression and alcoholism, problems he later conquered.

The man who emerges with most dignity from the moon landing and moon walk is Michael Collins, the third member of the Apollo team, the one who remained in the orbiting craft and never got to walk on the moon at all. Collins does have the minor distinction of being the third man ever to 'walk in space', in 1966 on Gemini X when he left the craft to perform certain 'extravehicular activities', but let's face it, a gravity-free space walk really isn't any kind of a walk, it's more of a float.

In any event, Collins had enough of the right stuff not to be disappointed, or at least not to let the disappointment spoil his life. No doubt it helped that he knew all along that he wouldn't be walking on the moon, and wasn't thwarted at the last minute the way Aldrin was. According to Collins, 'I think he [Aldrin] resents not being the first man on the moon more than he appreciates being the second.'

As Armstrong walked on the moon he fluffed his big line, made nonsense of it. He said, 'That's one small step for man, one giant leap for mankind,' when he should have said, 'one small step for *a* man'. Did anybody care? There is, however, footage in circulation indicating that Armstrong's initial reaction was far more colloquial and unscripted. On the soundtrack to a blurred bit of moon footage he's heard to say quite clearly, 'Jesus H. Christ, we're on the fucking moon.' And Houston, getting into the spirit of the thing, replies, 'You're cleared to hook up lunar equipment conveyor to walk, fucking walk, on the moon.' This has an air of believable authenticity about it, though for all we know it too may have been faked. Of course there are sources, not all of them certifiably insane, claiming that a man has never set foot on the moon at all. This too has been offered as an explanation for Buzz Aldrin's drinking. Having to *pretend* that you'd walked on the moon when you hadn't would surely create every bit as much angst as having been the second person to walk there.

Buzz Aldrin has been known to punch out people who accuse him of being part of a hoax, and while I'm not immune to the joys of a conspiracy theory, I find it hard to understand the pleasure some people take in believing that the moon walk never happened. Nevertheless, the not quite real walk, the walk that doesn't quite take place, that takes place largely or solely in the imagination, that contains an element of fantasy or fraud is a curious phenomenon and more common than you might suppose.

*

Albert Speer's imaginary walking was necessitated by his incarceration. Others have had less excuse. The fact is, a single lie may be all that's required utterly to destroy a walker's reputation and credibility. And, of course, he wasn't telling any lies, wasn't trying to deceive anybody. The same can't be said for Ffyona Campbell, a British walker (she now describes herself as a retired pedestrian) who first came to public attention in 1983, at the age of sixteen, when she walked the eight hundred and seventy-five miles from John o'Groats to Land's End, that old chestnut.

This was to be the first phase of a round-the-world walk that would take eleven years and cover twenty thousand miles. She crossed America, east to west. She crossed Australia, from Sydney to Perth, in ninety-five days, faster than any man had ever done it. She walked from Cape Town to Tangiers, about ten thousand miles, in a little over two years. And then she walked through Europe, from Algeciras in Spain back to London, to complete the trip. If you find yourself asking how a round-the-world trip can entirely avoid Asia, I share your puzzlement.

I don't remember Campbell being exactly front-page news in this period, though those of us who took notice of these things were aware of her two travel books *Feet of Clay* (1991) and *On Foot through Africa* (1994). However, I well remember, in 1996, when she published a third book called *The Whole Story*, that all hell broke loose and she became genuine tabloid fodder. Being a good-looking blonde was both a blessing and a curse for her; being by all accounts a thoroughly difficult and unsympathetic character made her toast.

This third book was a confession. She could no longer live a lie, she said. She revealed that early in her walking career, while she was on the American part of her journey, aged eighteen, she became pregnant by a member of her support team, a driver called Brian Noel, whom she was regularly 'bonking' (her word). Being pregnant slowed her down considerably. She could no longer complete the gruelling daily requirements to keep on schedule. She had commitments to a sponsor, Campbell's soup (no relation), that was organising events at stops along the way. So, by her own account, Ffyona Campbell rode in the truck with Noel for about a thousand miles of the journey, appearing on foot only at the beginning and end of each day when people were looking. The fact that she was able to get away with this certainly suggests that the American media spotlight wasn't trained on her with any great brightness.

Later, she terminated the pregnancy and continued walking round the world. Only after she'd walked another sixteen thousand miles or so did the guilt really hit her and turn her into a depressive and a user of heroin. Then she tried to exorcise her guilt by telling all.

The scorn and contempt poured upon her by the English press in the wake of her confession was truly staggering. The *Evening Standard* called her 'a self-serving ninny', which was the least of it. Campbell seems to have been surprised; I can't think why. To be conned is one thing, to have the confidence trickster then turn around and point out how gullible you were is simply unbearable. Revenge is called for. And naturally, once someone tells you they were lying about a certain part of their story there's no reason to believe they're telling the truth about any of the rest. That record-breaking Australian walk suddenly starts to look extremely suspect. Perhaps the confession itself is just another deception. Maybe Campbell really is a great walker, who told one lie and later suffered and made up for it. But by what means can we now tell whether or not that's the case?

The great contemporary British explorer Sir Ranulph Fiennes once called Campbell 'the greatest walker of them all'. I wonder what he calls her now. I also suspect that even at the time he was being uncommonly generous, since by Fiennes's standards very few people in the world are real walkers. Fiennes was the first man to cross the whole of Antarctica on foot, and in 2000 he attempted, but failed, to do a solo walk to the North Pole, losing his fingertips as a result. He cut them off himself because he was impatient with the doctors who were treating him.

*

Ffyona Campbell's title *On Foot through Africa* echoes, accidentally I suspect, that of a memoir written by James Augustus Grant, a Victorian explorer of equatorial Africa, and sometime companion of John Speke in his search for the source of the White Nile. Grant called his book, published in 1864, *A Walk across Africa*, but in fact he by no means walked all the way. For five months he had an excruciating condition in his right leg, what is now thought to have been Buruli ulcer, that caused abscesses, pain, swelling and foul discharge. He could barely straighten his leg, much less walk.

Eventually he was carried on a stretcher from the kingdom of Karague in Abyssinia to Uganda, where he was to meet up with Speke. Grant recounts that the stretcher bearers, members of the Waganda tribe, conveyed him at shoulder height, at six miles an hour, 'jostling and paining my limb unmercifully'.

Speke himself was no more merciful when Grant joined him. He was about to set off into the Ugandan interior and wanted to know if Grant was capable of making a 'flying march' of twenty miles a day. Grant knew he wasn't, and Speke knew it too. Speke travelled without him and therefore didn't have to share the glory of being the first white man ever to see the source of the White Nile.

The title of Grant's book may seem therefore at best an exaggeration, but given that Grant himself willingly reveals the fact of his incapacity in the book it would be churlish to object, especially since the title was inspired by Lord Palmerston, who greeted Grant on his return from Africa with the words, 'You have had a long walk.' Call it poetic licence.

It certainly seems more forgivable than the conduct of

Mao Zedung during the Long March of 1934/5. As ninety thousand Red Army troops retreated north from Jiangxi to Shanxi province, dwindling by ninety per cent along the way, Mao was one of only two people who did no marching, or walking, whatsoever. (The other was Otto Braun, a Prussian advisor, and an ideological opponent of Mao.) According to Dick Wilson's *The Long March*, 'He [Mao] would never march, and either rode a horse along the route or else, if it were a long stretch, would be carried on a wooden litter by four carriers.'

The Long March remains one of the great national myths of China. Writing in late 1935, Mao declared, 'The Long March is the first of its kind. It is a manifesto, a propaganda force, a seeding machine.' Well, only up to a point.

It wasn't until 2002 that anyone tried to repeat the exercise. In that year two Englishmen, Ed Jocelyn and Andy McEwan, retraced the steps of the Long March and although their, and apparently everyone else's, knowledge of the route depended on educated guesswork, they calculated that the march was some four thousand kilometres shorter than had generally been claimed. The Long March is said to have been ten thousand kilometres long (a nice round figure), but Jocelyn and McEwan only clocked six thousand. They covered the route in three hundred and seventy days, the Red Army took three hundred and eighty-four.

The two Englishmen were not iconoclasts, and they didn't set out to disprove or debunk the myth. Nevertheless, and not surprisingly, they've been denounced by Chinese officials. A spokesman for the Yan'an Foreign Affairs Department is quoted as saying, 'Can they change history? The whole world acknowledges these facts.' That's all right then. Print the legend.

*

Which brings me to one of the world's most enigmatic (and, let's face it, silly) walkers, an English playboy, womaniser and gambler called Harry Bensley. The story, and it comes in several versions, is that on 1 January 1908 Bensley set off from Trafalgar Square wearing a four-and-a-half-pound iron mask in order to test whether or not a man could walk round the world without being 'identified'. One version has John Pierpont Morgan and Lord Lonsdale debating the matter in the 'London Sporting Club', which was briefly the name of a boxing venue in Manhattan, though there were surely other places with the same name. Lonsdale said it could be done, Morgan said it couldn't. Bensley overheard the debate, and being a sporting man, offered to demonstrate that it could. He stood to win twenty-one thousand pounds of Morgan's money if he succeeded. Another version has Bensley, in enormous debt to the two men, being forced to do the walk as a forfeit.

There are problems with both these versions, and either way the whole proposition is surely an absurd one, and not much of a bet, since the matter of identification depends so largely on who the man is and precisely what parts of the world he walks around. But the real issue is the wearing of the mask, which seems to be a cheat in a couple of ways. Yes, in one way it prevents the wearer being recognised, but in another way it doesn't. After a while people might well see him walking down the street and say, 'There goes that guy in the iron mask,' which is surely a form of recognition. More crucially it means nobody could ever be certain it was actually Bensley inside the mask, and doing the walking. Perhaps this was his intention.

But even assuming there was a bet to be made, would anyone, however sporting, really be inclined to give up several years of his life to travelling round the world wearing a mask, even for that amount of money? If Bensley was doing it as a forfeit, that makes Morgan and Lonsdale a couple of very creepy guys indeed. Both versions do, of course, suggest that Bensley might have been thoroughly broke.

The conditions set down for the walk were extremely strict and occasionally bizarre, and could be read in a pamphlet that Bensley sold while travelling, in order to finance himself. They included details of how he was to dress, how much money he was allowed to spend (very little, though if he was broke this wouldn't have been much of an issue). He was to push a baby's pram in front of him, not a particularly onerous condition since he could carry his belongings in it, but far more problematically he had to find himself a wife *en route*, one who had never seen his face.

The conditions also dictated the route. It was an interesting version of 'the world'. Bensley had to visit over a hundred and fifty towns in Britain, fifty or so in Europe, three in Canada, eight in the United States, four in the whole of South America, eight in South Africa, six in Egypt (though none in central Africa), and a handful each in India, China, Australia and New Zealand. It was precisely the sort of route a son of the British Empire might take. Whether Bensley actually took it is anybody's guess.

He surely did go to some of the places dictated. A number of postcards were made depicting the iron-masked walker and messages on the back of some of the surviving ones indicate that Bensley covered at least some parts of England. Legend has it that he was arrested in Bexleyheath for selling his postcards without a licence, and that he once sold one to King Edward VII, for the staggering sum of five pounds. I find it hard to believe any king of England would pay one of his subjects so much for so little, but it's a story that does him credit.

Whether Bensley went abroad is more doubtful. The final

part of the legend has him in Genoa at the outbreak of the First World War, at which point he abandons the frivolous business of walking and enlists in the British army, to be invalided out a year later. In another version the start of hostilities moves Morgan to call off the bet, although since Morgan had been dead since 1912 this is a variant we can reasonably discount.

I suspect that Bensley wasn't much of a walker, and certainly didn't walk round very much of the world. Rather, I think he was a sort of showman and self-made fairground attraction, who had probably never set eyes on Morgan or Lonsdale. He'd turn up at gatherings around England on high days and holidays and make a spectacle of himself, be the centre of attention, sell some postcards and pamphlets, then go on his way. The walking, or the claim to be a great walker, was a way of drawing a crowd, part of the shtick, like the pram and the mask. He made a weird and improbable sight, and sometimes I wonder if the whole exercise wasn't just a photo opportunity, an excuse to make a zany postcard.

Bensley's round-the-world walk was, I think, imaginary, and it existed not so much in Bensley's imagination but in the minds of his public. Yes, Bensley was a sort of fake, a sort of conman, not a true walker, but he could see the appeal of being a great pedestrian, and although money was part of the equation, the invention of the walker in the iron mask must surely have appealed to some private need and fantasy of Bensley's. He may not have been a great walker, but he was one of the very greatest non-walkers. His imaginary walking had a perfection about it that remained unassailed by reality,

*

I realise that much of the above makes walkers appear to be a vain, duplicitous, lying bunch. Wasn't walking, especially walking straight and tall, supposed to be synonymous with honesty and plain dealing? Well, only up to a point. Perhaps all great walks involve the imagination to some extent and contain a nagging element of self-dramatisation and self-aggrandisement that may not have much to do with the facts. Perhaps if we're in search of perfection we need to look for something more local and less ambitious.

I have found one walk that strikes me as perfect and perfectly honest, the more so because it is essentially modest and small scale, and doesn't make any unnecessarily large claims for itself. One Sunday afternoon in the summer of 1948, George de Mestral took a life-changing walk in the mountains of his native Switzerland. De Mestral was an inventor by trade and an enthusiastic weekend hiker. He and his dog walked all the time, and as they set off that day he had no reason to believe that this walk would be different from any of the others, and in truth the walk itself was unexceptional enough.

It took him through brush and undergrowth, and when he got home he began the tedious process of removing the cockleburs that had attached themselves to his clothes and his dog's coat. Again, this was a common experience: it happened every time he walked. This time, however, as he picked off the burs, he found himself wondering, as he'd never wondered before, just why they stuck so firmly.

He took one of the cockleburs to his study, put it under the microscope and made the discovery that changed his and, to a significant if strictly limited extent, all our lives. He saw that the burs had hooks on them, and these hooks attached themselves to the fibres of his clothes and to the coat of his dog. He thought there must be some practical application for such a hook and loop system. There was. George de Mestral had made the discovery that enabled him to invent Velcro. The rest is social history.

De Mestral's walk has a genuine, unpretentious perfection about it. Something local and quotidian becomes the source for something ubiquitous even if not, in the more grandiose sense, universal. It's the simple domesticity that's so appealing. Almost none of us will ever know what it's like to walk on the moon or the North Pole. We won't walk around the world or across continents, we won't complete a ten-thousand- or even a six thousand-kilometre-long march. But most of us can imagine, and aspire to, a short walk in familiar territory that might provide us with our great idea, our great moment of inspiration.

And for a writer that's especially alluring. We know that for William Wordsworth walking and writing were pretty much synonymous. And I do believe that there's some fundamental connection between the two. In the broadest sense I've always found walking to be inspiring. When I need to solve a problem that's arisen in something I'm writing, to work out a plot point, to decide what character A might say or do if she found herself in a room with character Z, then going for a walk will usually clarify matters. The pace of words is the pace of walking, and the pace of walking is also the pace of thinking.

Both walking and writing are simple, common activities. You put one foot in front of the other; you put one word in front of another. What could be more basic than a single step, more basic than a single word? Yet, if you connect enough of these basic building blocks, connect enough steps, enough words, you may find that you've done something quite special. The thousand-mile journey starts with a single step; the million-word manuscript starts with a single syllable.

With writing, as with walking, you often find that you're not heading exactly where you thought you wanted to go. There'll be missteps and stumbles, journeys into dead ends, the reluctant retracing of your steps. And you have to accept that's just fine, a necessary, and not wholly unenjoyable, part of the process. It's an exploration.

Even the most determined and committed walker finds that there are certain walks he always intends to take yet never quite does. For instance, I have always meant to walk the length of the River Thames in London, crossing from one side to the other each time I encounter a bridge. In New York, I fully intend to walk the entire length of Broadway, but haven't as yet got round to it. A walk along the Great Wall of China remains an ambition, and obviously not an unrealisable one, though I haven't taken any steps to realise it.

None of these is a particularly original or unusual walk: they've all been done many times by others, but that shouldn't be a reason for me not to do them. And I tell myself there's plenty of time. I have plenty of years ahead of me: perhaps I will do these walks one day. Still, it is one of the intimations of mortality, to realise that we only have a certain number of walking miles in us. There are walks we simply won't make. We're absolutely guaranteed to end our walking days with certain routes and paths still untrodden.

For now, I continue to walk constantly, mostly in Los Angeles because that's where I live most of the time, but I also walk wherever else I am. Walking continues to be a great pleasure. It also continues to be a form of self-medication. It stops me getting depressed. It keeps me more or less healthy, more or less sane. It helps me write.

And so far I've managed to remain upright as I walk. Like anyone else I've occasionally tripped or slipped, lost my footing for a moment here and there, but so far I haven't fallen down again, not since that day when I was walking in the Hollywood Hills and broke my arm in three places. This is a small achievement but a real and welcome one.

Walking is not a risk-free activity, and we probably don't want it to be. We may fall down along the way. Something may get broken. People get lost, people walk into oblivion, some willingly, some not. Some return to tell lies about where they've been and what they've done, to create myths for themselves and others. This may not be strictly a good thing, but it's hard to see how it can be prevented. For many of us the perfect walk may simply be the one that we come back from in one piece. For a writer the perfect walk may simply be one he can write about.

Perhaps also, in both writing and walking, each word, each step takes you a little nearer to the end of things, to the last sentence, the last walk. Sooner or later everybody takes their last step. However, because walking is able to make us healthier, happier, very slightly fitter, certain steps in fact take us just a little farther away from the end, though we're absolutely guaranteed to get there sooner or later. The perfect walk, as Lao Tsu might have said, begins beneath your feet. It ends there too.

A Walking Bibliography

A bibliography of a thousand volumes begins with a single citation. But who would want a bibliography of a thousand volumes about walking? I've therefore limited this list to items that I've genuinely used in writing the book. Literary works mentioned in passing, like *Ulysses* or *Swann's Way*, are omitted; their bibliographical details are easy enough to find elsewhere.

I'd been planning to write a book about walking for a very long time, and before I started was aware of two well-known and well-received volumes on the subject: Rebecca Solnit's *Wanderlust*, subtitled 'A History of Walking', and Joseph Amato's *On Foot*, also subtitled 'A History of Walking'. Suffice it to say that if I'd thought these books contained the last word on walking I wouldn't have written one of my own.

I'm aware of two texts called *The Art of Walking*. One is a short piece by Christopher Morley from a 1918 collection *Shandygaff*, subtitled 'A number of most agreeable Inquirendoes upon Life & Letters, interspersed with Short Stories & Skits, the whole most Diverting to the Reader'. Morley writes, 'Now your true walker is mightily "curious in the world", and he goes upon his way zealous to sate himself with a thousand quaintnesses. When he writes a book he fills it full of food, drink, tobacco, the scent of sawmills on sunny afternoons, and arrivals at inns late at night.' Well, only up to a point.

There's also an anthology called *The Art of Walking*, actually rather slender, edited by Edwin Valentine Mitchell, and published in 1934. It contains works by many of the usual suspects, Dickens, Leslie Stephen ('In Praise of

Walking'), Max Beerbohm ('Going Out For a Walk'), as well
as a piece by Christopher Morley called 'Sauntering'. Thus:
'It is entrancing to walk . . . and catalogue all that may be
seen. I jot down on scraps of paper a list of all the shops on a
side street; the names of tradesmen that amuse me; the absurd
repartee of gutter children. Why? Because it amuses me and
that is sufficient excuse.'

It's interesting to compare the contents of that anthology
with those of a more recent one, *The Vintage Book of
Walking*, edited by Duncan Minshull, published in 2004.
Dickens, Stephen, Beerbohm, all hold their places, though
there's no room for poor old Morley. It seems that even in
the world of walking, of walking anthologies and walking
bibliographies, there are no such things as eternal *vérités*.

There's also a book by Michael Heher called *The Lost Art
of Walking On Water*. It's a wonderful title, and one that I
certainly wish I'd thought of myself. However, since its sub-
title is 'Reimagining the Priesthood', I don't think there's
much risk of the author and I stepping on each other's toes.

Abbey, Edward, *Desert Solitaire: A Season in the Wilderness*,
    New York, McGraw-Hill, 1968

—— *The Journey Home: Some Words in Defence of the
    American West*, New York, Dutton, 1977

Ainslie, Scott and Whitehill, Dave, *Robert Johnson: At the
    Crossroads – the Authoritative Guitar Transcriptions*,
    Milwaukee, Hal Leonard Publishing, 1992

Alstruther, Stephen, *The Mindful Hiker: On the Trail to
    Find the Path*, Camarillo, Ca, DeVorss Publications,
    2004

Amato, Joseph A., *On Foot: A History of Walking*, New
    York, New York University Press, 2004

Arturian, Judy and Oldham, Mike, *Movie Star Homes: The Famous to the Forgotten*, Santa Monica, Ca, Santa Monica Press, 2004

Aslan, Reza, *No God But God*, New York, Random House, 2005

Auster, Paul, *The New York Trilogy*, New York, Penguin, 1987

Banham, Peter Reyner, *Scenes in America Deserta*, Salt Lake City, Gibbs Smith, 1982

—— *Los Angeles: The Architecture of Four Ecologies*, Harmondsworth, Penguin, 1971

Baudrillard, Jean, *America*, translated by Chris Turner, London, Verso, 1988

Bean, J. P., *The Sheffield Gang Wars*, Sheffield, D and D, 1981

Bein, Alex, *The Jewish Question: Biography of a World Problem*, translated by Harry Zohn, Rutherford, NJ, Farleigh Dickinson University Press, 1990

Bellos, David, *George Perec: A Life in Words*, London, Harvill Press, 1993

Benjamin, Walter (1938), 'The Flâneur', in *Charles Baudelaire: A Lyric Poet in the Era of High Capitalism*, translated by Harry Zohn and Quintin Hoare, London, New Left Books, 1973

—— *The Arcades Project*, translated by Howard Eiland and Kevin McLaughlin, Cambridge, Belknap Press, Harvard University Press, 1999

Bradbury, Ray (1951), 'The Pedestrian', in *S is for Space*, London, Hart-Davis, 1968

Brinnin, John Malcolm, *Dylan Thomas in America: An Intimate Journal*, London, Dent, 1956

Brook, Stephen, *L. A. Lore*, London, Sinclair-Stevenson, 1992

Burton, Isabel, *The Life of Captain Sir Richard Burton* (2 volumes), London, Chapman and Hall, 1893

Burton, Richard, *Personal Narrative of a Pilgrimage to El-Medinah and Meccah* (3 volumes), London, Longman, Brown, Green and Longmans, 1855–7

—— *The Erotic Traveller*, edited by Edward Leigh, London, Ortolan Press, 1966

(The works of Sir Richard Burton are simultaneously much in demand and, with the exception of his translations of *The Arabian Nights*, *The Perfumed Garden* and *The Kama Sutra*, extremely hard to come by. The most accessible source for his voluminous travel and ethnographic writings is the website burtoniana.org which contains most of Burton's major works, either in facsimile or transcript.)

Burton, Robert (1621), *The Anatomy of Melancholy*, New York, *New York Review of Books*, 2001

Campbell, Ffyona, *Feet of Clay: On Foot through Australia*, Heinemann, London, 1991

—— *On Foot through Africa*, London, Orion, 1994

—— *The Whole Story: A Walk around the World*, London, Orion, 1996

Chandler, Raymond, *The Big Sleep*, New York, Alfred A. Knopf, 1939

—— *Farewell, My Lovely*, New York, Alfred A. Knopf, 1940

—— *The High Window*, New York, Alfred A. Knopf, 1942

—— *The Lady in the Lake*, New York, Alfred A. Knopf, 1943

—— *The Little Sister*, London, Hamish Hamilton, 1949

—— *The Long Goodbye*, London, Hamish Hamilton, 1953

—— *Playback*, London, Hamish Hamilton, 1958

—— *Selected Letters*, Edited by Frank McShane, London, Jonathan Cape, 1981

Chatwin, Bruce, *The Songlines*, London, Jonathan Cape, 1987

—— *What Am I Doing Here*, London, Jonathan Cape, 1989

Clark, David, *L. A. On Foot: A Free Afternoon*, Los Angeles, Camaro Publishing, 1972

Coverley, Merlin, *Psychogeography*, London, Pocket Essentials, 2006

Davis, Mike, *City of Quartz: Excavating the Future in Los Angeles*, New York, Vintage, 1992

—— *Ecology of Fear: Los Angeles and the Imagination of Disaster*, New York, Vintage, 1999

De Certeau, Michel, 'Walking in the City', in *The Practice of Everyday Life*, translated by Steven Rendall, Berkeley, University of California Press, 1984

Debord, Guy Ernest, *Panegyric: Volumes 1 and 2* (1989 and 1997), translated by James Brook and John McHale, London, Verso, 2004

—— *Society of the Spectacle*, translated by Donald Nicholson-Smith, New York, Zone Books, 1995

—— 'Theory of the Dérive', in *Guy Debord and the Situationist International: Texts and Documents*, edited by Tom McDonough, Cambridge, Ma., MIT Press, 2004

—— 'Introduction to a Critique of Urban Geography' (1955), in *The Situationist International Anthology*, translated by Ken Knabb, Berkeley, Ca, Bureau of Public Secrets, 2006

De Quincey, Thomas (1862), *Confessions of an English Opium Eater*, Harmondsworth, Penguin, 2003

Dickens, Charles (1860), 'Night Walks', Chapter XIII in *The Uncommercial Traveller*, London, Chapman and Hall, 1901

Drummond, Bill, *45*, London, Little, Brown, 2000

Dunaway, David King, *Huxley in Hollywood*, New York, Harper and Row, 1989

Duncan, Andrew, *Secret London*, London, New Holland (Publishers), 1995

Edmunds, Lowell, *Martini Straight Up*, Baltimore, Johns Hopkins University Press, 1998

Fletcher, Colin, *The Complete Walker*, New York, Knopf (various editions from 1968 to 1984)

Foster, Lynn, *Adventuring in the California Desert*, San Francisco, Sierra Club Books, 1987

Francis, John, *Planetwalker: How to change your world one step at a time*, Point Reyes Station, Ca, Elephant Mountain Press, 2005

Freeman, Judith, *The Long Embrace: Raymond Chandler and the Woman He Loved*, New York, Pantheon Books, 2007

Fuchs, R. H. *Richard Long*, London, Thames and Hudson, 1986

Gebhard, David and Winter, Robert, *Los Angeles: An Architectural Guide*, Salt Lake City, Gibbs-Smith, 1994

Gilden, Bruce, *Facing New York: Photographs by Bruce Gilden*, New York, Cornerhouse, N.D. (1992)

—— *Coney Island*, New York, Trebruk, 2002

—— *A Beautiful Catastrophe*, New York, Powerhouse, 2005

Grant, James Augustus, *A Walk across Africa; or Domestic Scenes from My Nile Journal*, London, Blackwood, 1864

Gray, Christopher, *Streetscapes: Tales of Manhattan's Significant Buildings and Landmarks*, New York, Abrams, 2003

Gross, Miriam (ed.), *The World of Raymond Chandler*, London, Weidenfeld and Nicolson, 1977

Harmon, Ruth and Minnis, John, *Sheffield*, New Haven and London, Pevsner City Guides, Yale University Press, 2004

Harrison, Jim, 'Westward Ho', in *The Beast God Forgot to Invent*, New York, Grove, 2000

Henson, Matthew (1912), *A Negro Explorer at the North Pole*, New York, Invisible Cities, 2001

Hiney, Tom, *Raymond Chandler: A Biography*, London, Chatto and Windus, 1997

Herzog, Werner, *Of Walking in Ice: Munich–Paris 23 November–14 December 1974*, translated by Marje Herzog and Alan Greenberg, New York, Tanam Press, 1980

—— *Herzog on Herzog*, edited by Paul Cronin, London, Faber, 2002

Jakle, John A. and Sculle, Keith A., *Lots of Parking: Land Use in a Car Culture*, Charlottesville and London, University of Virginia Press, 2004

Jarvis, Robin, *Romantic Writing and Pedestrian Travel*, London, Macmillan, 1997

Jasen, David A, *P. G. Wodehouse: A Portrait of a Master*, New York, Mason and Lipscomb, 1974

Jencks, Charles, *Post-Modern Triumphs in London*, London, Academy Editions, 1991

Joyce, Julie and Firmin, Sandra Q., *Mudman: The Odyssey of Kim Jones*, Cambridge, Ma., MIT Press, 2007

Kayton, Bruce, *Radical Walking Tours of New York City*, New York, Seven Stories Press, 2003

Kazin, Alfred, *A Walker in the City*, New York, Harcourt Brace, 1951

Keaton, Buster, with Charles Samuels, *My Wonderful World of Slapstick*, Garden City, New York, Doubleday, 1960

Kerouac, Jack, *On the Road*, New York, Viking Press, 1957

—— *Dharma Bums*, New York, Viking Press, 1958

Klein, Jim, *The Complete Films of Buster Keaton*, New York, Citadel Press, 1993

Lawson, Kristan and Rufus, Anneli, *California Babylon: A Guide to Sites of Scandal, Mayhem, and Celluloid in the Golden State*, New York, St Martin's Griffin, 2000

Lelyveld, Nita, 'He Has His Walking Points: Neil Hopper navigates the LA area with his feet', *Los Angeles Times*, 16 September 2004

Lewis, Percy Wyndham (1928), *The Childermass*, New York, Riverrun Press, 2000

Long, Richard, *Walking the Line*, Thames and Hudson, London and New York, 2002

—— *Richard Long: Selected Statements and Interviews*, edited by Ben Tufnell, London, Haunch of Venison, 2007

—— *Walking and Marking*, Edinburgh, Scottish National Gallery of Modern Art, 2007

Lopate, Phillip, *Waterfront: A Walk around Manhattan*, New York, Random House, 2004

MacShane, Frank, *The Life of Raymond Chandler*, New York, Dutton, 1976

Machen, Arthur, *The London Adventure: or, The Art of Wandering*, London, Secker, 1924

Mahoney, Erin, *Walking L. A.*, Berkeley, Ca, Wilderness Press, 2005

Meegan, George, *The Longest Walk: An Odyssey of the Human Spirit*, New York, Paragon House, 1989

Minshull, Duncan, *The Vintage Book of Walking*, London, Vintage, 2000

Mitchell, Edwin Valentine (ed.) (1934), *The Art of Walking*, Great Neck, New York, Core Collection Books Inc., 1978

Morgan, Bill, *The Beat Generation in New York: A Walking Tour of Jack Kerouac's City*, San Francisco, City Lights, 1997

Neil, Charles Lang, *Walking: A Practical Guide to Pedestrianism for Athletes and Others*, London, C. Arthur Pearson, 1903

O'Hara, Frank, *Standing Still and Walking in New York*, Bonias, Ca, Grey Fox Press, 1975

—— 'Let's take a walk' in *Selected Poems*, edited by Donald Allen, New York, Knopf/Vintage, 1974

Olson, Brian and Olson, Bonnie, *Tailing Philip Marlowe*, St Paul, Minnesota, Burlwrite, 2003

Peiper, Albrecht, *Cerebral Function in Infancy and Childhood*, London, Pitman Medical Publishers, 1963

Poetzsch, Markus (13–17 August 2005), 'Walks Alone and "I know not where": Dorothy Wordsworth's Deviant Pedestrianism', presented at the 13th Annual Conference of the North American Society for the Study of Romanticism: Deviance and Defiance

Porter, Roy, *London: A Social History*, London, Hamish Hamilton, 1994

Radford, Peter, *The Celebrated Captain Barclay: Sport, Gambling and Adventure in Regency Times*, London, Headline, 2001

Rice, Edward, *Captain Sir Richard Francis Burton*, New York, Scribner, 1990

Rousseau, Jean-Jacques (1782), *The Reveries of The Solitary Walker*, translated by Charles E. Butterworth, Indianapolis/Cambridge, Hackett Publishing Company, 1992

Rubenstein, Raphael, 'Snap Judgements: Exploring the Winogrand Archive', in *Art in America*, February 2002

Sacks, Oliver, *A Leg to Stand On*, New York, Harper and Row, 1984

Sardar, Ziauddin, 'How Mecca Became a Death Trap', in *New Statesman*, 26 March 1999

Sebald, W. G., *The Rings of Saturn*, translated from German by Michael Hulse, London, Harvill, 1998

Self, Will, *Psychogeography*, pictures by Ralph Steadman, London, Bloomsbury, 2007

—— *Psycho Too*, pictures by Ralph Steadman, London, Bloomsbury, 2009

Saward, Jeff, *Labyrinths and Mazes: A Complete Guide to Magical Paths of the World*, New York, Lark Books, 2003

Sinclair, Iain, *Hackney: That Rose-Red Empire: A Confidential Report*, London, Hamish Hamilton, 2009

—— *Lights Out for the Territory: 9 Excursions in the Secret History of London*, London, Granta Books, 1997

—— *London: City of Disappearances*, London, Hamish Hamilton, 2006

—— *London Orbital: A Walk Around the M25*, London, Granta Books, 2002

—— *Lud Heat*, London, Albion Village Press, 1975

Snow, Sebastian, *The Rucksack Man*, London, Hodder and Stoughton, 1976

Solnit, Rebecca, *Wanderlust: A History of Walking*, New York, Penguin Books, 2000

Speer, Albert, *The Spandau Secret Diaries*, translated from German by Richard and Clara Winston, New York, Macmillan, 1976

Stisted, Georgiana M., *The True Life of Captain Sir Richard Burton*, London, H. S. Nicols, 1896

Sutherland, John, 'Clarissa's Invisible Taxi', in *Can Jane Eyre Be Happy? More Puzzles in Classic Fiction*, London, Oxford University Press, 1997

Tatley, Roger, 'In the Studio: Richard Long', in *Art + Auction*, February 2006, pp. 40–4

Thom, Walter, *Pedestrianism: or, An Account of the Performances of Celebrated Pedestrians during the Last and Present Centuries; with a Full Narrative of Captain Barclay's Public and Private Matches; and an Essay on Training*, Aberdeen, NP, 1808

Thomson, David, *The Big Sleep* (BFI Film Classics), London, British Film Institute, 1997

Thoreau, Henry David, 'Walking', in *Atlantic Monthly*, June 1862

Turner, Jack, *The Abstract Wild*, Tucson, University of Arizona Press, 1996

Underhill, Paco, *Call of the Mall*, New York, Simon and Schuster, 2004

Van Ash, Cay and Rohmer, Elizabeth Sax, *Master of Villainy: A Biography of Sax Rohmer*, edited by Robert E. Briney, Bowling Green, Ohio, Bowling Green University Popular Press, 1972

Van Dyke, John C. (1901), *The Desert*, New York, Gibbs Smith, Scribners, 1980

Waldie, D. J., *Holy Land: A Suburban Memoir*, New York, W. W. Norton, 1996

—— *Where We Are Now: Notes from Los Angeles*, Santa Monica, Ca, Angel City Press, 2004

Ward, Elizabeth and Silver, Alain, *Raymond Chandler's Hollywood*, Woodstock, New York, Overlook Press, 1987

Westbury, Virginia, *Labyrinths: Ancient Paths of Wisdom and Peace*, Cambridge, Ma., Da Capo Press, 2001

Westerbeck, Colin and Meyerowitz, Joel, 'Afterword: The Sidewalk Never Ends', in *Bystander: A History of Street Photography*, London, Thames and Hudson, 1994

White, Edmund, *The Flâneur: A Stroll Through the Paradoxes of Paris*, London, Bloomsbury, 2001

Williams, George, *Guide to Literary London*, London, Batsford, 1973

Wilson, Dick, *The Long March: The Epic of Chinese Communism's Survival*, New York, Viking Press, 1972

Winogrand, Garry, *Figments from the Real World*, edited by John Szarkowski, New York, Museum of Modern Art, New York, 1988

—— *1964*, edited by Trudy Wilner Stack, Santa Fe, Arena Editions, 2002

Wood, Dennis, *The Power of Maps*, New York, Guilford Press, 1992

Woolf, Virginia, *Mrs Dalloway*, London, Hogarth Press, 1925

—— 'Oxford Street Tide' (1931), in *The London Scene: Six Essays on London Life*, New York, Ecco, HarperCollins, 2006

Wordsworth, Dorothy, *Journals of Dorothy Wordsworth*, London, Oxford University Press, 1971

Wright, Thomas, *The Life of Sir Richard Burton* (2 volumes), London, Everett, 1906

Wrigley, J. R., *A Hillsborough Camera*, Sheffield, Pickard Publishing, 2003

Ziegler, Philip, *London at War 1939–1945*, London, Sinclair-Stevenson, 1995

Zochert, Donald (ed.), *Walking in America*, New York, Alfred A. Knopf, 1974

Some online sources

http://web.wits.ac.za/Academic/Humanities/SLLS/Holistic/BibliographyWalking/

A serious academic bibliography on walking, though with some unexpected and very welcome quirks, by Andie Miller of the University of Witwatersrand, Johannesburg.

*

http://www.walkinginla.com/

Neil Hopper's website recording his walks around Los Angeles.

*

http://www.egreenway.com/wellbeing/walk.htm

A bibliography and a collection of links and quotations compiled by Michael Garofalo.

*

http://walkart.wordpress.com/bibliography/

A weblog about the uses of walking in art, including a bibliography, initiated by Tate Modern, run by Ana Laura.

*

http://temporarytraveloffice.net/main.html

The people behind the walking tours of the parking lots of America. I'm still uncertain whether this is art pretending to be urban studies or vice versa, but the uncertainty is all part of the fun.

*

http://www.flickr.com/photos/32373413@N00/
A small number of images I assembled while writing this book.